The Human Condition In Biblical Perspective

Messages On The God-Human Encounter

Harold C. Warlick, Jr.

CSS Publishing Company, Inc., Lima, Ohio

THE HUMAN CONDITION IN BIBLICAL PERSPECTIVE

Library of Congress Cataloging-in-Publication Data

Warlick, Harold C.
    The human condition in biblical perspective : messages on the God-human encounter / Hal Warlick.
        p.   cm.
    Includes bibliographical references.
    ISBN 0-7880-1292-4 (alk. paper)
    1. God. 2. Man (Christian theology)   I. Title.
BT165.W37   1998
233—dc21   98-11288
                                                                    CIP

ISBN 0-7880-1292-4   PRINTED IN U.S.A.

This volume is brought forth in the academic term of the completion of physical additions to the Chas. E. Hayworth Sr. Memorial Chapel, High Point University, High Point, North Carolina. Thanks for the leadership and generosity of President Jacob C. Martinson, David R. Hayworth, Pauline L. Hayworth, and the late Charles E. Hayworth, Jr.

This book is dedicated to the alumni, students, and staff, both past and present, whose commitment and support have enabled their university's chapel to remain a vibrant place of worship.

The Human Condition In Biblical Perspective

Part One — Origin, Fall, and Grace

I. Origin

II. Fall

III. Grace

Part Two — Responsibility and Character

IV. Responsibility

V. Character

Part Three — Wholeness and The Future

VI. Wholeness

VII. The Future

Acknowledgments and Introduction to the Volume

The task of compiling a thematic anthology from one's published writings covering two decades proved more difficult than initially anticipated. As the project unfolded, it became abundantly clear that each and every piece had to be rewritten, edited, and expanded.

The idea of attempting such a collection originated with Thomas Lentz, Acquisitions Editor, CSS Publishing Company, Lima, Ohio. His encouragement and vision provided the needed impetus to get this project started and rushed to completion. A number of my books had been out of print for over a decade, eventuating in readers, clergy, and teachers having to rummage through used bookstores to find them. Several college professors and churches had to group some of the writings under a single theme and duplicate them in-house for use in their respective classrooms.

Consequently what follows is a **revised collection of previously published material, organized in a thematic format with an updated and recast focus.** Not only are the messages organized in a new format, but their individual contents, from most recent to oldest, have been substantially reworked in light of theological reflection, new educational approaches to the study of ethics, and recent exegetical insights. It is hoped that the volume reflects both the resiliency and the elasticity of the Divine-Human encounter.

In this, my thirtieth year of ordained ministry, the task of sifting through two decades of published works, to discern which messages proved to be timeless and worthy of inclusion and which proved to be time-conditioned and fit only for exclusion, has been at once sobering and stimulating.

The format for the volume has been designed to be of service to a wide audience. Scripture references have been included at the beginning of each piece to enable the preacher and teacher to expound upon the text and material in their classrooms or pulpits.

The grouping of the messages into three distinct parts should enable preachers and teachers to utilize the material in either a deductive or an inductive manner.

Preachers and teachers should find the number of messages under each heading to be particularly helpful. Often when one seeks to research a particular topic or text, two less than desirable types of homiletical resources are available. The first is the "entire tome on a single subject" reference. What busy preacher or teacher has the time to read an entire book on a subject to glean but a few usable illustrations?

The second, equally frustrating, resource is the "stand alone" reference. When working with a lectionary text for a sermon, a lecture topic for class, or a theme for a discussion, one often discovers but little material and wastes precious hours tracking it down. In fact, many preachers and teachers probably feel like small-game hunters as they surf the sermons and lectures available on the World Wide Web or labor to uncover the needle in the haystack from a lectionary reference book or a college textbook. In order to find more than a single sermon, illustration, case, or writing on the matter at hand, we small-game hunters have to hit many sites, consult many books, and/or sift through numerous magazines, journals, and collections. I hope the effort to provide five or six different messages under each subtopic, complete with a dozen or more textual options, will allow the reader or researcher to combine completeness with economy of time and effort.

Few apologies need to be made for the revised nature of the offerings in this volume. We live with revised weather forecasts, revised economic indicators, revised budgets, and a revised standard version of the Bible. God's word is, indeed, both timeless and time-conditioned. Perhaps the greatest gift of the Holy Spirit is bringing God's word into compliance with the needs of a particular place, time, and people. Soren Kierkegaard is correct: "Life must be lived going forward but it can only be understood by looking backward."

I must confess that, like all preachers and teachers, I cannot easily claim the ideas being published herein are mine alone. Without my own teachers, preachers, colleagues, and students, most of these ideas would have perished on the vine or been less effectively communicated to a contemporary world.

Colleagues would have difficulty keeping a straight face upon hearing me referred to as an "academic." I merely try to make connections between biblical concepts and emergent human conditions. Whatever I write and teach is fleshed out in normal, everyday language, grammar, and sentence structure. The underlying desired effect is to be comprehendible for a wide audience. Yet the faithful preacher or teacher can take some comfort in the fact that the enclosed messages are backed up by sound biblical exegesis and considered theological and philosophical reason. It is those underpinnings which I must now acknowledge. In this effort, I fully realize that any shortcomings or faulty applications are mine and mine alone!

The approach to Scripture reflected in these messages is dependent on the historicist perspective handed to me in my earliest training by the late G. Ernest Wright at Harvard. As my first faculty advisor, G. Ernest taught me that there is such a thing as a canon of Scripture which is still theologically meaningful. In spite of recent attempts to discredit and deconstruct the perspective that history is the ultimate arbiter of theological validity, I cling to it. While recognizing the contributions of narrative, metaphorical, process, and postmodern theologies, I still regard God as "one who acts"!

Scholars will recognize at once the theological biases toward the perspectives of H. Richard Niebuhr and Paul Tillich. Niebuhr's emphasis on responsibility and his caution against substituting Christ for God have kept many of these messages from slipping into a form of Christological "superstition" which is not necessarily a help for understanding faith. Tillich's efforts to become a theologian of synthesis, as he sought to formulate the Christian message in the thought-forms of his generation, have had an impact on my effort to reconcile opposites. While I have not attempted to interpret or illuminate Christian concepts by using existential language, as did Tillich, the wording "the human condition" in biblical perspective is not by accident. Religion cannot relinquish the absolute and culture cannot allow truth and justice to be sacrificed in the name of religion.

11

All readers will, I hope, affirm the inclusive language contained herein, as well as the effort to recognize the distinctive Western nature of our faith. My claim that tolerance is the essential ingredient in Christian character owes its origin not only to informed teachers but also to life experiences working with and for two dear friends, Constance H. Buchanan, Program Officer for Religion, the Ford Foundation, and George Rupp, President of Columbia University.

Preachers will, perhaps, with a breath of kindness, find some of these messages to be "preachable." The effort to couch religious material in modern issues, compelling stories, and specialized needs owes a debt to mentors in the field. Thanks to Peter Gomes, Plummer Professor of Christian Morals and Minister of Memorial Church, Harvard University, and John Killinger, former Distinguished Professor of Preaching at Vanderbilt. These two have suffered my presence in their lives for two decades and have kept me an honest preacher.

Every time I finish a book, I say, "That's the last one!" Two special friends, William Brown, Distinguished Professor of Music, University of North Florida, and Robert Blocker, Dean of the School of Music, Yale University, always pull me back to the task of writing. Were these two accomplished musicians less interested in religion, my life would be less hectic *and* much less fulfilled.

Finally, a special debt is owed to the following: Shirley Connor, whose life as a secretary would be smoother without having to type, scan, and computerize manuscripts; Diane Warlick, whose life would be calmer without a husband who writes at odd hours; Carole Stoneking, Berry Crawford, Clint Corcoran, and Akin Akinade, whose access to their Chair would be greater without his innumerable projects.

Harold C. Warlick, Jr.
High Point, North Carolina

I. ORIGIN

Point Of Origin

Genesis 1:1-5

The beginning of the world's story is our story. This magisterial word "create" suggests no point of origin other than God. This creation is an absolute new beginning which carries profound implications for what it means to be a human being. For the universe and humankind to be created by God demonstrates the surprising and uncontrollable power of God. For humankind to be created in *the image of God* indicates a uniqueness that leads to a significant purpose in life.

Despite the first five verses of the Bible being among the best-known in all of scripture, their significance is often overlooked. The perspective that the universe and human beings are *created* sets the biblical perspective apart from other, competing perspectives in life.

Consider other perspectives of human development which often translate into practical consequences. The way we theorize about our origin and purpose often shapes the way we treat others. If we view human beings solely as highly-developed animals, we can find much to back up our claim. Certainly a biological or anthropological perspective has the weight of research behind it. We humans, indeed, still share 98 percent of our genes with chimps. We are indebted to *Homo erectus* as our *Homo sapiens* ancestor. Perhaps a magic twist in 0.1 percent of our genes within the past 60,000 years did create the anatomical basis for spoken complex language. Certainly as long ago as Charles Darwin's *The Descent of Man,* it has been pointed out that we are similar to other animals in being subject to the same laws of development from primitive forms in nature, passing on variations by inheritance from individual to individual, reproducing in greater numbers than can survive, and possessing body parts we no longer use, such as a tail bone to carry a tail, an appendix to store food when we ate only plants, and wisdom teeth with which to crush bones.[1] If we believe that humankind is solely a part of nature, a species of animal and nothing more, then we are likely to treat the people we encounter as highly developed animals. Those we like we view as pets. If they love us and remain faithful to us, we cuddle them as we would any friendly and lovable dog or cat. We will bring them into our household circle of friendship and even try to curry the favor of others as we, too, seek to be friendly animals. To those who are unfriendly, we act as if they are a swarm of flies at a picnic or a beast of burden. We ask our schoolteachers, our police, and our courts to protect us from these pests. We organize our labor force and our economy to enable us to take advantage of these beasts of burden, paying them lower wages and creating social programs to see that they are fed, watered, and sheltered. While all this is quite unconscious, it still reflects an understanding of humankind as animal: **pets, pests, and beasts of burden.** That is a perspective upheld by many.

Other thinkers view the human being as simply a unique creature that knows it's going to die. If, indeed, we are the only animal that knows it's going to die, what value is love, if we only return to common clay? The existentialist perspective raises genuine questions about the meaninglessness of life. If life ends for us as individuals and eventually for the cosmic scheme, why bother? Why marry? Your spouse is going to die anyway! Why even bother to preach this sermon? All of you are going to die anyway! We are helpless victims. The older we get the more aware we become of the impending end. Consequently, perhaps the best we can hope for is existence today as we eat, drink, and be merry and a painless suicide tomorrow when self-consciousness and good health begin to wane. The human being as **a helpless victim** of life's forces is a perspective upheld by many.

Finally, consider the perspective that the human being is more like a machine, a complicated but efficient machine. This perspective animates education and industry. In a computer age we tend to view people for their functions. This perspective doesn't pay much attention to "feelings" as long as the machine produces the goods. As long as the machine functions well it gets rewarded with merit raises and job security in the business world and good grades in the educational institution. We don't hand out bonuses or *cum laude* honors based on "feelings." When the machine becomes older or weaker and falls behind in production or starts making poor grades, we try to repair it. Retraining efforts, continuing education courses, tutoring centers, counseling agencies, and quotas abound. We even have affirmative action programs to make certain every machine gets its chance to perform or be repaired. When the machine stops going altogether and stops performing, we get rid of it, flunk it out of the institution, or dispose of it in some suitable way in a retirement center on the edge of town. That the human being is a **machine** is a perspective upheld by many.

The first chapter of Genesis is an irreplaceable portion of scripture because it gives us an analysis of the human predicament. It maintains that the universe and the humans within it were ***created*** by God. It upholds the goodness of this creation and proclaims a vision that all human beings, the ones we see on the street and others we never see, whether in hospitals or prisons, are something like God. If we hadn't heard this scripture so many times and thought about it so little, we would see how blasphemous it sounds against other practical perspectives of life.

The Genesis text is more than God bringing order out of a surging chaos. It is more than the wind (*ruah*) which gives life and restrains the waters. It is more than the voice of a ruler on a throne who speaks in a sovereign voice. It is more than a God who calls into existence things that do not exist. It is a new beginning, a new perspective which continues to be blasphemous. ***God created!*** The order and the goodness presented in the first five verses move symmetrically toward a grand climax. The order in the universe finds its climax in the freedom bestowed on human life.

The good priests in Babylon who compiled the account with striking resemblances to the Babylonian story of creation, the *Enuma elish,* moved beyond the details of Babylonian order to view humans not as slaves or machines, not as unique creatures, not as animals, but as very "images of God." Genesis 1 defines an element of goodness and freedom. The "images of God" are called upon to exercise dominion and care and finish off the creation.

That is the *biblical* perspective of our origin: the human is a created co-creator. The human is no pet, no pest, no beast of burden, no machine, no victim. The human being is a co-creator in a created universe. The human self is holy. It lives in dialogue with its world, its creator, its fellow humans.[2] It shares in creation. It has the freedom to create its own history. Among all the animals it is most helpless and unfinished at birth. It creates things from the materials of its universe, from the words you read to the paper on which it is printed. It creates time through memory and imagination. And it co-creates itself. It overcomes handicaps and blows great opportunities. For seven or eight hours each night it dies through sleep and must rise the next morning to create again.

Each night you and I die. And each morning you and I rise from the dead to create, almost literally. We exist, to be certain, but as for the world we live in, our family and friends, the work we are committed to — we are dead for a while. Then, without even a hallelujah chorus, we wake up in the morning.

Each day we all enact the familiar biblical metaphor of death and creation, of sleeping and waking. Each year we all enact the metaphor of creation, of standing at bay the chaos of past experience and bringing to birth a new historical recognition. January is the time when we mark a new beginning, a new creation, on our calendar-conscious minds.

The Genesis 1 text calls us to reflect on a strange Christian term, "epiphany." The word means "to make known." Essentially, it's when something is recognized for what it is. When the wise men saw Jesus and knew what he looked like, that was an epiphany. Actually, Jesus was not the Messiah or the Savior until somebody recognized him as the Messiah. As in sleep, it's perfectly possible to be unaware of what's going on around you. Each year Epiphany is celebrated on January 6. It's the time after Christ's birth when people recognize him not as the babe in a manger, but as the Lamb of God. Only when people recognize Jesus as the One who can take away the sin and despair of the world does Christmas mean anything.

A student made his first A in a course in graduate school. The school was on a British-type system. It had a reading period in January for two weeks and then students took exams. After the exams, everyone took off for home or snow skiing or warmer climates. When students turned in an exam, they gave the professor a stamped, self-addressed postcard. The professor would mail the grade. The day before this student was to leave for home, he received the postcard in his dormitory mailbox. It said A. He was an A student. Well, actually he wasn't quite. You see, all the others had departed on their trips. As the dormitory proctor, he had to stay there and lock up. There wasn't anyone for him to show his postcard. He was not recognized yet. He was just a guy from South Carolina standing in the middle of a dormitory in Massachusetts with a postcard in his hand. Consequently, he caught a bus to Arlington, Massachusetts, where he was on the staff of the Park Avenue Church. He went into Park Florist and showed the card to the owner. "Wonderful," the owner exclaimed, as he showed the card to his daughters. Then he pulled in to visit the owner of the funeral home. And finally, when a friend came in to the local bank to handle the now mangled card, he was really an A student. After the hugs, he felt for the first time like an A student. It doesn't matter what you are if other people don't recognize you for it.

Only when we recognize the created nature of our origins can we truly recognize the fullness and wonder of our humanity. It is through that recognition of who we are and what we are about as human beings that we are beckoned into an awareness of what we could become through Jesus Christ.

In 1931, the National Broadcasting Company invited the great musician and conductor Arturo Toscanini to conduct a concert tour of Latin America. The orchestra for the tour was made up of select professional musicians from around the United States.

The group came together on a hot and humid afternoon for their first rehearsal. They began rehearsing Beethoven's Sixth Symphony in a rehearsal hall that was not air-conditioned. These professional musicians had played the piece so many times that they could almost play it from memory. They knew exactly when to come in and when to rest. Usually during rehearsals they could get up and go out for a smoke or a soft drink and still be back in their places in time to play their parts.

If you've ever been to initial rehearsals for a Broadway play, a movie, a musical, or a great symphony, it's somewhat disappointing to be backstage. A card game is going on in one corner. The lead actor is in a room watching the New York Mets. People come running up the steps with a sandwich in hand, throw it in the trash at full gallop, and walk in on cue to give a dramatic performance in their sweatshirt and bluejeans. These people are pros. They can lay down their cards in a gin rummy game and rush out and play a torrid love scene. They can turn it on and off in an instant. That's why they are called professionals.

But something happened that day when Toscanini began to direct. Everyone could sense it. By the end of the first movement no one was daydreaming. Each person was intent on the music. They played it flawlessly. At the end of the final movement the maestro put down his baton. The members of the orchestra rose to their feet in applause. Toscanini stood there until they ceased. Then he said, "That was not Toscanini. That was Beethoven. You just never heard him before."[3]

Perhaps you and I are so familiar with the style and characters of the Genesis 1 account of creation that we can almost recite it from memory. Perhaps these first five verses of the Bible have been subject to more minute examination than any other opening verse of any book, religious or secular. But just maybe a recognition will take place in our lives this year. "In the beginning God created...."

The biblical text which follows those words is not a scientific attempt to answer questions as to how life got going. The chapter is not a repudiation of the sexist passages in the other Genesis creation story of Adam and Eve which some have used to demean women. The chapter is not even just a radical break with myths in other world religions which put all the real action with the gods and goddesses. No, the chapter is a statement which governs how we relate to one another today. It is a theological statement about what it means to be a human being.

"In the beginning God created ... it was good." Those are not the words of this preacher. They are not the words of the priests in Babylon who compiled them. That's Word from God. And perhaps we need to recognize that we just never heard God before in those words. So be it!

1. James Rachels, *Created From Animals: The Moral Implications of Darwinism* (Oxford: Oxford University Press, 1990).

2. See Reinhold Niebuhr, *The Self and The Dramas of History* (New York: Charles Scribner's Sons, 1955), especially pp. 3-5.

3. Thanks to Charles Carter, Forest Hills Presbyterian Church, High Point, North Carolina, for calling my attention to this story told by James Harnish in an article, "What Will You Do With King Jesus?"

Creation

Exodus 2:23-25
Luke 12:56

An issue very much in the news in recent years is the repair of America's bridges. It seems that many of our country's bridges are in disrepair and need to be upgraded. The issue is a lively one as Congress wrestles with the repair of these numerous spans which connect one bank with another bank in our country.

I think of the need for effective bridges when I think of where we stand each day, wanting to effect a tie between today's world and the world of ancient Bethlehem in order to understand our human condition. The shore of America in our technological society seems far removed from the Bethlehem of Christ's birth. And the bridge of our non-scientific Bible-thumping childhood seems to be in permanent disrepair. Consider the opposites over which we and our children have to traverse.

We stand on the banks of a scientific culture. We live in a world of computerized technology. Santa Claus leaves under trees various assortments of software, cellular telephones, and compact disks. On Christmas day as church bells ring and Luke's account of the birth of Christ is read, many children will be trying to download their presents and get on the Internet to talk with friends. And when that lengthy day has passed, they will cuddle up in bed not with a pocket version of the New Testament, but with a remote control for their television or CD player. Even we adults wonder at the ever-increasing possibility that one day the heart which beats in our body will have been made in Japan. That's the shore on which we stand, my friends. In some ways we probe deeper, fly higher, and understand more than any generation before us.

And we look across an ever-increasing chasm to a distant shore. On that distant shore we see the world of the Bible, with its primitive understandings of science which seem so strangely out of place to our consciousness. We witness people who speak of water being

22

changed to wine; a stick that becomes a serpent; and wise men, lonely figures against the eternal sand motivated by some impulse they could but dimly understand, journeying day after day, month after month, following a star to a stable. These people believe that somehow the child they found was linked with God. They believe that this child grew up to become a man who preached love and that when he died his spirit slipped out of this earth into something greater than the body which held it.

So here we stand, between two seemingly irreconcilable shores. We see the scriptural accounts of the creation, the exodus, and the birth of Jesus. But we see those accounts from the vantage point of a culture that is instinctively scientific, mistrustful, and cautious.

Some people tell us there is no bridge we can build between our generation and ancient Bethlehem; we must choose one of the two shores and stay there. These people stand in the biblical accounts, found schools and churches where the Bible is taken literally as a science book, and argue that we should disregard evolution, and the twenty-first century.

Still others tell us we must stand in the scientific world and throw out the biblical accounts as mere products of the active human imagination in pre-scientific, superstitious cultures. "The Bible," they say, "is outmoded for our times and can't stand up to the evidence."

So we stand and look at the two apparently distant shores and say, "I want to find out how I got here and who I am before I die." *Can we build a bridge between modern society and ancient Bethlehem that answers the primal cry for understanding in terms that will make sense to our children and ourselves?* Can we reconcile the cherished notion of a Savior with the realties of modern science?

That seems to me to be a need our faith ought to be able to satisfy if our hope is to be well-founded. If the reasons behind the birth of Jesus as the Son of God cannot stand the tests of scientific discovery and intellectual inquiry, few people, in my opinion, should even believe in God. If God does not make sense in our time, God will not make sense at all. If our hopes are not based in some scientific possibility, they are not hopes. They are *illusions*. We have no less an authority on this than Jesus himself. Jesus said the *truth*, not superstition, would make us free. He had little patience with those who could not discern the presence of God in their own times. You, hypocrites," he asserted, "you can understand the weather and science ... how is it you do not discern this time?" (Luke 12:56).

Consequently, I believe Jesus demands that I build a bridge for my children and myself between the scientific and the biblical world-views, in order to bring together ancient Bethlehem and modern America. How can a Christian believe in a scientific creation?

Scientists tell us our universe had a birth fifteen or so billion years ago in what they call a "black hole." Before that, there was nothing. How our universe came out of a black hole is a mystery. We think we know that a fireball came out of an exploding black hole fifteen billion years ago. When the fireball cooled down, stars and our sun were formed. Finally, the dense nova stars blew up and formed our solar system. It took billions of years and incredible vastness of space. The question is obvious: why did it take so long and why is the universe so large? The only way to answer that is to say that *human life had to be the ultimate purpose of creation*. If, fifteen billion years ago, human beings were the idea in mind when the black hole exploded, the universe would have to be this old and this large. A younger and smaller universe could not have created human life. The universe would have to be at *least* nine billion years old. Five billion years would be necessary just to produce DNA and RNA codes. Another four billion years of ever-increasing complex evolution would be necessary to get a man and a woman. The human being is the most complex organism that has appeared so far. Scientific discoveries of the incomprehensible age and vastness of the universe cause us to rejoice. It had to be this old and this large if human life were the purpose for its creation.[1]

Consider also when the fireball began to be our universe, three constants were built into the process. Three items were constant. The speed with which light travels is always 186,000 miles per second. That is a given in our universe. Secondly, the electrical charge of an electron is always constant.

24

Finally, there is a unit called h cross (h) by scientists. An electron as it rotates always jumps by that unit. Its angular momentum always *jumps* by h. Now those three constants blew out of that black hole. Scientists have devised a formula using those three constants (E^2/hc) and have come up with the stable figure 137.06 for our universe. They have played with that figure greatly. Suppose the speed of light were 185,000 feet per second? Suppose the unit of angular momentum were just a little different? If we had 136 or 137.05 or any other figure instead of 137.06, our universe could not have produced human life.

When our universe was created, somebody or something set those constants so human life could eventually be created. You can't explain it any other way. Humanity was the purpose for our universe.

The scientists phrased it this way: "Humankind was created in the image of God. Humankind is more than the fortuitous combination of atoms." C. S. Lewis, in *Christian Reflections*, says it like this:

> There are no ordinary people. You have never talked to a mere mortal ... It is immortals whom we joke with, marry, snub, and exploit ... Next to the Blessed Sacrament itself, your neighbor is the holiest object presented to your senses.[2]

The one born in ancient Bethlehem told us that the greatest thing in life is to love God with all our being and love our neighbor as we love ourselves. The essential thrust of Jesus' ministry was the *radical concept that the neighbor is holy*, because the human personality is the purpose for creation.

That radical concept, to my mind, is our bridge with ancient Bethlehem.

I once knew a man who stood by his daughter through two difficult marriages and a five-year bout with drugs. Even through some of the worst human conditions I have ever been exposed to, this man kept hanging in there, performing one incredible act of love and kindness after another. When she had attained stability, someone asked him what strength he had drawn on. He said, "I helped give her life and had invested 21 years in her. I just wasn't going to let her kill herself without at least a glimpse of some goodness."

The author of the scenario of cosmic evolution, the one who spent five billion years just producing DNA and RNA codes, the one who set the speed of light, the quantum of angular momentum and the electrical charge of an electron — *the one who had expended so much time and energy getting us to life — was not willing to let the summation of creation destroy itself without at least a glimpse of its holiness*. Jesus Christ was born to enable a fallible struggling creation to gain a glimpse of its creator. Even when this creation rejected that glimpse and nailed it to a cross, God in the death event continued to enable the world to have a peek at its holiness.

I am afraid our world has a tendency to reverse the issue. The issue is not trying to understand the angels, the accounts of miracles, and the scene in ancient Bethlehem in terms that make sense scientifically. The issue is this: we cannot understand science, the age and vastness of the universe, and the three constants of existence without ancient Bethlehem. Without understanding humankind as the intended purpose for creation, our world just doesn't make sense.

What a profound ramification that is for the way we should treat life. It means *a woman is holy*. A woman is more than the sum of her childbearings and miscarriages. She is more than years and years of standing at the sink developing popped veins as the symbol of weary worlds of work. A woman is holy. She is more than the source of a second income or a professional who hammers out a career or a single person living contentedly in singleness. *A woman is holy.*

It means a *man is holy*. A man is more than a once-young person who has a particular job and whose original physique has waned into flabbiness or grayness.

It means a poor person is more than a poor person. A poor person is holy. It means that a diseased and infirmed person is more than one whose best years are spent. *A person is holy.*

From the shepherds, to the lepers, to the rich and haughty, to the demonic, to the fishermen, to the tax collectors, to the publicans, to the thief on the cross, to the technicians, to the nuclear scientists, to the businesspeople, to the homemakers, to the children playing with their computers, *the message comes cascading over the tumults of time — God is with us.*

The wisest people of the world are not those who have delved into the great libraries of the world; nor are they those who have sat at the feet of the great teachers. *The wisest people in the world are those who can look to ancient Bethlehem and catch a glimpse of its holiness.* That glimpse can not only fire our eternal hopes, but when coupled with the crucifixion and resurrection, it can enable us to live by faith in a world of chance.

---

1. Information gained through a visit to the Atomic Energy Commission facility at Oak Ridge, Tennessee, 1980.

2. C. S. Lewis, *Christian Reflections* (Grand Rapids: Eerdsman, 1967), edited by Walter Hooper, p. X. The quote is from Lewis' sermon, "The Weight of Glory."

The Personal Touch

Exodus 33:13-23
John 10

Each year certain congratulatory letters arrive in our home. One of these letters begins like this: "Congratulations, you have been recommended for biographical and pictoral inclusion in a volume of the *International Who's Who*. Please send a small paragraph for publication when you return your completed questionnaire." The computer-written form letter is accompanied by another letter notifying me that for "only" $150.00 (U.S.) I can obtain a royal edition of the book and read the small paragraph about myself. A cheaper paperback copy is available for "only" $50.00 (U.S). Having learned my lesson two years ago, I immediately dispose of such letters. You see, a few years ago I kept receiving a questionnaire every few months from a Who's Who publication that I did not wish to respond to. I kept throwing the inquiries in the trash can. Then, after some months had passed, I noticed the correspondence had ceased. I casually mentioned to my secretary at the time that I was delighted we were no longer receiving that "junk mail." "Oh, yes," she remarked, "I grew tired of handling that material, so one day about six months ago, I completed the form for you. I simply fabricated some data, in order to keep them from soliciting us."

Well, in panic, I ran to the telephone and started calling my family. Alas, I was too late. My father had already purchased the $50.00 paperback. My aunt had also sent in her check. And even my wife's parents were contemplating a favorable response to the smashing news from the company.

In the United States local newspapers have had to run editorials warning high school students and their parents about such enterprises. One venture, *Who's Who Among High School Honor Students*, has made millions of dollars by simply deeming any student who responds to their questionnaire an "honor" student.

The success of such offers points to a salient fact in our world: regardless of our position or influence in life, at the basic level of existence, *all of us cry out for recognition*. It is a natural craving of the human heart to want to amount to something in the eyes of the world. We want to have the tap of recognition on our shoulders. We want the world to know that we are more than the sum total of our x-rays, blood tests, and urinalyses. We want the world to know that we are more than the sum total of our work and child bearing and rearing. We want a little feeling of being touched or tapped or set apart or written about by somebody or some group that recognizes and affirms our importance.

In our day of computers and identification numbers set within the sprawling mass of big business, big government, and international communication, we are in some ways more isolated from meaningful human contact than any generation before us. Chores are no longer social events. Most of us do not buy commodities, food, and services from personal friends. And the product of our increased mobility has been a mixture of freedom and uprootedness. The average adult now moves fourteen times in his or her lifetime. Consequently, never have there been so many books on the market dealing with intimacy and loneliness. We shout the loudest where we hurt the most.

In the midst of such a world, it behooves us to go back to the record of the human discovery of the God we worship. In the 33rd chapter of Exodus, Moses is worried and goes before God. The people in his charge have just constructed a golden calf. They have sinned. And Moses doesn't know what's going to happen. Maybe God will leave them forever. Or, even worse, God might destroy the whole lot of them. So Moses seeks some assurance that God will stay with the people in spite of their foolishness. In response to the request, God gives this earth-shaking reply, "Moses, *I know you by name*."

In that simple sentence comes a new concept of God. A promise was made that the people of God would have a *personal* relationship with God. "I know you by your name." In an antiquarian society of dreams, visions, demons, and awesome terror came a powerful new message. God is not detached from and uninterested in his creation. God can make God's self small enough to know God's children by name.

A particular insight into the personal aspect of God's nature was brought to us by Jesus Christ. Most of Jesus' teachings focused on the availability of a *personal*, caring God for each and every one of us. To be without the personal touch, whether by physical illness such as the lepers, by accident like a lost coin or a lost sheep, by willful action such as the Prodigal Son, or by anonymity such as the woman reaching for the garment, was the worst fate Jesus imagined for anyone.

A gentleman by the name of Fynn captured the essence of Moses' discovery and Jesus' teaching. He wrote a book called *Mister God, This Is Anna*. Anna was a special little five-year-old girl whom Fynn had met. She possessed the incisive idea that Mister God, as she called him, did not at all mind making himself small. Her words were profound: "People who think that Mister God is very, very big make a big mistake. Mister God can be any size he wants to be." To be certain, my friends, we make a mistake if we assume that God is always to be found in size and power. God has throughout human history evidenced the concern and the love to become very small and personal. God is a God who lives at our elbow and knows our name.

In this world of much loneliness and despair through feelings of lack of importance, there is a message for us. In a capsule, Jesus' message is that God's *nature is to love each of us as if there were but one of us to love*. We are all included in God's *Who's Who*. No one is left out.

We constantly concern ourselves a lot about "what we believe about God." Of equal importance is what God believes about us. God knows our name. Most people value Christ for his ethics, or his sacrificial death on the cross, or his extension of hope for eternal life through his resurrection. These emphases, of course, are of unquestionable importance. But it is also true that *no one has come to God as Father except in Christ*. Nowhere in Islam or Buddhism, Hinduism or Marxism do we find affirmed the ultimacy of the personal relationship of humans with God.

God indeed knows our name and prepares a personal place for each of us to live eternally with God. John's Gospel quotes Jesus as saying, "I am the good shepherd; *I know my own sheep and they know me ...*"(10:14).

God as our loving shepherd is one of the key concepts of the Bible. An incredible amount of personal love for sheep goes into being a good shepherd. I once went to the home of a friend who owns some sheep to take a look at what's involved in being a shepherd. It's amazing how close and personal a relationship is involved in caring for sheep. Sheep are so docile they will not drink from swift running water. You can place sheep in a field near a roaring stream and they will die of thirst. They will let the life-giving water flow past them and never touch it, out of their fear. In such cases the shepherd must either build a still-water pool or hand-carry water to them in pans or bowls. If that were not incredible enough, consider this: a mother sheep will walk away from her babies and not feed them. The shepherd has to pick up the baby and hand-carry it to the mother for it to eat. I watched a young lamb, born that morning, stand bleating for food while the mother stood a few feet away looking placidly at something else. The little lamb would have starved to death if it had had to depend on the mother to move over a few feet. Finally, sheep are so docile that they don't even put up resistance when another animal attacks them. A dog can destroy an entire herd and the sheep won't even run.

For me, that backdrop is far more than the lifting of an agrarian motif from the past to the present. It is life as we know it. It is the human condition. We sit in a pasture called earth with all the options available for living that anyone could ask for. Through the center of our existence runs a life-giving resource. But left on our own, running with our insecurities and fears, we would sit down and die of thirst only inches from real nourishment. So God, the good shepherd, brings the drink to us in a form that is more acceptable to us, a human being of peace and calmness, the Christ.

Likewise we stand in a world of riches, where we have so much to offer one another and so many resources of food, clothing, kindness, and love to offer those less fortunate than we. Those countless folk stand only a few feet from us, bleating their heads off for a little of the life-giving resources we possess. If they had to depend on the natural goodness of our hearts to move us over a few feet to them, they would surely starve to death. So God says, "I will send you a shepherd to teach you that when these bleating lambs are carried to you, you'll know that when you feed the least of them you are really doing it unto me."

Similarly, we are left like sheep in the midst of a world of raging dogs. When the snarling teeth of greed, ugliness, pettiness, prejudice and warped religious leaders come running up to us, we often find it easier to offer no resistance than to fight. Any of these mad dogs of selfishness can clean us out and often we find our entire herd of fellow humans just standing there waiting with us for the ruin. Again, the good shepherd comes to our aid and puts up a fence called the "church." Inside this protective device we are supposed to find at the least a place to gather for a brief time each week, somewhat removed from the snarling hounds of a secular world.

The purpose of much of our New Testament is to tell the good news about this place where loving intimacy and personal relationships can develop between people. We are a Kingdom community, a place where every name is known by the good shepherd and every person is held equally precious. That's a strong affirmation to carry into life's trenches, isn't it? Affirmation carries responsibility. We who are affirmed must carry the personal and caring touch to the desperate, hungry people who have been smitten by the world's greed and prejudice. To Simon Peter, Jesus posed the question, "Do you love me?" Then he offered the advice, "Well, if you love me, then feed my sheep."

What an affirming glimpse you and I have received into the personal love God has for us. From Moses through Christ it has shivered its way over five thousand years of human history. I thought of it most recently in hearing some events that transpired in a university city.[1]

A certain college was observing Visitors' Day and the parents were invited to stay on the campus for some weekend activities. The local merchants were vying for the anticipated increase in business. A favorite watering hole among the students there was Larry's Tavern. That popular establishment also served a marvelous Sunday brunch. So two days before Visitors' Day, a huge advertisement appeared in the local paper. Its headline read: "Bring your parents to Larry's Tavern for Sunday brunch." At the bottom of the ad were these words: "P.S., I'll pretend I don't know you. Signed Larry."

The very next day, another huge ad appeared in the same paper. It was headlined: "Bring your parents to the college chapel for worship tomorrow." At the bottom of the ad were these words: "P.S., I'll pretend I know you very well. Signed, the Chaplain."

To the prodigal sons and daughters, the lepers, the demoniacs, the disciples, the rich young rulers, the ill-spirited, and to each of us comes an advertisement which still thunders its way across the gaps of recorded time: "Come to me all of you who are heavy laden and I will give you rest."

"P.S., I don't have to pretend I know you, for I know you by name. Signed, God."

This, too, is a part of our origin as a human being.

---

1. I am grateful to my friend, Sydney Hall, former Chaplain of Hampden-Sydney College, Virginia, for sharing this story with me.

Power

2 Corinthians 5:16-17
John 19:19-30

For generations many people have told us that the driving force behind us human beings is the will to power. Power is everything. In fact, God has often been viewed as one who gives power to God's special people. Ancient people prayed for God to give them power over the antelope and the buffalo, whose pictures they drew on the walls of caves. The ancient mariners prayed to Proteus for power over the sea. In our day and time, money is power. So we have prayed for that power and tried to help God along by having power lunches, dressing for success, and majoring in business. From age to age the perspective is the same: God is powerful and certainly God can help us get some power, as well. Is this not our true human condition?

You learn much about life and power from living in a college dormitory. I've always had a special place in my heart for resident assistants, those students who are paid to help manage a floor in a dormitory. Blessed are the peacemakers. I once served as a dormitory manager in Harvard University. It would have been an easy job, except for a student named Dan. Dan was a little scrawny guy with a long red beard. But he made up for his small frame with his oversized mouth.

Dan's apparent goal in life was to become the world's biggest pest. He was an expert in irritation. When Dan found a chapter he needed to read in a library book, he'd just tear it out of the book, fold it up, stick it in his pocket, and walk out of the library with it.

Dan's most annoying trait was late-night use of the pay telephone in our hallway. His girlfriend lived in California. Several nights a week, around 1:00 a.m., he would pile umpteen quarters and dimes into the phone and converse with her in a loud voice.

Most everyone would pour into the hallway, yelling at me to make Dan get off the phone and give them a chance to sleep. Each time Dan would look up at me and say, quite boldly, "You don't have the power to tell me when to use the phone. Only the telephone company has the power to tell me not to use their phone."

One night while Dan was chattering away with his girlfriend and laying that "You don't have the power" speech on me, Bob walked out of his room. Bob had been an All-American tackle in football at the University of Michigan. He weighed 260 pounds. Without saying a word, Bob ran ten or fifteen feet toward the phone, aimed his shoulder, and knocked the phone completely off the wall. Wires whipped everywhere. One of them caught Dan under his armpit, drew blood and knocked him to the floor. Bob looked down at Dan and said, "Now, Dan, *that's power!*"

Believe it or not, at times that's exactly the way some humans have viewed God's use of power. The nation Israel at one point viewed God as a deity who would take all he could stomach of human nature, let Israel's enemies push her almost to the brink, and then knock everything off the wall and start over. At other times God would take all the irritation he could handle from Israel herself. Then he would use another nation to knock Israel off the wall. Power! Certainly power is the ability to effect a change forcefully.

One of the critical issues in the ministry of Jesus Christ was this issue of power. He contended that most of us do not understand the way God uses power. We often ask, "Why does this powerful God allow so much evil in the world?" Why doesn't this God do things differently? While all those Jews and Christians were praying, why didn't God strike down Hitler much sooner?

I would have.

If I had all that power, I would have removed Stalin much earlier. I would have ended slavery much sooner and without a civil war. I would show people how to prevent cancer. If I were all-powerful I wouldn't just hear the prayers of people who became rich rather quickly, or scored the winning touchdown.

I would have run Marcos out of the Philippines years before he left and eliminated Qaddafi long ago. Now that would be power. Or would it?

Jesus Christ maintained that it takes far less real power to act like that than to use power the way God actually exercises power.

Jesus said, "God is love." God bears our griefs and carries our sorrows: not just at Calvary but all the time. That is certainly a sobering thought. It means that God's power is love and not might. It also means that *God's power is directed toward a purpose: the whole world coming to understand that love is greater than force.* As such, if love is God's goal, God cannot rush to God's end by using the shortest possible means. For example, a teacher could have a great class if he or she simply excluded all the lazy, tiresome, and below average students. If you threw out all the non-A students, you'd have a rather exclusive and wonderful class. I've known some teachers who use their power in that manner. The very first class they throw out a mile-a-minute lecture and a reading list that would terrify all but the best students. It just knocks all the below-average students right off the wall. They drop the course and all that's left are good students. It's quite a power play. You can make certain your teaching is evaluated only by good students.

But if your purpose is to reach all the students in your class, it's quite another matter. If your purpose is to educate all the students, you can't use power that way.

If God must operate with our world in a similar manner, you and I must ask: Well, then, what power comes to me as a human being when I pray to God? What does prayer do for me? What power can I claim?

Prayer gives us the power of an identity that goes back farther than our own life and extends beyond our death. It is amazing how human beings can lose their identity. To forget who you are is called amnesia. A spiritual amnesia seems built into our human condition.

I'll never forget the time Big Al Geddie forgot who he was. Big Al was from Mount Olive, North Carolina. He was the biggest athlete recruited in my class at Furman University. Since our colors were purple and white, we had purple helmets with a big white stripe down them. That is, everybody but Big Al. Big Al's head was so big he could not wear one of our helmets. The helmet company had to make one especially for Al, and it was white. Big Al looked funny out there in his white helmet.

One day, Big Al did not come to class. Then, for a whole week, no one saw him. Nothing in Big Al's room was out of order. His bed was made and his clothes were all there, even his wallet. But no one knew where Big Al was — no one in Greenville knew and no one in Mount Olive, North Carolina, knew. Big Al was lost. Police throughout the South searched for Big Al. Three weeks later Big Al was found. The Atlanta police found him walking around the streets of Atlanta. Big Al didn't know who he was. He had amnesia. Nobody, least of all Big Al, who did not know he was Big Al, knew how he got there or where he stayed or how he ate. They took Big Al back to Mount Olive and reintroduced him to his family. They said, "Big Al, meet your mother. Big Al, this is your daddy. Big Al, this is where you came from." Al just looked at them and said, "I don't know you."

Well, after a year, Big Al's memory finally returned. He remembered who he was and came back to finish college. Big Al didn't forget who he was anymore and eventually graduated.

It must be a horrible thing to forget who you are. Fred Craddock believes that we humans have a residue of our memory of the Garden of Eden. We have a faint reminiscence of a closeness to God. We are all born, created, with this faint memory in our minds. Consequently anyone who cannot attach himself or herself to a memory that stretches back before his or her birth is in real trouble. In essence, prayer gives us the power to tie ourselves to a life that precedes our birth and extends beyond our death. We are enrolled in a story that is beyond our personal story.

The roots of who we are lie with the ancient Jews. From them came the Christ. You and I were in Egypt. We were with Abraham. We were in Jerusalem. We saw the star in the east.

If we do not absorb all that into our awareness, our identity is not complete. We are left orphaned in our space and time. We become victims of amnesia.

Spiritual amnesia can strike anyone. It is amazing how quickly we human beings can forget we are children of God and should live by love instead of force. I've forgotten that at times in my life and had to be reintroduced to my heritage.

The president of a bank can forget who he is. The president of a college or dean of a college can forget who he or she really is. Students can come to college and forget who they are. It happens all the time. We get orphaned without memory of our heritage.

I've seen some horrible cases of amnesia. A mother raised her child among the rats in a Houston, Texas, ghetto. There were rats coming in and out of the room where they slept and ate. The mother held two jobs — by day she was a teacher's aide; at night she worked in a laundry, folding clothes. With every dollar not needed for the bare necessities, she purchased books for her son. This kid made a perfect score on the SAT — 1600. He went to the University of Texas and made all A's, a 4.0 GPA. Every major graduate school offered him a full scholarship. Yale wanted him. Harvard wanted him. Stanford wanted him. Finally my university sent me and our director of minority recruiting to interview this phenomenon. "Offer him a full scholarship," we were told. "Everybody else has."

We met with him in the lobby of a hotel in Austin, Texas. He began the interview by discounting completely his childhood, dumping on the very environment that had raised him. He let it be known in no uncertain terms that he was going to grab it all. He was going to become a millionaire.

In four years of college life he had not been back to see his mother even once. "I'm beyond that," he said. "We don't have anything in common, intellectually or socially."

We asked him if he'd gone to church or the university chapel or belonged to any service organizations there at UT. "Oh, I'm way beyond that, too," he asserted. "I'm long past that simplistic emotional stuff. That pie-in-the-sky by and by stuff is for poor and unintelligent people."

Rather sadly the recruiter said, "Son, we don't need to offer you a scholarship. We don't want you. Go somewhere else. You don't even know who you are. Your memory is too short if you have one at all. It would be a waste of the school's money to educate you. This suffering, hurting world isn't going to be helped by one more selfish millionaire."

The boy jumped up and angrily spit the words into the face of the recruiter like hot rivets being pounded into a steel girder: "That's okay, one day I'll have the power to bury sentimental saps like you."

I had a strange sense of *deja vu* as he walked angrily away from us. In terms of knowing who he was, his amnesia was as great as was Big Al Geddie's when he aimlessly walked the streets of Atlanta. He was paralyzed by a memory that reached back no farther than his own current life.

The disciples went to Jesus one day and asked, "Teach us to pray. It seems to give you a power we don't have." It was one of the few things they ever asked Jesus. And Jesus told them. "When you pray, say, 'Our Father who art in heaven ...' " or "our parent" and the meaning would be the same. Our father — father of those before our birth and father of those beyond our death. Our father. Our parent. The power of prayer enables us to be placed within a human stream of existence that is eternal. It is identity-forming. It gives us the power to be connected *to an identity that goes back farther than our own life and extends beyond our death.*

Can there be any greater power, any more lasting security? The New Testament clearly crystallizes this new identity of ours. Jesus is called the "angel of the bottomless pit" (Revelation 9:11) — King of all kings; the Lord of all lords; the name that is before and beyond every name. As they moved and breathed, loved and served, Peter and John were asked by the rulers this question: "By what power or by what name do you do this?" In defense, Peter responded, "There is no other name under heaven given among humanity by which we must be saved" (Acts 4:7, 12).

With an identity that began before his own birth and extended beyond his own death, Paul could sweep away every lingering doubt in the believer's mind as to God's power with his series of paired opposites:

neither death	nor life
nor angels	nor powers
nor things present	nor things to come
neither powers from on high	nor powers from below

<pre>
        nor height   nor depth
               nor any other creature
</pre>
shall ever be able to separate us from the love of God.

This power is built into our human condition from the very beginning. It is a part of our created possibility from birth.

Pain And Promise

Hosea 2:14-20

One of the amazing claims of the Judaeo-Christian heritage is that God takes on the attributes of humans. God's essence is unknown, but the Scriptures claim that God's actions are known. God experiences what humans experience. In the Old Testament God *walks* in the Garden of Eden. God *closes* the door of the ark. God *smells* the fragrance of sacrificed animals. God *chases* Moses in the wilderness.

In like manner Hosea describes God as a wronged husband who seeks to recover his wife who has gone chasing after other lovers. Hosea's own marriage to Gomer is a prophetic symbol of the pain and promise in the heart of God in the face of Israel's faithlessness. Like a brokenhearted husband, God woos back God's bride.

Like an eager and joyous young groom, God had married Israel in the wilderness. The relationship was pure and uncomplicated. Israel had relied solely on her God, and God had figuratively made love to Israel in that time of few, if any, competitors for God's affections. But, alas, like a faithless spouse, Israel became a wayward people, leading to the pain of a broken relationship and subsequent divorce.

Hosea begins with a long poem of divorce in which the husband, Yahweh, casts out the fickle spouse. With the image of God as a pained, brokenhearted husband as a backdrop, Scripture describes Hosea's vision of a resumed marriage between God and God's people. Hosea paints a picture of God's incredible desire to live with this wayward partner.

Perhaps hundreds of sermons are preached each week in our nation on the topic of Hosea and his relationship with Gomer. Unfortunately, the text easily opens itself up to the preacher's whim, allowing the preacher to define as sin whatever in his/her congregation or civilization raises the particular hackles of the moment.

41

To understand truly this Scripture as a word from God to us about the human condition today, we must cling to history. This word from God through Hosea bears a pain and a promise unlike any other. Hosea is the only prophet who preached to the Northern Kingdom of Israel who was actually born and brought up there. There is no greater pain and promise than preaching to your own people about suffering and hope. To be certain, outside intervention is often necessary to jog a recalcitrant people into action. But it is also less risky and much less intense to deal with other people. We can always tell other people how *they* should respond to *their* children and *their* domestic problems much more easily than we can gain a hearing in our *own* household.

The same is true for the church. The story is told of a preacher in Vermont who was running into some difficulty with his congregation over the strident nature of his sermons. He had lambasted the lack of racial diversity in the town, the high property taxes, the insensitivity of the merchants, and the lack of caring present in family relationships. This was too much, so an *ad hoc* committee was quickly assembled to meet with the young man to "set him straight." The gathering took place in the church parlor right after worship. The chair began, "Preacher, we are a little worried about the effect your preaching is having on the congregation. When you rail against materialism, the bankers and the merchants find that hard to take. And when you talk against the television preachers pursuing religion for profit, a lot of our folks send money to those people. And when you start talking about family values, why, a lot of our people are busy and commute to Boston and can't just communicate with their children like you envision. And, heck, you make us feel bad about being white and wealthy. Can't you find something else to preach about?"

Totally exasperated, the preacher asked: "Well, what do you people suggest I preach about?"

From the back of the room came a clear voice: "Why don't you preach about the communists?"

"But we don't have any communists in our town, in Vermont," he answered.

"Exactly. Preach about them!"

42

Hosea has avoided that easy transference. Not only is he speaking to his own people, but his oracles elaborate the theme of the relations between Israel and Yahweh in terms of those between Hosea and his wandering spouse. Hosea's acutely personal experience is used to illumine a conception of a spouse's forgiveness as indicative of Yahweh's ability to reconstitute the entire people of God.

One of the amazing features in the book of Hosea is the notion that words, even The Word, are not enough to turn pain into promise. As Hosea's life unfolds, the prophet's obedience is contrasted with Gomer's disobedience. His faith is shown over and against Gomer's unfaith.

The Old Testament story in all its concrete reality is not removed from our world of harlotry with other gods of wood, stone, and metal, our world of the pursuit of religion for profit, and the political intrigues which consume our national leaders. We must cling to history in order to see specifically that the Old Testament story of Hosea ends at a table surrounded by thirteen men, in an upper room, with one of them holding a cup and saying, "This is the new covenant." The story also ends with some women running from tomb to tomb and telling disbelieving disciples, "He is risen."[1]

Hosea's vision of God as an actor, who in reality turns "not my people" into "my people" again, began to wane in *importance* after his day. After the fall of both kingdoms and the deportation of Judah to Babylon for exile, the majestic qualities of God began to fuel the imaginations of suffering people. Israel began to place her trust in priests who stressed the unapproachable nature of God. They stressed the holiness of God rather than the activistic, approachable nature of God. They stressed dreams, temples, and angelic visions. In the priestly writings God was spoken of as "holy" or "separate" 161 times! One had to go through a professional priest to experience God, much as one today must use a lawyer to go to court or a pharmacist to secure prescription drugs.

Have you noticed our generation's recent infatuation with angels? If you go to the religion section of major bookstores you'll find that angels are making a big comeback in the world of the unapproachable television-priests. The spoken word of the sound and stage studio has become the new temple beamed into your living room each day. And satellite religion has enabled us to become farther removed from the point of origin of the word that comes through to us. We take our faith over the cable from people we most likely will never see in person. When we cling to history we see that this is not a new phenomenon. Just as Hosea challenged the remoteness of God from God's people, so did Jesus undo the remoteness of his generation.

After long centuries of having fallen prey to an overemphasis on angelic visions and unapproachable holiness, God's humanity, indeed, God's remarriage to the world, was brought back into focus in the life of Christ. The word became flesh, just as it had when Hosea's life served as the vehicle. The God of Jesus Christ walked beside humans, listened to prayers, knew the number of hairs on human heads, welcomed little children to his lap and prodigal children to the kingdom, and even referred to himself as the bridegroom come to remarry the *world*.

These actions of God in Christ, like God in the symbol of Hosea's marriage, are not just for individuals. So often we become duped into thinking of sin as an individual phenomenon. But the Bible, from Hosea through Jesus, doesn't always make a sharp distinction between the individual and society. We tend to sin as a group. We tend to be "not my people" as much as we are "not my person."

Hosea is right. God divorces God's people. We live on an earth where, with all its abundance, over twenty million people die of starvation each year. Over twelve million of those are children under the age of five. In addition to the 30,000 children who starve to death each day are those whom hunger does not kill. Since the brain accomplishes eighty percent of its growth in the first three years of a child's life, no amount of food *later* in life can repair the damage.

What if you were God and your spouse (our world) was doing that to your children? What if your rich spouse, the United States, whom you'd loved in a special way, was spending $24 million an hour on defense? Wouldn't you have a great pain in your heart and want a divorce?

Wouldn't you say "Amen" to that judgment on Golgotha where God says decisively, "You are *not* my people," in light of Jesus Christ illuminating our destructive, rejective ways? Hold to history, then and now, and see the pain in the heart of God.

But see also the utter foolishness and passion of God, from Hosea to Christ to the present, in the reversal of the prophecies of doom. Yahweh forgives, Christ redeems, not just the individual, but the world God is married to. The people of God are reconstituted. That's the good news of Christ. We have received mercy. The spouse still stands by us and wants us back. We cannot know the promise of Jesus Christ apart from the proclamation of the Old Testament. We cannot know the magnitude of the reconciliation without an awareness of the divorce.

All of us are disobedient, orphaned children who have rejected our marriage vows to God and are sure to die. The Fall is a part of our human condition. And yet — and yet! Like Gomer and ancient Israel and first century Palestine, it is not we who get what we deserve. Christ woos us with love and kindness. Like an eager lover he turns our duty into a joyful affair. Consequently no message of creation can stand alone without an understanding of some of the depths of our shattered lives and need for God's grace.

---

1. See Elizabeth Achtemeier, *The Old Testament and the Proclamation of the Gospel* (Philadelphia: Westminster, 1973), for fuller treatment.

II. FALL

The Search For Self-Esteem

Mark 4:1-20

Can you remember the first time your *actual* self, with your abilities and circumstances, did not measure up to your *ideal* picture of yourself? I can. When I was a child the church to which my family belonged held a Christmas pageant every year. All the choirs sang and certain members of the oldest children's choir provided a live nativity scene. The highlight of the year for those children in the choir came when they voted on who would play Mary and Joseph. Anyone could play the wise men. And the director had to beg children to play the shepherds. But Mary and Joseph, now they were the prizes. Since I held the dubious distinction of most hyperactive choir member and grandest fraternizer, I assumed the voting to be a mere formality. Obviously I would play Joseph and my self-perceived girlfriend, Susan, would play Mary. I even had in mind which bathrobe I would wear and which towel I would drape over my head.

But a strange thing happened. Susan was, indeed, elected to play Mary. But after a run-off, a new boy in town was elected to play Joseph. It was the first time I *remember* having experienced a loss of self-esteem. I felt as if something deep inside of me had died. And in a way it had.

Obviously that was not the last election I ever lost. And it certainly was not the last time I lost my self-esteem. You see, self-esteem is the meshing of our actual selves with our desired selves. *When our actual self does not measure up to our ideal picture of ourselves, we have a hard time accepting ourselves as we really are.*

Our actual self is then perceived as less worthy than our imagined self. How do we handle ourselves when we find an impassable chasm between our actual self and our desired self?

It's a tough question because all of us face the gulf between actual and desired self or between actual circumstances and behavior

49

and imagined circumstances and behavior. This imperfection is part of our *fallen* nature. If we were created in the image of God, we are certainly no longer that way. Whether in the Garden of Eden or recently acquired, such innocence has long since fallen from us.

Homemakers constantly face the tension between *actual self* and *imagined self* as they raise children and lose themselves in preparing meal after meal and doing thousands of washloads of clothes. The actual behavior of a child can conflict with our imaged behavior of a child. And a person in business, stitching time and life together in the performance of tasks, faces conditions ripe for touching off the civil war between actual self and desired self. This war within us is not always an obvious war. Sometimes it becomes buried deep inside our psyche where it gnaws away at our personality for a lifetime. In our fallen condition we can become people of despair.

Think with me for a moment. *How do you develop love for a child?* When the child is in the mother's womb, the parents engage in grandiose expectations. Every child is, to a degree, expected to be something that it cannot possibly be. Unconsciously we expect our children to be beautiful, healthy, talented, well-mannered, loving, intelligent, and athletic. Is not love the giving up of the unrealistic expectations, the myth of perfection, which cannot possibly be accomplished by the child in favor of constant encouragement and affirmation of the child's *actual* self? It's the difference between loving an actual person and loving a projection of an ideal. The story of the fall of humankind in the garden of Eden depicts a God whose children pushed the limits and fell from an ideal relationship. Yet the story becomes one of love, not abandonment, as God's love continues to be present.

The true test of life is a person's ability to change his projected picture of himself and other fallen beings in the world. The human condition requires us to go on and make a creditable and serviceable use of the self we really have. To make the choice between healthy ambitions and unrealistic demands for perfection is to accept the human condition and the possibilities God gave us from the very beginning of time.

Jesus the Christ encouraged us to have self-esteem. "Love your neighbor as you love yourself" were his words. Not loving your real self or being out of touch with yourself can make you sick. Worth comes from within a person, not from the outside.

Sometimes something drastic happens to bring us back to our actual selves: an accident; an illness; the loss of a job; a divorce; a failure in business or school; an insight gained through prayer or religious experience; a sense of desperation like that felt by the prodigal son when he finally "came to himself" and decided to go home. *In a sense Jesus' whole ministry was an invitation to people to get in touch with their truest selves again.* When he said we must become like little children to enter the kingdom, he asserted that we must get beyond the imagined complications and paraphernalia of life to the job and worth of our actual selves.

Perhaps Jesus' most poignant message on self-esteem is to be found in the parable of the sower. The parable was spoken to Jesus' disciples. These men were having a horrible battle between their actual life with Jesus and their imagined life with Jesus. The Galilean campaign was not going well. Their hope was flickering dim. They left their jobs and families in a sense of euphoria and wild-eyed idealism to follow the new king. But the Pharisees resisted the authority of Jesus. He and his disciples became unacceptable in the synagogues and often met hostility. The disciples were discouraged by the ups and downs. Some of the Galilean crowds were very small. Much of their work had come to nothing. They wondered if their effort had not been wasted. They had scattered widely like the farmer with the seed and their actual situation had fizzled in comparison with their imagined harvest.

Jesus' parable faces failure head-on. There is much in life that has no depth. The wind can blow it away. And sometimes you can throw out your truth and expectations on open ground and gossip or inconvenience can come and eat them up like a bird. And sometimes who you are and what you have to offer in life can get thrown among the rocks. The rocks of cynicism can crush most anything. And sometimes the thorns and the seeds wind up in a place vying for the same nourishments.

All that is true. *But the disciples had become so mesmerized by the apparent failures they could see in their desired selves that they lost sight of the colossal harvest beyond expectation, there for the taking if they would but use their actual selves.*

It is as if Jesus were saying, "The key to success is an initial self-acceptance, as though to say, I, Matthew; or I, Mark; or I, Luke, hereby accept this life with its inherited handicaps and endowments and with the elements in my environment I cannot alter or control, and so accepting myself, I will see what I can do with this *actual* Matthew, Mark, or Luke in this *actual* situation."

"Do this," said Jesus, "and the harvest will be a hundredfold in your life and in God's work. There is no get rich quick scheme. Focus on the good ground and the harvest will far exceed that which is lost on the rocks and thorns and barren ground."

What a marvelous parable. *If you cannot envision the harvest in your actual situation you can't find it anywhere.* If there is no hope to be found in your circumstances, there is no hope.

Jesus also left that parable for the church. Churches possess a lack of self-esteem. The Church, too, must accept its fallen, or imperfect, nature. Churches always have to encounter the tension between what they are and what they want to be. Sometimes the disproportion between actual and imagined ideal is great. This is especially true in an era of mass communications and increased mobility. Everyone knows what other people have and what they do not have. There is more capacity to focus on the ideal situation and become so mesmerized by the shortfall of the actual than ever before.

One year a minister had quite a transition. He left a position as Senior Minister of a church of 416 members to go to be the Senior Minister of a church with 2,600 members. Strangely enough, the church of 400 members in many ways lamented the fact that it wasn't like the church of 2,600. And, strangely enough, the church of 2,600 members was desperately trying to acquire some of the imagined traits, like intimacy and fellowship, of the 400-member church. For example, the large church felt it needed more intimacy to be successful. Consequently it secured a professional designer and a television communications person to work on improving its "image" as a "family church." Not enough people knew one another. Two of the great things the 2,600-member "family" decided to do were to switch to homemade loaves of bread for communion and have people tear off pieces as they do in a smaller church and then to join hands and sing "Blest Be the Tie." *Do you know how long it takes 900 people to pass around and tear off pieces of bread from loaves?* Thirty-seven minutes! The huge church never found how long it took to circle 900 people for "Blest Be the Tie" because that got scratched on the spot.

Now, the church of 400 decided it would become more "professional" in orientation and outreach, just like a huge church of 2,600. It wanted to improve its self-esteem because it was small and always had to look up to the big programs of other churches. It collected professionally printed bulletins and newsletters from larger churches. Fearing it was missing out on something, the smaller church hired a professional designer to construct a printed format for its materials. Then, it reasoned that the church would mail these bulletins on a weekly basis to the membership. As part of the process it discovered that you must mail a minimum of 200 pieces under a bulk rate permit. Unfortunately the church only had 150 families. So for two years it mailed out 200 bulletins. Some people received one at work and another at their home address. The minister's dog received one. A pharmacist's cat received one. And the city attorney's gerbil, Buster, always got one. Finally, the smaller church decided that in the time it took it each week to be like a big church and mail a bulletin to 165 member units plus eleven dogs, two cats, and nine infants, it could visit seven new families a week in their homes. So it ceased. When the church accepted itself with its inherited handicaps and endowments, and decided to see what it could do with its actual self, it multiplied in membership.

That's life, my friends. It is as true for individuals as it is for institutions. *God made us. If we do not accept ourselves, how can we accept the God who sustains us?* When we get in touch with ourselves at the deepest level, we find out that we are sons and daughters of God, not perfect but real. We must never get carried away from our origins, our actual selves. The Son of God died for each one of us while we were fallen. His blood was shed, that you and I might know how important we are to God. That is the basis of our self-esteem. No earthly king ever inherited more than a human male has inherited. No earthly queen has ever had more royal blood than a human woman possesses.

We humans are not perfect creatures. We have a fallen and imperfect nature. That is our actual self. If we will accept and turn over to God and God's church that actual self we are now, right now, not what we think we might be or what we think we ought to be or what we think we used to be, our lives will be used to multiply blessings a hundredfold.

The Search For Intimacy

Luke 8:21; 19:41-42

An Intimacy-deprived World

Several decades ago, Erich Segal, a professor of English in Yale University, wrote a simple little volume about love. Amid the complex, abstract movie scripts replete with symbolism that flood contemporary movie offices, his seemed to be quite absurd. He simply produced a story of the intimate relationship between a Harvard hockey player and a Radcliffe coed. Equally simple and trite was the title applied to both the book and movie — *Love Story*. *Love Story* became a box office bonanza. This story of love, intimacy, and death rivaled *Gone With The Wind* in cash receipts. Many reviewers predicted that it would revolutionize the movie industry. It did not. Producers and directors did not flock to the melodramatic theme in moviemaking. Like a breath of fresh air, *Love Story* blew across the horizon and was gone.

As one who stood in a line two blocks long to see the movie, I contributed to the phenomenal financial success of *Love Story*. Oh, I did not relish the personal characterizations in the movie. As a Harvard grad myself, I realized that Ryan O'Neal little resembled the average Crimson hockey player. And suffice it to say that Ali McGraw had little affinity with the Radcliffe coed! Yet I came; I wept; I was moved.

Our world needs a *Love Story* every so often. As we move about in a country that possesses destructive nuclear forces equal to 35,000 pounds of TNT for every human being alive, we grope for emotional foods. Intimacy is the one thing we crave. We need it to survive; we need recognition that we are alive, that we are essentially worthy in being the unique selves that we are.

Most of us exist alongside other people, but not really "with" them. We are truly the parallel generation. That humans could fall from a tight little world as depicted in both the creation stories in

Genesis back into today's chaos is an ever present reality in our condition.

Luis Bunuel, who won an Academy Award nomination for *The Discreet Charm of the Bourgeoisie*, offers a profound critique of our society in another of his movies, *The Exterminating Angel*. This imaginative movie revolves around eighteen wealthy, influential people who attend an elegant dinner party. During the course of the evening they discover that, for some inexplicable reason, they cannot leave the room. As the days pass, they run out of food and water. The tinsel facade of their social existence is abruptly shattered. They discover that they have absolutely nothing in common. In fact, they despise each other. Before long these wealthy, powerful, cultivated people have fallen openly into the superstitious, malicious savages they have always been.

Our parallel existence, however, is safe. It is highly unlikely that we will become trapped with our "friends" without food and water. Our masks are not in danger of being dislodged. Thank God for that. But our search goes on — a search which has been ours since the beginning of time. We wish to relate, not in just a superficial way, with some other human beings. We are influenced throughout our lives by the fact that we came into this world with a unique heritage of humanness. Carl Sandburg has noted this in the prologue to *The Family of Man:*

> *The first cry of a newborn baby in Chicago or Zamboango,*
> *in Amsterdam or Rangoon, has the same pitch and key,*
> *each saying, "I am! I have come through! I belong! I am*
> *a member of the family."*

Indeed, member of the family or nothing are we. We recognize that loss of intimacy is loss of everything. Perhaps our greatest challenge in the coat-and-tie world in which we live is that of achieving intimate relationships in a fallen, intimacy-deprived world.

Rollo May has noted how strange it is that, in our society, sharing tastes, fantasies, dreams, hopes, and fears makes people more shy than going to bed with someone. Perhaps we are more afraid of the tenderness that goes with psychological and spiritual nakedness than sexual relationships and physical nakedness. Indeed, whereas Adam and Eve wore the fig leaf to cover their private parts, we may well have moved it to cover our faces. We are afraid to cry in public. We flinch at displays of weakness. We sit emotionally starved. We live in the same house with other human beings for decades without ever experiencing a joining or a linking of thoughts, feelings, fears, dreams, or delights. We are together, yet we are in absentia.

The Intimate God

As we reflect upon our need for intimacy, we can, perhaps, gain new insight into the life of Jesus of Nazareth. "And when Jesus drew near Jerusalem and saw the city he wept over it, saying, 'Would that even today you knew the things that make for peace' " (Luke 19:41). We can imagine that there is no greater feeling of aloneness than recognizing that other people do not sense the tremendous importance of what we are doing. How painful it is when our wish to share falls flat upon preoccupied ears or ears that want to make fun of us.

Most theologians value Christ for his ethics, his sacrificial death on the cross, or his ushering in eternal life and eternal hope in resurrection. These emphases are of unquestionable significance. *Yet it is also true that no one has come to God as Parent except in Christ.* Nowhere, in Islam or Buddhism, Hinduism or Marxism, do we find affirmed the ultimacy of the personal relationship of humans with God. Jesus capitalized on the Old Testament concept of God as lovingkindness [*Hesed*]. This parent-child relationship terminated in a covenant binding on its members.

Perhaps we need to look afresh at the *imago Dei* or image of God. *Is not the image of God the human capacity for intimacy?* Humans are intimacy-needing beings. A dog does not recognize its own puppies once they become grown. Fish eat their babies. Certain female insects eat their mates to provide food during pregnancy. Alone among the animals, humans need emotional food to exist. Humans need other humans in order to be truly human. George Albert Coe described religion as "the discovery of persons."

Indeed, we can only make the "good news" come alive in valuable human relationships. Our capacity for intimacy is no assurance that it will be achieved.

Perversions Of Intimacy

Many of us have misunderstood the nature of intimacy. Frank A. Clark, author of *The Country Person*, once said, "To enjoy a friend, I need more in common with him than hating the same people." So much of what we call friendship or intimacy is based on common hatreds. Our logic tells us that if John Doe hates Bob Smith and I hate Bob Smith, it follows that John Doe is my intimate friend. This is not true in relationships between men and women, and it is not true in relationships between humans and God. Some of us study the Scriptures and find what we think God is against. We then stand in opposition to these same forces in life and feel that we possess an intimate relationship with God. But such thoughts neglect the God of compassion, love, and forgiveness.

Another misconception is the belief that intimacy means you scratch my back and I'll scratch yours. Intimacy, however, involves genuine caring for the other. It is that power to love someone and receive him in the very moment that we realize how far he falls short of our hopes. There are touchy spots in everyone's psyche. And this knowledge gives us a responsibility to respect these spots. This is a by-product of an intimate relationship.

The Joy Of True Intimacy

Sometimes I think we ministers contribute to the decline of intimacy in our society. We often emphasize the hard work involved in achieving intimacy and totally neglect the joy and spice of life which accompany intimate relationships.

One of the ambivalent tasks of a minister is preaching at funerals. While sadness is certainly a part of it, joy and ecstasy are also. To see a person, who has graciously given of her life to her friends, living on in the lives of those present at her final laying to rest is a beautiful experience. There is nothing greater than the development and nourishment of intimate relationships. Bertrand Russell declared:

I have sought love first because it brings ecstasy — ec-stasy so great that I would often have sacrificed all the rest of my life for a few hours of this joy. I have sought it, next, because it relieves loneliness — that terrible loneli-ness which one's shivering consciousness looks over the realm of the world into the cold, unfathomable, lifeless abyss.

Camus is right — "Destiny condemns us all to death." Behind our search for intimacy is the consciousness that we must one day die. Deepening our relationships with other people will not elimi-nate our anxieties about death, but it will make it possible for us to live without panic.

Ours is a personal God. Christ has set the example. He has touched us and commissioned us to touch others. Christ has recog-nized and redeemed our fallen world. That from which we have fallen, right relationships, is more than a personal quest. It is an essential part of the human condition.

Who's Going To Get What?

Matthew 12:18-25
Genesis 16:15; 17:18-21; 21:8-20

The worst fight I ever saw, much less participated in, occurred on a football field. It did not occur between hostile fans. In fact, it did not take place between two *opposing* teams. It took place between members of the same team, our Furman team. We were playing Davidson College in Charlotte, and their quarterback, Jimmy Poole, now a prominent physician, was completing pass after pass. Our defensive backs were of the rather strong opinion that our linemen were not putting much of a pass-rush on that Davidson quarterback. Little comments like "Poole could write a letter to his mother or drink a cup of coffee while he is waiting to see if his receivers get open" were verbalized between the backs. On the other hand, our linemen were of the strong opinion that they couldn't rush because our backs were leaving the receivers wide open. Finally, John Briscoe, a huge tackle, turned around to me and screamed, "Warlick, are y'all gonna start covering those guys?" I *might*, I don't remember exactly, have said something unpleasant to Briscoe about his size and lack of speed. Well, the next thing I knew, our strong safety, Andy Hancock, had slugged Briscoe upside the helmet. Quick as a flash, our other tackle leveled Hancock. For five or ten minutes it was the worst argument you ever saw. The coaches couldn't stop it.

When order was finally restored, penalty flags littered the field. But the referees were at a loss as to what to call. You can't call a personal foul when it is against members of the same team. The best they could come up with was an unsportsmanlike conduct penalty and a delay of game penalty. Needless to say, as those grudges were nursed through the rest of the season, ours was very much a house divided for some of the remaining games.

The worst fights which ever take place are those between members of the same family. In our history, more American lives were

60

lost in the Civil War than in all the other wars we have fought in *combined*. And look at our world today. The great battles are not between invading and defensive nations and superpowers but between warring members of the same national family. South America, Korea, Lebanon, you name it. Family fights are the worst kind. The worst fights are between family members over who is going to get what. If you cannot understand that, you cannot understand the Bible and the true miracle that was Jesus Christ. What's more, *you can never have peace of mind, true emotional and mental stability, until you understand the human race as part of your family and stop worrying about who's going to get what in life.* Perhaps in this regard our Bible can be of genuine help to us.

The place to look is in the life of a man of faith who was not always a person of perfect character. The Bible is realistic about our father, Abraham. He was a human being, not a perfect saint. Occasionally he, like perhaps all of us, had some serious letdowns in his usual uprightness. The Bible tells us that there was a famine in the land, so Abraham went down to Egypt to live where he could obtain food. As he journeyed, he began to worry. His wife, Sarah, was very beautiful. He feared that the Pharaoh might kill him and take his wife. So he decided to lie to Pharaoh and tell him that she was his sister. Abraham then sold Sarah to the Pharaoh. Fortunately, Pharaoh learned the truth, gave Abraham a good lecture on ethics, and let her go. To say that Arab and Jew are interrelated is an understatement. If not for God's power and Pharaoh's ethics there would be no children of Israel.

Well, Abraham's family problems had just started. Abraham and Sarah grew older and they became painfully aware of their inability to have children. Sarah often cried over her plight. She knew God had blessed Abraham and had promised him that he would be the father of a great nation. So she came up with a scheme. She suggested to Abraham that he have a child by Hagar, their Egyptian servant. That was quite proper for the Bronze Age culture. Sarah reasoned with Abraham that "since Hagar is part of our household, it's the closest we can get to having our own child." There were no adoption agencies. So, Sarah directed the whole affair out of her own insecurity. When Hagar became pregnant,

Sarah told Abraham that the purpose had been accomplished and he was to go no more to Hagar. Of course, you know what happened. Sarah began to resent Hagar and abused her. Hagar fled to the wilderness and there God promised her a healthy baby, to be named Ishmael, and told her to go home in spite of Sarah. As the oldest son of father Abraham, Ishmael was the child of entitlement, the rightful heir of Abraham and God's promises. In fact, Scripture says that God had a special commitment to Ishmael.

As so often happens when people who can't have children make arrangements to secure a child, Sarah herself became pregnant. She gave birth to a boy, whom she named Isaac. Of course, Sarah abruptly ordered Hagar never to hold or touch her son, Isaac. All of Sarah's pent-up resentment came to a boil one day.

To show off their new son, who was then at the crawling stage, Abraham and Sarah threw a huge lawn party. Sarah was moving among the tables talking and laughing with the guests when she stopped in horror. She noticed that Ishmael was kneeling at Isaac's crib. He was waving a banner to make Isaac smile. And when Sarah heard Ishmael call him "little brother," she exploded. She ran into the house and pointed her finger in Abraham's face and screamed, "You drive out that slave and her son. I'm worried about who's going to get what. Listen. No son of that slave is going to share the inheritance with my son Isaac."

Well, Abraham was greatly distressed. He went out in the backyard and prayed. God told him to calm down. God told Abraham that God was well inclined toward both boys. God told Abraham that the descendants of Isaac would bear his name. But God also promised Abraham that God would make a great nation of Ishmael also since he, too, was Abraham's offspring. So the next morning, in great sorrow, Abraham gave the young Egyptian woman, Hagar, and their mutual son, Ishmael, some water and bread and sent them out into the wilderness.

After a few days, Hagar and Ishmael ran out of food and water. Hagar thought they would die. But God heard the little boy's cry and sent a messenger who pointed out a well of water.

Finally, Abraham died. Ishmael returned for his funeral and together with Isaac, his half-brother, they buried old Abraham in a cave. Now Abraham left a will. Even in death he apparently continued his imperfection. You see, although he had seven children, Abraham left everything to his son Isaac.

Abraham's choice between Isaac and Ishmael resulted in a relentless feud of warring cousins which has lasted 7,000 years to this very day. The Jews trace their origins to Abraham through Isaac and Sarah. The Arabs go back to Abraham through Ishmael and Hagar. The children of the freeborn woman and the children of the slave girl have never recognized each other as brothers and sisters. They are still fighting in the Middle East over who's going to get what.

After 5,000 years of watching his fallen, warring children, God sent God's only son down among them to try to make them see that the human race is all one family under a living God. God had this son born a Jew and raised a peasant. Paul said it correctly, "God was in Christ reconciling the world back to himself." And do you know what the world did with this Jesus? They started arguing again over who's going to get what. He gave a commandment — "Love God and neighbor." So they said, "Who's my neighbor? Who's going to get this love?" He preached the resurrection. But the Sadducees came up to him and said, "Master, Moses said if a man dies, having no children, his brother shall marry his wife, have children, and raise up children. But suppose the man has seven brothers and they each marry the woman, die in turn, and leave no children. In the resurrection whose wife will she be?" Who's going to get what? Jesus answered, "You do not understand, in the resurrection they neither marry nor are given in marriage, but are as the angels of God in heaven." In other words, you don't have to worry about who's going to get what because everybody gets it all. Jesus told James and John to follow him and they started talking with their parents. Finally, their mother came up to Jesus and asked if maybe her boys couldn't sit at the right and left hand of Jesus in heaven, in favored places, since there were twelve disciples and that's quite a crowd. In other words, who's going to get what? Finally, a Samaritan woman was impressed with Jesus by a well one day. So she said, "Sire, there are three temples, one in Samaria, one in Jerusalem, and one in Egypt. Which one is the true one?"

Who's going to get what? Jesus replied, "None of them. The true worshipers worship one Father in Spirit and in truth. God is a spirit. We are all one family." Now, what do we make of all these family feuds?

What is the Bible trying to tell us? In the first place, it means that God chooses us not because we are truthful, honest, and dependable. Do we merit God's choosing us and sending his son? The answer given from Genesis to Revelation is a resounding NO! We Christians, Baptists, Methodists, Americans, or whatever, are not righteous but sinners. We are not just created but fallen. The Son of God comes not to call the righteous but the fallen, fighting sinners. It's a gift.

Secondly, our history has proven that the Scriptures are right about what it takes to get peace of mind. Look at the Bible and all the misery caused by those who fought over who's going to get what. See how that fallen state affects our human condition even today. The sociology department of Duke University did a study on peace of mind. They isolated the factors which create emotional and mental stability. They were:

1. The absence of suspicion and resentment. Nursing a grudge is the major factor in unhappiness.

2. Not living in the past. Who got what doesn't matter if you trust God. Do not be unwholesomely preoccupied with old mistakes and failures. Everybody gets everything in the long run.

3. Refuse to indulge in self-pity when life hands you a raw deal. Accept the fact that nobody gets through life without some sorrow and misfortune. (Abraham didn't. Sarah didn't. Isaac and Ishmael didn't. Joseph and Mary didn't. Jesus didn't. And you won't either.)

4. Find something bigger than yourself to believe in. Self-centered people, who are always worrying about who's going to get what, score lowest on tests for measuring happiness.

Can you imagine how powerful your life would be if you stopped worrying about who's going to get what? Can you imagine what a world would be like where everybody stopped worrying about who's going to get what? Jesus said there is such a power and there is such a place. It is called the Kingdom of God. And there is no greater peace, no *greater* peace, than accepting his invitation to walk out of your present condition into that kingdom. It heals. It restores. It is the only thing that can heal anxiety, worry, bitterness, and fear.

Terminal Illness

2 Kings 5:1-14

Imagine, if you will, two children walking down a hallway at school. Neither one of them is paying close attention to what he is doing. Consequently, they bump into each other. One child pushes the other down and makes a fist. "He bumped me. He bumped me," the child screams. He is ready to fight.

The other child is headed toward class, realizes there is a class to attend, and that the hallway is plenty big enough for both of them to pass. So he wants to go around and continue on his way. The first child is still screaming, "He hit me," and wanting to fight.

Now, we commonly think of the first child as ill-tempered, hyperactive, and incorrigible. Consequently, we are tempted to believe that the difference between the two children is that one is a bad child and the other a good child. Actually, the problem or the difference, most likely, is that the first child has an attention deficiency and the second child does not. His attention can only focus on the moment and it stays there: "He hurt me. He bumped me." The attention is deficient. It cannot see beyond the moment. In a way, it's egotistical. But it is certainly a deficiency in attention. Adults even have attention deficiencies. The person who is angry most of the time doesn't have to be a child. "He hit me. She bumped me. I suffered." You perhaps know a person who reacts instead of responds to an event or a situation. You *react* to a sudden discomfort but you *respond* to life as you focus your attention on something beyond the discomfort of the present. You realize you've got places to go and that the world is large enough for you to walk around that discomfort.

Amazingly enough, Jesus Christ used as an illustration in his very first sermon a man who possessed an attention deficiency disorder and was healed of an incurable disease because he overcame it. Jesus stood in his home synagogue and said, "Many lepers were

66

in Israel in the time of Elisha the prophet; and none of them was cleansed, except Naaman the Syrian" (Luke 4:27).

Apparently there was something in Naaman's life that had universal appeal. Perhaps he was similar to many of us. Naaman was a person who wanted healing on his own terms. He could not focus his attention on matters greater than his own life. He was a man of the highest social position. Everyone held him in greatest esteem. Naaman was a victorious general. Life seemed to have poured all its treasures into his arms. Naaman only had two faults: he was afflicted by leprosy, an incurable disease; and he had a bad temper, always wanting life to be on his own terms. Naaman's home was not a very happy place despite his good showing in public. Those two faults, being a leper and an egotist, are not small faults. Naaman's wife must have cried a lot and his children probably did, too. If wealth and luxury lived in that place, so did suffering and fear.

One day a little slave girl told Naaman of a prophet in Samaria named Elisha who perhaps could cure leprosy. "Oh, he's never cured anybody," she asserted. "But nobody has asked him, either. I think he could do it for you."

At that point, the king got involved. Naaman was too valuable a soldier to lose if there was even a thousand-in-one chance someone could save him. "Go, Naaman, go," said the king.

So Naaman did what any of us would do. He made travel plans and set off with as much money as he could cram into his travel bags, about $125,000 in today's currency, to pay for the exotic treatment. He knew that physicians, treatment, and religious healers cost a lot of money. But they are worth it, he thought.

Naaman finally arrived at the prophet's house. What happened then threw him into a complete rage. He was mad because the prophet did not visit with him. Naaman was an important man. But Elisha sent some nameless servant out of the house to tell him to dip in the Jordan seven times. Even today fund-raisers and most preachers know that the wealthy like to be visited personally. Elisha didn't do that. And Naaman grew madder than a wet hen. He was insulted. His attention deficiency rose to the surface. "He didn't visit me. He sent a nobody out to see me." Then, to add insult to injury, the prophet did not heal Naaman the way he imagined a prophet ought to heal people. Naaman had an attention deficiency relative to the manner in which he could be healed. Surely the prophet would call on God, touch the disease, and it would be quickly over. That is what preachers do, don't they? Well, Naaman really got hot then. This dipping seven times in a river was humiliating. He had to do all the work. Finally, the crowning insult was to be commanded to dip in the river Jordan. "If it's only a matter of dipping in a river, why did I have to get up and travel way over here? I can dip in beautiful rivers in my own land. Why do I have to dip in this muddy little Jordan?" In today's idiom, he would say, "Man, I can stay home and watch better stuff than this on television!"

In a rage, Naaman turned to leave. He decided that he would not surrender his heart. If he could not have healing on his own terms, then he would not have it at all. Better to go home and rot and still have your pride than to be humiliated and get well. Now that's a real deficiency in one's attention, isn't it? Naaman's bad temperament almost killed him. "The guy is a fake!" he replied. "He made me angry. I'm mad at the prophet. I'm mad at religion. I'm mad at God. I'd rather go home and rot! He bruised my ego. And insulted me. Better to be a non-insulted leper than a humiliated well person."

Fortunately for Naaman, his servants saw his attention deficiency. They came near to the ranting, raving general and said, "Sir, if the prophet had demanded something great and exciting, you would have done it in order to be healed. Suppose the prophet had demanded $125,000? You were prepared to give it. If he had asked you to crawl back home on your hands and knees you would have done it."

The good sense of Naaman reasserted itself and he began to focus his attention on the big picture. He went down to the Jordan. Can't you just see and hear him dipping himself a few times: "Embarrassing. Boring. This is humiliating. Crummy, little, muddy river. I'm just as leprous as I ever was."

"Keep going. Keep dipping," yelled the servants. Finally he came up the seventh time after he had taken the final plunge. He looked and his flesh was as smooth as the flesh of a little child. It's a great story of healing, isn't it?

We can resonate with that story. Many times in life, we prefer to be a non-insulted leper, in our own way, than a humiliated well person. It's just easier to remain fallen, but proud! Sometimes our own attention deficiencies get in the way of our love for life. We want to stay and fight, put up the defense, instead of moving on to the rest of life and walking around the bumps and bruises that have come our way in a world that has plenty of room in which to do just that.

Look at the biblical narrative that way. Consider the little slave girl who first told Naaman about Elisha. She was a war casualty. The Syrians had swooped down on her helpless nation. She had been carried away into a strange land. In one fell swoop she had lost her mother and father, her home, and all of her possessions. She had even lost her freedom. You can't lose much more than that. Then she discovered that the man who was to blame for all that was deathly ill. In all honesty, place us in that situation and most would say, "Let him suffer. I'm glad for every pain his body feels. I'm glad he is getting paid back. He hurt me; now let *him* get hurt. It's God's way of paying him back. He bruised me."

Fortunately, her attention was not limited to finding pain for pain, evil for evil. She had been robbed of everything in the way of outward possessions. But there were some values, thank God, that force and violence could not touch. She still possessed a vision of God and love for neighbor that made life worth living. She had something even Naaman did not have. She tried to help a person that she had every right to hate.

That is so rare to find — so hard to do. But she knew that a bad temperament can kill you worse than leprosy. Each day of life we can see women who have been wronged by men, lying in wait for some suffering to beset those who have wronged them. We see men who have been wronged by women, hoping that they suffer, hoping that they get paid back. We see children who have been wronged by their parents actually glad of every pain of body that the parent experiences. Meet hate with hate. Let evil be returned for evil. What a way to live. Stay fallen but proud. They've hurt us, and one day we're going to be there when the house comes falling down. Let's hope our attention, like hers, can be focused on something beyond "he hit me," or "she bumped me," or "I suffered." It is a tough decision, deciding whether to be a non-humiliated and proud sick person or a humiliated, surrendered well person. Maybe we could take the plunge once but not seven times.

Finally, consider old Naaman. Ever been in his shoes? Many have. Life never ceases to amaze us. Suppose the doctor pointed his finger at you and said: "You are terminally ill with cancer. We can see it in your body. You are going to die very soon. But if you will crawl out of here to your car and come back Tuesday with $125,000 for us, we'll cure you." Well, most of us would crawl out of there and somehow beg, borrow, or steal the money. We'd even do that for our spouse or children. You know we would.

Well, Jesus is right on one score. *We are all terminally ill. We are all dying.* Not a single person here is going to get out of life alive. Not one. But there is a cure. Jesus said, "I am God's son. I know where you can be cured. I can't visit all of you, all the time, but you know where my house is. Come down there as often as you can, on the one day a week set aside for that. It is where the treasure is. There may even be some people there that you don't like. But dip yourself into my word and into my values. You have to dip yourself more than four or five times to even notice a change. I don't want all your money. You give what you want to. It's that simple. It is not spectacular. But you will find the cure there to your terminal illness. *You can be saved.*"

Sometimes our attention deficiency gets in the way of seeing a greater vision of life. We are important people. We've got important things to do. If all we have to do is dip into a Sunday School lesson, some prayers and hymns, listen to a choir, be with other people in a small building, and listen to a preacher preach from the Bible for eighteen minutes, we can stay home and do better stuff than that. Why do we have to come over here? Better to be a proud, well-slept, enjoyable leper than a surrendered, faithful, and humbled well person. You know, a bad temperament can be fatal. It can cause us to embrace a fallen but proud state of existence.

Children Of Cocaine

Romans 7:14-25; 8:35-39

Unfortunately, today's world is not a world particularly concerned with the future. We live in a generation that has been characterized as the "Generation of the Egoist." Egoism is a philosophy that focuses on doing what will be in one's long-term best interests. The egoist generation is the generation of "give me my pleasure. Let me indulge only in my own pursuits. I want to consume all I can consume. What's right is what serves my own best interests."

Many in a capitalistic economic system are convinced that money is the root of all good. We tend to define ourselves by what we want rather than what we are. Consequently, if some people want to be a doctor, it can be because doctors make lots of money, not because he or she is committed to medicine. And once an egoist becomes a doctor, the main concern is how much money he or she "put on the books" today instead of the relationship with the patients. Likewise, if an egoist wants to be a lawyer, it is because of the money a lawyer makes, not because of any desire for public service or representing the widows or the orphans like the biblical imperative. God's standard of fairness and compassion has no place in the economics of an egoist.

You can easily see why the drug cocaine is the ideal chemical for the current generation. Cocaine can separate you from the present. If you are bent on being an assertive egoist, cocaine appears to help you. Pre-existing shyness and feelings of inferiority tend to disappear with cocaine. You can go for days without sleep.

Cocaine also increases the blood pressure by fifteen percent and the heart rate by fifty percent. Ah, but remember, you cannot separate yourself from your future. Paranoid and suspicious thinking also accompany cocaine use. A semi-break with reality occurs.[1] Draw a line out twenty years and, after twenty years of fifteen percent blood pressure increase and fifty percent heart rate accelerations, go up to room sixty in the years of life and visit the wreck of a human being you would have to live with.

In like manner, spend the next six or seven years of your life concerned only with money, power, and prestige. What kind of society will you create? Better still, go up to room forty or room fifty in the years of life hotel, and it may be the most expensive room in the hotel, and visit the wealthy, selfish, empty, spoiled, unfriendly, unsociable, frowning person who depends on his or her money and power for satisfaction. Are you going to like living with that person? Proudly value the world of conspicuous consumption and greed and disregard the timeless message of Christian sharing as just boring rot. Then extend those lines out and visit the person you will be stuck with in twenty years. You cannot separate yourself from your future. The impact of a future is part of the human condition. This is why some of the Bible's messages are *timeless* and not just *time-conditioned*.

Fortunately, there is another thing you can never separate yourself from, and that is the love of God. Paul is right:

> *Who shall separate us from the love of Christ? Shall tribulation, or distress, or persecution, or famine, or nakedness, or peril, or sword? ... No ... I am persuaded that neither life, nor death, nor angels, nor principalities, nor powers, nor things present, nor things to come shall be able to separate us from the love of God, which is in Christ Jesus our Lord.* (Romans 8:35-39)

Like the prodigal son, you may grab your money from society and run away totally to the cares of the world. Like the lepers and the lame, some unfortunate illness may overtake you. Like so many persons in Scripture, you may lose loved ones. But you cannot lose God. You cannot be separated from the love of God.

God has shown us God's nature. In Bethlehem's child, God gave us what was not deserved. Instead of reacting with anger and hostility to the wayward children, God came down and was crucified among us. We humans could not and cannot separate ourselves from the love of God. Even in a fast-track world, our effort to find the way home depends upon conviction as much as conversion. In a simpler culture, religious symbols provided the dominant ordering of an agrarian society. The terminology "follow me" enabled a person to participate totally in a corporate religious life.

Today's world, with its emphasis on individual identity in the midst of increased secularization of the culture as a whole, creates a delicate and often frightening seesaw. We try to find stability and meaning in a world that is becoming increasingly complex and frantic.

"Follow me." Jesus Christ said, "Follow me. Take up your cross and follow me!" In short, that was the sum of what Jesus had to say to us. "Follow me." Eighty-one times the command occurs in the Gospels, that we are to follow him. We may choose not to obey this order but we are not at liberty to change it, regardless of the speed of our culture. Our faith begins with attachment to a person, not with subscriptions to a creed. "Follow me."

That's a difficult command. In fact, we know more about believing in Jesus than we know about how we are to follow him. There's always the tension between conversion to a person and the conviction to follow that person.

I once knew a man who changed his life, but I couldn't tell if it was for the better or not. He needed to become converted to something. He was missing something in life. There was no joy, no spark, no self-assuredness. Sam was president of one of South Carolina's largest banks, a leader in his political party, and the social friend of a thousand people. But there was a big void, an emptiness. He needed a cause to support, something to reach out and grab his emotions, that would eventually transcend his regular world and justify his life in terms of obedience. Sam was sixty years old when he became converted. He was converted to the football program at Furman University. He became a personal admirer and friend of the head coach. He purchased a purple blazer and a purple tie. He pumped thousands of dollars into the program. He followed the coaches around on their speaking trips and probably recruited more new members to the athletic boosters club than anyone in its history. His life had a new purpose, a new direction. He possessed meaning instead of emptiness. He came to practice sessions regularly and even sat on the bench with the team during the games. Jesus had Peter and our team had Sam. Sam memorized all the players' names, backgrounds, and numbers by carefully studying the media guide. We knew him and he knew us. At one point, sitting on the bench was not enough for this zealous disciple, so he began to accompany the team into the locker room at halftime.

Well, at that time in the flow of life, our biggest rival was Davidson College. All those games were played in Charlotte. Sam started riding the team bus with us to Charlotte each year. My senior year was the year Sam lost his conversion. The game was a brutal one. And true to form, Sam followed us into the locker room at the half. He stood there, by the door, just watching as the trainers taped and retaped ankles, the doctors checked the wounded, and the individual coaches met with their selected groups. Then our silver-tongued orator of a head coach blew his whistle and called everyone together. He launched into his best sing-song cadence about loyalty, effort, and victory. Sam's eyes grew larger and he started squeezing the program in his hands. Sam hung on every word the coach delivered. As the coach's voice rose to a crescendo, Sam rolled his program into a tight little roll. Finally, as the coach screamed his final plea, Sam literally left his feet as he yelled in response, "I'm ready; follow me!" Then he threw open the door and sprinted out into the night for the field. With fifty athletes running behind him, he turned his head back over his shoulder, waving his program in the air, and yelled again, "Follow me!" Then, before he could turn completely back around, he ran headlong, in full stride, into the goalposts and knocked himself unconscious.

We had to leap over and sidestep Sam's limp body to get on the field. The ambulance, which is at every football game in case of injury to the athletes, had to drive the length of the field to get Sam. They carried Sam to Charlotte Memorial Hospital where he stayed two days. His wife was so embarrassed she wouldn't even drive to Charlotte to transport him home. So poor Sam, with a bandage on his head and his rumpled purple and white outfit, had to catch a Greyhound bus back to Greenville.

We never saw Sam at any of our practices or games after that. There just wasn't enough conviction to make him stick beyond the conversion. He hadn't attended our college so there wasn't that knowledge of historical tradition to keep him close. And it was the coach's last year, so his hero left. And Sam really didn't know that much about the game. He had memorized the media guide but he didn't understand enough about a game he hadn't played to really appreciate it. He was a lost convert. In his embarrassment and his pain, he found that there wasn't enough conviction to keep going.

We modern Christians have a hard time with conviction. We have problems maintaining momentum in our journey toward "home." We are touched and pulled by our faith at both the feeling and response levels. Then, that which has sustained us in our hour of need becomes relegated, out of necessity, to live a compartmentalized lifestyle, to only one facet of our existence. As a result, we are always on the lookout for new plans, new pathways, and new programs which quickly degenerate into formal religious programs.

Many Christians are like old Sam, *converted but not convicted.* Sometimes memorizing the Bible and recruiting other converts in a frenzy of activity becomes the be-all and end-all of the enterprise. There is no history developed, no knowledge of the lifestyle, no lasting effects that will carry them beyond the embarrassments, doubts, and headlong dashes into stone walls that are a part of every emotional experience. So they quit the enterprise. "Conversion" is thrown overboard because it is now a part of the past.

Secondly, we humans, I think, have tended to separate conversion to the person of Jesus from the conviction to follow him because we live in an age of proxy. We tend to turn over to others the carrying out of some of our obligations. We send people to Congress to govern for us by proxy. We want to be associated with good government without having to be directly involved in it. We create social agencies to take care of our needy by proxy. We can be associated with bettering the welfare of others without having to be directly involved in it. We truly live in an age of proxy. In some ways it is helpful, but in some ways it is harmful. We often confuse autonomy or independence with living by proxy. Some churches live by evangelism and turn conviction over to churches which are judged to be more socially and educationally inclined. And sometimes churches with conviction try to give proxy to other sectors of the community judged to be more evangelistically inclined. Such living by proxy hurts the churches. "Follow me," said Jesus. We cannot contract out to others essential parts of that challenge. "Follow me." It is an imperative for all of us. It is Jesus we must follow, not a scissors and paste picture of him presented by the denomination or popular sentiment or even a media evangelist. What does it mean to follow Jesus in an age of proxy?

First of all, we must be converted and convicted to having a life of prayer. We must be open to God and his will for our lives. Again and again Jesus took the disciples aside to pray, to be alone in their thoughts with God. He made people of prayer out of them. They were transformed by the practice of regular prayer. If we would follow Jesus, if we would walk in his steps, we too must learn to be with God in prayer. When people are praying when a church member is having a problem, a miracle happens. You can feel a strange power. But it took the disciples years to learn how to pray like that. We certainly cannot become sanctified overnight. Now, this is not a popular word in a culture that worships the instant way of life: instant coffee, instant tea, microwave ovens, remote control television, and instant communications. Prayer is the work of a lifetime. Follow Jesus by becoming converted to beginning a life of prayer. Start someplace. Say, "Now, today, I'm going to begin learning to pray." But become convicted to it for a lifetime.

A second aspect in following Jesus is taking this life which is turned over to God in prayer and letting it be led toward a ministry of reconciliation in the world. In short, to follow Jesus is to become committed to the poor, broken, and despised of the world. His ministry was not just to the wealthy and the comfortable. We can't follow Jesus by proxy in that regard, my friends. Jesus wasn't just a decent sort of fellow with his eyes blindfolded to the depravity of human existence. Jesus withdrew often to have his cup filled. But always so he could not only supply his own needs but share the power and love of God with others. George Bernard Shaw once observed that Christian congregations are not to become as groups of hermits coming into the sanctuary, each person bringing his or her own cup of self-satisfaction to be filled and then carrying the filled cup back to his own cave to be devoured. Become converted to taking your love to the parts of the city and to the people in the congregation who confront the greatest pain and humiliation. And become *convicted* to stay with it. "Follow me," said Jesus.

Finally, following Jesus means your willingness to give up something. "Take up your cross and follow me," said Jesus. Not your featherbed. Not your lounge chair. Not your lawn chair. But your cross. Have you ever become converted to giving up something, surrendering anything, to be a real follower of Jesus? I want to ask this honestly: what would this world be like if we could get Christians to show the church the same conviction and commitment they give their civic responsibilities, their businesses, and their community service organizations? There is pain and there is cost to following Jesus. Do you surrender anything to be a part of Christ's church? Or do you give Christ's church what you have left over after everything else in your life is taken care of? "Take up your cross and follow me." Jesus is not the church. Nor is the minister the church. The minister is not supposed to be the one that makes the church go.

In his farewell sermon a minister once told his congregation why he was quitting. "For years now," he said, "I have been like a pump by the side of the road, with a sign on me that said, 'take my handle and pump me, and I will slake your thirst.' It made me feel good for people to use me that way. Then one day, there wasn't anything left in me. I had been pumped dry. I didn't have anything left to give."[2]

Many Christians feel like a pump by the side of the road in our fast-paced society. Many of us fail to get on the path toward home because we have little left to give the journey. When we have been pumped dry by a consumer-oriented society, there is little conviction left for beginning an arduous religious pilgrimage. The speed at which our society moves outraces our ability to recognize direction and purpose as we grope on that fast track. Fortunately our human condition includes more than a state of being created and fallen. God's Grace is a critical element in what it means to be a human being.

1. From "Cocaine Today," by Sidney Cohen, M.D., Department of Psychiatry, UCLA School of Medicine. Quoted in *Drug Enforcement*, Fall issue 1982, pp. 10-12.
2. John Killinger, "How to Treat a Minister," November 27, 1983.

III. GRACE

Cynicism And Optimism

Ecclesiastes 1:12—2:11
1 Peter 2:9-10

For three years I belonged to a little circle of friends in Boston who took an annual winter pilgrimage. There were four of us — a banker, a florist, the owner of several funeral homes, and myself. The funeral home man owned a farmhouse in the White Mountain range in New Hampshire. Around early March we would all become stir-crazy from the confinement of winter, so we would go on our three-day breakout. The old farmhouse would be freezing until we had built our fires in the fireplaces. We would unload our provisions, cut a hole in the ice over the river, and lay in some drinking water. Then we would be off on snowmobiles under a full moon. We would stay out all night, zooming through the trees at full speed until dawn. It was always an exhilarating event. Then, after a few hours of sleep, we would awaken at noon and go up to the toboggan slide. The toboggan slide was actually an old logging road that started in a clearing on top of the mountain and wound its way through a dozen or more curves to the main highway. The road would be iced over with huge snowbanks on either side. You could get on a little one-person sled with large runners and literally fly down that road. It was wonderful to feel the wind blowing around you as you took that all-out, head-first plunge down the mountain. The trick, of course, was to bail out and leap into a snowbank just before you got to the highway. Otherwise, you might get hit by a car! Now, the ride down the mountain took approximately three minutes. The walk back up the mountain took 25 minutes. It was "pssst — and walk back; pssst — and walk back." After three or four trips on the sled, you began to wonder if the "pssst" was worth the walk back. After the fifth trip you decided that it was easier just to stay down at the bottom.

That happens to a lot of people in life. Some people decide that it is just easier to stay down at the bottom in life than it is to walk

81

back up the hill. You and I get that way sometimes. The "pssst" isn't worth it. Cynicism seems to be the dominant attitude in our human condition.

Apparently this is what happened to the writer of Ecclesiastes. He set himself to the task of doing things that the world says give you the most exhilaration. He became a builder. He built homes and palaces. He accumulated rental property. He constructed gardens. He amassed a vast fortune. He heaped up silver and gold. He had hundreds of people working for him. But when he completed all those enterprises he looked back in disgust and said, "The 'pssst' just isn't worth it. All is vanity. You're just as well off staying at the bottom."

Next he tried wisdom. He went to college. He taught himself. He educated himself. But he discovered that the more you learn about life the more complicated it makes your decisions. He studied religion and philosophy and decided that wisdom was exciting. But he also discovered that because the wise person knows more than the fool, the wise person also suffers more mental anguish. Consequently he decided that it is better to be a happy fool than a wretched wise man. The "pssst" just isn't worth it. You're just as well off staying at the bottom.

In other words, there is always the possibility of arriving at a fatal moment "where we survey where we have been and are forced to the reluctant and devastating conclusion, 'I've been had.'"[1] All is vanity. The "pssst" just isn't worth it. We call this human condition being cynical. It is an attitude of disbelief in the trustworthiness of humans and the reality of a good God. Because of the disappointments and long uphill climbs in life, the cynic loses the optimism necessary to keep on trying. Sometimes it's just easier to stay at the bottom and keep to a view of the human race as reflected in the doctrine of original sin. Since the cynic believes that evil rather than goodness is at the heart of the human condition, he questions the motives of everyone: "People only give to the church because they want an income tax deduction or they want to control the pastor. Or the pastor only does this because they give a lot of money to the church." Or they stay away from church because hypocrites go there. It works that way in life outside the church, too. I doubt that anyone has escaped having at least one moment when he or she felt that the "pssst" wasn't worth the long walk.

You work for hours cleaning up a house and the children come home and fifteen minutes later it looks like it hasn't been cleaned. You invest years of your life in raising children and in they walk with bad grades, a wrecked car, or an ungrateful posture. You spend five years with the company building up a business and you move to something else. They hire someone else at more than your salary and he messes up all your gains. The company winds up right back where it started from. It's true. Thirty people can labor for eleven months building a beautiful home. One idiot with a sledgehammer can destroy it in twenty minutes. Sometimes a pastor looks back on churches and sees years of work ruined by an in-house personality clash or a poor situation with a successor and wonders if all the "pssst" was worth it. If humans are fallen, totally absorbed with themselves, why not just accept the imperfection in the human condition and stay at the bottom in terms of expectations?

Your every utterance can become sarcastic and biting. Now, maybe you have never felt that way. I wouldn't want to impute feelings to you as a reader or hearer. I, at least, can attest to the fact that cynicism can lay hold of the mind. All of us can become cynical at one time or another. The problem occurs when the anxiety, despair, or the depression of the day or the month becomes the permanent state of our life. We heard it in Jesus' day in those haunting words, "Can anything good come out of Nazareth?"

To fully appreciate God's Grace, we have to realize that Jesus was born into a rather cynical society. The Jews had affirmed their faith for four thousand years, that God cared for God's people — and millions of them had been overrun and exiled all over the world. Believers had affirmed their faith that God has a purpose for every life — and children were running around with leprosy and begging in the streets. Moses had affirmed his faith that on the other side of slavery was a promised land — and now after the exodus the people were still under the Roman eagle. By all rights the disciples of Jesus had every right to say, "Vanity of vanities, all is in vain. The basic rule of thumb is trust no one, not even God." The race is a fallen one. And, to a degree, that is what they did when the going got tough during the events that led to Easter: Peter sliced off someone's ear; Thomas ran and hid; and Judas cashed in his faith for some money that he could spend in the here and now.

The essential question is this one: Is our universe in the control of a God of love and goodness, or of a satanic prince of darkness? We must decide — are we cynics or optimists? Is there more good in life or more evil? Is there more kindness in life or more despair? How reaching is God's redemption? We must choose. We cannot serve disbelief and belief at the same time.

It is a rather grand leap of faith to hold to the Judeo-Christian belief that light and goodness are the dominant forces in the human condition. The Christian faith teaches that all creation is fundamentally good. Christianity says that what darkness there is in life is due to the sin and ignorance of men and women. Life is essentially good. That takes real faith to believe. You see, there is no "evidence" so coercive that it will ultimately force us either to believe or disbelieve. Woody Allen once said that if only God would give him some clear sign, like making a large deposit in his name in a Swiss bank, then he would believe in God.[2] I don't think God is going to do that. Robert McAfee Brown is correct: "Discovering whether or not we have been 'had' is not something that just a little more evidence, or an ongoing open mind, will finally determine for us."[3]

All we can do is take Jesus at his word that evil is a tunnel, not a prison. The light outshines the darkness and blessed are those who mourn, for they shall be comforted. Evil is a mystery to be lived with. It is not a problem that we shall ever solve. One has to choose to be an optimist or live the sad world of the cynic.

The Apostle Paul wrote these words to the Corinthians: "We are afflicted in every way, but not crushed; perplexed, but not driven to despair ..." (2 Corinthians 4:8ff). In other words, even though we are afflicted, we do not give up and stay at the bottom of the run; even though we are perplexed we do not give up and stay at the bottom of the hill. Yes, life is indeed "pssst and walk back, pssst and walk back, pssst and walk back." But the "pssst" is worth the walk because one day we will live in a land where there is no walking back up the mountain, where there are no more tears, where there is only the eternal downhill ride in the bosom of the one who created us.

Somehow in the death and resurrection of the Son of God, the disciples caught the vision. Virtually overnight those caustic cynics became the greatest optimists the world has ever seen. You see, if you can believe that God is good, then you can believe that God's world and the men and women in it are basically good.

Perhaps the dearest way to explain it is in a powerful illustration from history. Beethoven doubted that the keyboard instruments of his day had reached mechanical perfection. He believed in the capacity and goodness of the human race. He felt in his heart that creation would keep on growing and learning about beauty and music. Consequently, he wrote piano music that could only be played properly on instruments not yet built. Now that's faith. Can you imagine a deaf man believing enough in future generations and ultimately in God to write music that could only be played properly on instruments not yet built? All is not vanity. One is indeed not better off just staying at the bottom in spite of all the evidence to the contrary in a solitary lifetime.

That is what happened to the disciples. They doubted that the human race had reached perfection in its understanding of God. They loved and left us Gospels that could only be played properly in communities and churches that were not yet built. Indeed, they are still not built. Now that's faith in God.

My friend Will Willimon tells of the birthday of a little boy named Clayton. Clayton was four years old. His mother told him he could have any kind of birthday party he wished.[4]

So Clayton said, "I want a party where everybody there will be kings and queens." His mother granted the wish. She created a score of golden paper crowns, royal blue crepe paper robes, and cardboard scepters. As the guests arrived for the party, they received royal crowns, scepters, and robes. Everyone at the party was indeed either a king or a queen. They had a royal procession up to the end of the block and back. All the children were delighted. And they even behaved like kings and queens.

When the guests had all gone home and Clayton was being tucked into his bed, he said to his mother, "I wish everyone in the whole world could be a king — not just on my birthday, but every day."[5]

That's what happened at Calvary. The nobodies became somebodies. We who were once no people became somebody. God lifted the veil not only in the temple but in front of the eyes of his children. He gave us royalty not only in the temple but in front of the eyes of his children. He gave us not only a glimpse of his goodness but a glimpse of our own royalty. That's who we are and that's what life is all about. Grace is a vital part of the human condition.

Pssst and walk back. Pssst and walk back. That's life, isn't it? Is it all in vain? Or are we really kings and queens? Cynic or optimist? Thank God for Grace! May we accept our royal blood and start living from this day forward as the kings and queens we really are.

---

1. Robert McAfee Brown, *Is Faith Obsolete?* (Philadelphia: Westminster Press, 1974), p. 89.
2. *Ibid.,* p. 87.
3. *Ibid.,* p. 95.
4. William H. Willimon, *The Gospel For The Person Who Has Everything* (Valley Forge: Judson Press, 1978), p. 76. I transposed some of this material. This is not an exact quote.
5. *Ibid.*

Innocent Suffering

Job 38:1-18
John 19:30

In the town where I was raised there is an intersection in a residential area which I have skillfully avoided for the past eighteen years. Even when a trip would be made shorter by going directly through that intersection, I still go around.

There are two houses at that intersection that I haven't laid eyes on in eighteen years. Haven't wanted to, really. In one house lived a childhood friend of mine named Ed Arnold. When I was engaged in high school athletics, young Ed was the up-and-coming superstar in baseball and basketball. At age sixteen, Ed stood 6'5" tall and weighed 205 pounds. He was a gentle, lovable, fine Christian fellow. Everyone loved Ed. Then, Ed developed cancer. Within six months he was dead. At the age of seventeen, he still was 6'5" tall, but he weighed exactly 68 pounds when he turned over and died.

In the other house, directly across from Ed Arnold, lived Jane Eddins. Jane and I were the best of friends in high school. There were few people as pretty, kind, and fun-to-be-with as Jane Eddins. We went to ball games together, always saved at least a page for each other to write on in our high school annuals, and even went together on a trip to the Rocky Mountains, over 1,500 miles away. One night she and her brother were returning to our town from the University of South Carolina. A car driven by a person under the influence of alcohol careened out of control, smashed into the Eddins' car and decapitated Jane. She, like Ed, was seventeen years old when she was buried.

So I avoid that intersection in my old hometown. It's more than a place where two residential roads intersect. *It's the place where my belief in a kind, loving God, to whom I pray and in whom I believe, intersects with the randomness and suffering in the world which prompts me to question even the existence of a caring God.*

87

Now I suggest that all of us have such an intersection in our lives. If God's grace is available to humankind, it must be available to us as we seek to understand the apparent injustice of our common lot. Some of us are able to avoid the reality of innocent suffering for long periods, but that still doesn't make it go away. Others among us have to live very close to that reality all our days because of its ever-present claim on our lives through events in our own families. Harold Kushner is perhaps correct: "There is only one question which really matters: why do bad things happen to good people?"[1]

Can we really believe the world is good and that God is a kind and loving God? The world is certainly not a neat and just place. Any grace we are given must be grounded in a just God.

I do not intend to give a pat answer to the problem of suffering. Far from it. But I firmly believe we can strengthen our faith in order to live *with* the sufferings we must all face.

To be certain, there is a randomness in the universe. We do live in a world of chance. Although we are born with biologically inherited characteristics, no moral intelligence decided for us which of the millions of sperm would fertilize a waiting egg. We were born as we are, by chance. There are accidents, weather conditions, and failures that are also apparently randomly determined. And God appears to take a hands-off approach to this randomness. On the other hand, life surely must be more than a gigantic game of Russian roulette. If God is personally interested in what happens in the world and loves us as he says he does, then there ought to be some explanation for the suffering we face. If God is powerful and good, it did not do Ed Arnold and Jane Eddins any good. Did it? Did it do their friends any good to hope for their well-being?

The Old Testament presents us with a clear example of the question about good and evil in the form of a man named Job. Here was a godly man who suffered calamity after calamity. He lost his property, his health, his children, and the love of his wife. Yet people not as good as Job were prospering. It really wasn't fair. Job didn't deserve his fate. So in utter defiance he finally asked of God the ancient question: "Why me?"

In typical fashion, some counselors came to Job and offered him ridiculous answers. First, they said the world makes sense so there must be some reason for your suffering. Job didn't buy that. The world doesn't make sense and there isn't any *reason* for it. Then Job was told that life is tough and not to be surprised when things go wrong. Fortunately, Job didn't buy that either. Life is tougher for some folks than it is for others. Next, they told Job simply to "be patient." What ridiculous advice. So finally they gave Job the age-old cop-out for God, "suffering is good for you." Job didn't buy that either. *Suffering is not good. It is bad.*

Finally, there came a whirlwind, and out of that terrible windstorm God answers Job with these words: "What do you know about how to run a world?" God's response is to live with the mystery. There are mysteries that will always remain. But God responds that his love and concern operate in this world of change. God cares for a sparrow and even keeps track of the gestation period of the mountain goat.[2]

My God! How do we interpret that response? First of all, it means that God allows pain and misery in the world but does not deliberately inflict it. God has created a free universe with morally free creatures. *God can allow something to happen that God doesn't will to happen.* Not everything that happens is God's will. *God has set limits on God.* God will not intervene to take away our freedom, even the freedom to hurt ourselves and others. We have a wrought iron fire poker by the fireplace in our den. I could use it to hit someone on the head. I could kill someone with it even if he is a morally better person than I am. God could have created a world so that our iron poker would become as soft as bread when I unjustly used it as a weapon. But that would leave me with no responsibility to use it properly. In like manner, cancer will eat up an Ed Arnold even if he is a better person than someone who is free from cancer. And an out-of-control automobile will kill indiscriminately. Unlike other animals we humans have the capacity to understand both the indiscriminate nature of God's creation and our own eventual death. It's quite a burden for humans to carry as we contemplate our human condition.

89

Perhaps you have read or seen the television account of Colleen McCullough's novel, *The Thorn Birds*. It chronicles the life of a family in the harsh "outback" lands of Australia. As I peeped in on that family from my vantage point as a reader, I had an overwhelming urge to play God. I encountered a little girl whose personality was scarred forever by an elementary school teacher. She was treated with less dignity, because of her poverty, than the children of people who rode to school in big cars and donated buildings and organs to the town church. I wished I could have reached down into the book, picked the little girl up, and placed her in another school with another teacher, but I could not.

I encountered a son fighting with his father. He left home in helpless anger. He fell in with the wrong people who turned his life into violence and landed him in prison. I wished I could have reached into the book and placed him with different friends. But I could not. *I could not go into the lives of these people and manipulate them at will if the chief intent in their creation was their freedom to make their own history.* They must be free to live long or short lives, suffer innocently or deservedly, and choose their own responses to living in a world of chance and freedom. That is God's dilemma in relating to us humans.

If you were God, how would you handle life? Imagine, if you were a loving and caring God, what would you do, if the chief intent in our creation was to give us the freedom to make our own history?

I, frankly, can imagine only five things a loving God could possibly do to intervene in our process of life. If I were God, first of all, I would have to *intervene once* and for all for everyone, born and unborn. I could not respond to three or four billion human requests a day. What one human would want would negate what another human would want. The whole system of freedom of choice would go down the drain. It would have to be a one-time, inclusive shot, if I intervened. Secondly, this reconciliation with a suffering world would have to deal with more than one chapter of the human existence. If I loved humans I would have to cover more than just their years on earth, because all humans aren't given the same number of years to live on earth. It would have to be an *alpha and omega* intervention. Thirdly, if I really cared for these humans, I would have to intervene in such a way as to *share their suffering*. Fourthly, this once-and-for-all, alpha-and-omega, shared-suffering intervention would have to be done in such a way that they could *help one another* bear the burdens of suffering. And finally, I would have to leave behind something that would enable those humans always to have *access to personal communication* with me, to remind them constantly that I know their name and will remember them forever.

Now, that, in my opinion, is what a loving God would do to redeem the tragedies of this world from senselessness. Apparently that's what humankind came to see over a 4,000-year period. The Old Testament raised those questions. The Old Testament wanted answers to the unfair, unjust, God-awful tragedies that occur in human existence. It's full of curses against God. The Psalms hoped for a new sovereign who might bring in a new reform movement to champion the poor, weak, and oppressed. But the hope was unfinished. No God showed up to do that. The first Isaiah hoped God, if God was good, would at least cause a representative to be born on earth. Maybe a young woman could give birth to an ideal king who would be a wonderful counselor, a mighty God, a prince of peace. But it did not happen. Then, Jeremiah, two centuries later, looked out on his people shut up like birds in a cage with Babylonia ready to pounce and break what they understood to be a covenant with God. So Jeremiah cursed God and said if God was really good there would be a new covenant not on tablets of stone but on the eternal hearts of people, a covenant not just for one race but for all people. But it never happened. In this world of chance, Nebuchadnezzer crushed Jeremiah and put his people in exile for 500 years.

Then a second Isaiah wrote a message from that horrible exile: "Why do we suffer? If God is so great, so all-loving, let's hope he'll do the miraculous and send us a suffering servant to identify with our pain. Wouldn't a really good God comfort his people and suffer alongside of them?" But, friends, it just did not happen. Another writer from exile, the author of the book of Job, just came out and said it: "Why do the innocent suffer if God is so good?

91

Why do we have such a disease-ridden, non-loving, unjust, ca-lamitous, slop-bin existence if God is so good?" Why, indeed, is there not a once-and-for-all, all-inclusive, forever-intervention by a God who is good and will know our suffering to the extent something can be left behind to account for all the tragedies of random existence? Like a tidal wave the rush of human history shouted its bewildered cry. Hope after hope seemed to come to naught.

If the life of the human race from its creation to the present could be captured on motion picture film, *all the frames in that film combined would not add up in importance to the one where this Jesus of Nazareth cried, "It is finished," and pitches his head forward in the death on the cross.* That crucifixion took nearly nine hours. It was a slow death, the muscles degenerating into knobs of agony. There was nothing civilized about it. Paul tells us, "God was in Christ reconciling the world ... " (2 Corinthians 5:19). Think of it. God — *hanging like a slab of meat on some spikes.* Most of the faithful never showed up. Those who came were for the most part ignorant hecklers who spat and cursed. God in Christ looked down on a scene of madness, cried, "It is fin-ished," and slumped over into eternity. But God stuck to the rules when the Son cried out. God didn't unpin him. God did not play games with Pilate's freedom of choice, or negate the power of the Pharisees. It is indeed a random existence, a world of chance. *But it was finished!*

God knows our pain and becomes completely approachable even as we walk through the valley of the shadow of death. God sent us the strength to cope with existence. Existence is still something we should get angry at. At times it is rotten, unfair, and undeserved. *But it is finished!*

God always has the *last* word in human affairs. The Apostle Paul records these words from God when he sought help for his thorn in the flesh: "My grace is sufficient for you, for my power is made perfect in weakness."

I have seen some incredible tragedies redeemed from sense-lessness through the love and power of God. It is finished and there is a grace sufficient for our living in a sometimes rotten, unfair, and untimely world of chance.

It was finished long before you and I were born. And it is finished for others who will be born long after our death.

I think the next time I go back to my hometown I'll ride through the intersection again. Maybe I'll even get out of the car and walk around. When the issue is decided and there is a grace that penetrates the randomness of human existence, a person can see beyond the shadow of the present. *You can live by faith in a world of chance.*

Once one encounters the possibilities of a life of hopeful living, the possibilities are powerful beyond belief. In spite of our modern dilemmas, one can lift the psychological ceiling on one's hope in order to embrace the unseen, reconcile cherished notions of peace with uncherished facts about violence, embrace scientific inquiry and live by faith in a world of chance. Jesus certainly thought it possible. In fact, such hopeful living is our only hope. We can actually serve as lights of kindness in a rough world. Our lifestyles can reflect, and indeed must reflect, those internal characteristics which evidence the redemptive grace of God in Christ which sustains us in this world of innocent suffering.

---

1. Harold Kushner, *When Bad Things Happen to Good People* (New York: Avon Books, 1981), p. 6.

2. Daniel J. Simundson, *Faith Under Fire* (Minneapolis: Augsburg, 1980), contains a helpful analysis of Job.

The Mothering Side Of God

Lamentations 4:1-5
Luke 1:67-80
Ephesians 1:3-12

His name is Harold and he lives near Atlanta. Harold is a child who very much wanted to be in his church's Christmas pageant. Harold wasn't selected for one of the larger parts. He was selected to be just a shepherd. Harold's sister, however, landed a big part. She was chosen to play an angel. During rehearsal, the director of the pageant marked an "X" on the stage floor to show each character just where to stand. Harold knew exactly which "X" was his.

On the afternoon of the pageant, Harold dressed in his robe and slippers in just ten minutes, while it took his sister most of the day to get on her white dress with hoops and wire-up her halo and wings. Obviously, Harold was disgusted with his lesser role.

As the pageant began, the angels took their places in great splendor. Now, the director's only oversight was a failure to realize that the hoops in the angels' dresses caused the spread-out dresses to cover completely some of the X's. When Harold entered, he could not find his X. It was under an angel's dress. He walked all around the stage but could not find his spot. Finally, he walked to the center of the stage, lifted his arms as though to lead in prayer and shouted, "The dumb angels have covered up all the crosses!"[1]

Sometimes it is like that in our religious perspective. The angels can indeed cover the crosses. When that happens we tend to miss one of God's greatest gifts to our human condition: God's mothering side.

There already existed in that story of the birth of Christ in Bethlehem a foretaste of the sufferings and crosses that he would have to bear in his lifetime. In fact, the story of the birth of Jesus has all the ingredients to be a horror story, even if we do tend to cover them with angels' dresses. We can't let the angels cover up those crosses or we miss God's gift to us.

94

Imagine what the Christmas story would be like if you filmed it or made a video of it. A young teenage girl named Mary received word that she was pregnant. In those days you could be stoned to death for being pregnant before marriage. There was little romance about the events which happened to this woman named Mary. Foreign soldiers occupied the land and everyone was required to return to his home city to re-register for taxation. Mary was well into her pregnancy and had to ride on a donkey's back many weary miles. Then all the places to stay were booked, so she had to set up residence in an animal shelter and have her baby there. It was a dangerous time. Birthing was a crude process. And once the child was born, the dangers were everywhere. One of the "signs" given to the shepherds was that they would find the child "wrapped in swaddling clothes." The mother had to wrap the child in swaddling clothes lest he freeze to death in that little cave in the hillside. Then, the mother heard that King Herod had ordered all male babies slaughtered. So she and her husband had to take the small infant and flee many, many weary miles to Egypt.

No, we must not let the angels' dresses cover the many crosses that were in the Christmas story for that brave mother. And we Protestants, in our valid attempt to revolt against the excesses of Mariolatry and Catholicism, must not lose the mothering side of God.

The late George Buttrick used to say that there is no such thing as a "self-made" person. For every great self-made person some brave mother went down in pain and discomfort to get him or her here.

If there is something which keeps the Christmas story from being a horror story, it is not the presence of angels. It is the mothering nature of God. God is not only powerful and almighty; God is so tender and caring that no person is so forsaken and homeless in this world that God cannot see him and come to him and take care of him with real tenderness.

The mother and the child hold the story together, don't they? We never escape the need for a mother, do we? The mother cannot be written out of the picture. All else can be removed from the Christmas story and it is still the Christmas story. The mother who

95

sang praises to God for giving her such a son; the mother who wrapped him in warm clothes and loved him; the mother who remained close by him during his ministry; the mother who stood by the horrible cross when her son was executed. The mother cannot be written out of the grace of God toward humans. The angels' dresses cannot cover up all the crosses that the mother stood on.

What a powerful message it is! In the Old Testament we see a God who is a powerful and tremendous force. God is accompanied by loud and awesome trumpet blasts. God's messages were so terrible that people begged God to stop speaking. Moses became so frightened at the sight of God on the mountain that he shook with a terrible fear. In addition, the Israelites believed that anyone who touched the Ark of God, other than the most holy, would surely die.

We need a powerful God. And we have one. But we need a caring God, too. That is one of the clues toward finding Grace in the human condition. *God has a mothering side.*

When Jesus grew to be a man he told us that in his father's house are many mansions and that he will not leave us as orphans, struggling alone in the world. There is a mothering, caretaking side to God's nature that the trumpet blasts and the angels' dresses cannot obscure.

One of the greatest pastors in this century was the German, Martin Niemoller. In 1938, Niemoller was arrested and placed in solitary confinement as Adolf Hitler's personal prisoner. Three years later he was sent by the Nazis to the Dachau concentration camp where he preached to his fellow prisoners for four years. On Christmas Eve in Dachau in 1944, he spoke of the great joy that came precisely in these unromantic aspects of the first Christmas: "God, the eternally wealthy and almighty God, enters into the most extreme human poverty imaginable. No person is so weak and helpless that God does not come to him in Jesus Christ, right in the midst of our human need; and no person is so forsaken and homeless in this world that God does not seek him, in the midst of our human distress."[2]

That is powerful. There is a tender side of God that does not leave us as orphans. In spite of the most brutal of human conditions, God has a mothering side that comes into our midst.

God can come. There is no situation so bleak that God cannot come and wrap tender arms around us and love us. There is no place that can shut God out; no cold that can freeze God away; no tyrant that can murder God's comfort; no journey that can conquer God's resolve; no disease that can blot God's grace.

The Marys of our world can still feel God's blessedness. I know a woman named Mary. She is 97 years old. Her crippled body is folded awkwardly into a wheelchair. She will spend the rest of her life in a nursing home. She has no family. She resides in a room at the end of the hall where the smell of urine is stronger and the people look like zombies. The Salvation Army occasionally brings her a package containing a toothbrush, a comb, some candy, and Kleenex. A church group or some Girl Scouts often walk perfunctorily down the hall, stealing glances into Mary's room. It seems so lonely as their voices rise above the moaning and crying. Don't worry. Unto her a Savior has come and the dumb angels' dresses can't obscure the smiling face of God standing on Mary's crosses.

Somewhere in Ethiopia, a mother pulls a rag over the face of her starving child. The baby's body shakes one last time and then it gives up its spirit to death by famine as we sit down to our VCRs, home computers, and compact disc players. Don't worry. That child has had a Savior born unto it who will pick it up in his arms, and wrap it in swaddling clothes and hold it to his heart. Our dumb angels' dresses can't obscure the smiling face of God standing on the crosses, pointing the way toward home for those who suffer poverty and death in ways we cannot begin to imagine.

Somewhere a body racked with pain, processing chemotherapy treatments, laboriously makes its way to a table for one last dinner with the family before the cancer drains its life from it. Don't worry. Unto it a Savior has been born and the dumb angels' dresses can't obscure the smiling face of God standing on its cross.

Isn't that wonderful news? *God has a tender side.*

That's a great gift of hope for our human condition. There is no weakness, no pain, no amount of tragedy and horror that can come into our lives that is so extreme that God cannot seek us and find us right in the middle of our human distress. Look for it. Expect it. Count on it. There is so much more to God than the gift of power and angelic visions. There is the tenderness of love and grace.

There is the adoption of the human race by a God with a mothering side. In our system of patriarchy, we often tend to focus on the experience of being born into a home. It strikes us as somewhat foreign to conceive of a God who prefers to *adopt* children into an eternal home. Yet the mothering side of God comes from a tradition in which adoption by a tolerant and impartial parent into an eternal home stands at the core of its assertion.

Children are marvelous creatures. They can love and hate one another and their parents at the drop of a hat. My sister and I experienced the usual sibling rivalry when we were growing up. Our parents had to exercise care to give us presents that were exactly alike when we were small. Then, as we grew older, they could get away with purchasing different items, as long as they both cost the same.

On several occasions in our childhood my sister and I voiced questions to each other relative to our natural or adopted relationship to our parents. These occasions were when we overstepped our boundaries and were punished by our parents. More than once, after my mother and father had yelled at me over a "C" in conduct on a report card or over one of my displays of bad temper, I would go into my room crying. I would whisper to my sister, in utter sincerity and complete confidence, "Mary Jo, I think I'm adopted. Really. Nobody that mean could be my real parents. I think I'm adopted."

Obviously, I did not know much about adoption then. It takes as much love to care for something or someone you've adopted as it does to care for something you've made.

The writer of Ephesians made a powerful statement to the effect that none of us are natural-born children. We are all adopted — that is, if we want to be adopted. He stated that God, as an act of love, decided before time began to adopt everyone on earth through Jesus Christ and freely give those people the inheritance of his kingdom. Most of us probably do not understand the seriousness of those adoption papers. Our lack of appreciation perhaps comes because we confuse our privileges with rights. That wasn't the case with the first Christians.

Under Roman law, adoption was a serious step. It was not uncommon to adopt a child to ensure that your family would not become extinct. The ritual of adoption was very impressive. Copper and scales were used. Twice the real father sold his son and twice he symbolically bought him back. Then the sale was held a third time, and at the third sale the son was not bought back. After this, the adopting father had to go to the magistrate and plead his case for adoption. When the adoption was complete, the adopted son had all the rights of inheritance in the new family. All his debts and obligations connected with his previous family were abolished as if they had never existed.[3] You, obviously, were quite lucky if someone adopted you. In fact, you were doubly rich. It was a powerful image of a state of grace.

For the early church, God, through Jesus, adopts us from a worldly family of sin and death and gives us full rights of inheritance in his heavenly kingdom. It is a great privilege to be delivered from a situation from which you could have never delivered yourself. Ezekiel depicted Israel as an illegitimate child who, on the day of her birth, was cast into an open field and left to die of exposure. But God came by and adopted that foundling into God's family and left her a great inheritance. That, said the writer of Ephesians, is what God did for the whole world, not just one nation, in Jesus. We were lying exposed in an open world of sin, with all kinds of human obligations. We were not going to make it. Death was the lot to which we were born. But Bethlehem's God adopted us, bought us with God's only son, and gave us a rich inheritance. That is tremendous news, isn't it? We're all illegitimate children, but God loves us anyway!

Sometimes we have a difficult time accepting our state as adopted children because we confuse rights with privileges. For example, most of us attend church because we, or a member of our family, can drive a car. No one has the right to drive an automobile. Driving is a privilege that is granted by the state in which you drive. If you do not obey the laws, that state can take that privilege away from you. If you do not possess certain information and driving skills, the state will not even grant you the privilege in the first place. One can't simply go down to city hall and pound his fist on the desk and scream, "I demand the right to drive." A privilege is given. It is not owed to you.

In like manner, we did not have a right to be adopted by God. We did not have a right to the birth of Christ. No one has the right to be adopted by anyone else. It is a privilege. That's the good news of our human condition. We march toward an eternal home at death, not out of a right but a privilege.

It is amazing to me that the Apostle Paul could grasp that idea in his situation. Paul was in prison in Rome, awaiting trial before Nero. He was allowed to stay in a house which he himself had rented, and his friends had access to him; but day and night he was chained to the wrist of a Roman soldier whose duty it was to see that he never escaped. Amazingly, Paul considered it a privilege to be a prisoner for Christ. Just because he believed in God and had perhaps a closer relationship with God than any of us ever will, he did not demand that he had a right to be set free and live an easy life. He knew that God had adopted him and given him everlasting status as a son. God had bought him through the blood of Jesus, and he had full rights of inheritance of all that his adopted parent possessed. He concluded that that was a privilege that far outweighed the sufferings of his present time.

One of the great success stories in our country is that of Booker T. Washington. He was born a slave. But with his courage and his bare hands he founded Tuskegee Institute and lived to see it evolve from a henhouse and an abandoned stable to a world-renowned educational center. He raised most of the money needed to build and staff this first teachers' college for his race. His autobiography tells us that he never had to resort to begging. The genuinely generous people felt privileged in being in a position to support a worthwhile enterprise. It is a privilege to be able to help a good cause, to have a share in something worthwhile. Not many people have that privilege.

Someone once asked me, "How do you get a person to be generous? How can you make an ungenerous person into a generous person?" I only know of one way — that person must recover a sense of privilege in being an adopted child of a tender, mothering-fathering God.[4] The key word is learning to appreciate the privilege of your state as an adopted child of God. Frankly, I'm tired of preaching on people's duty to come to church; their responsibilities as a Christian; their obligation to do certain things; their need to sacrifice for something. You rarely hear the word "privilege" used around a church. But we are a very privileged people.

Parents complain about all they sacrifice for their children. No one has a right to have a child. I know a young woman, 36 years old, who has had five miscarriages trying to have a child. Twenty percent of the funerals I have done as a minister have been for children less than one year old. I have visited with people who have been waiting seven years to adopt a child. It is a privilege, not a duty, to be entrusted with the upbringing of a child for a few years. You will never be generous with your time to your children until you understand that.

We hear about sacrifices people make to go to school. Few people in this country sacrifice anything to go to school. It is a privilege not everyone in the world has. There are 600 students in a school in Kenya who have four textbooks among them. When they go home and it becomes dark, they can't do homework even if they wanted to because there is no electricity in their homes. Our children don't have an obligation to do their homework in order to get a good grade. Every time they go in that room, open a book, and turn on a lightbulb, they are participating in a privilege, a privilege not everyone has. I once served as director of ministerial studies at Harvard University. I saw a young man walk to that university from Minnesota. He lived on a small farm, which had just been repossessed. His family lost everything. So he packed what he could into a backpack and odd-jobbed his way to school, literally walking 1,000 miles when he couldn't catch a ride or hop a slow train. No, most of us did not go to college because we were sacrificial and responsible. We went as the acceptance of a privilege.

The writer of Ephesians hammered home a great awareness of a general privilege that Christians possess. He said that it is a privilege to know something that other people don't know. He said that the Christians know a secret that not everyone knows:

"God has adopted the world. We are God's children and through the ministry, death, and resurrection of Jesus, we have become heirs of God's estate." Therefore, life is worth living. That is a secret that has been unveiled to Christians which not everyone knows yet.

As we march toward our death, we do so as adopted children of a tender, if not mothering, God. We participate in a common condition with the entire human race.

———————

1. The story is told by Thomas Are, Shallowford Road Presbyterian Church, Atlanta, Georgia. Reprinted in *Disciples' Diary*, Disciples United Methodist Church, Greenville, South Carolina, December 1984.

2. From *Dachau Sermons* by Martin Neimoller, trans. Robert H. Pfeiffer (New York: Harper & Row, 1946), pp. 1-14.

3. William Barclay, *The Letters to the Galatians and Ephesians,* revised edition (Philadelphia: Westminster, 1976), pp. 79-80.

4. See Leonard Griffith, *Ephesians: A Positive Affirmation* (Waco: Word Inc., 1975), p. 49.

The Lord's Response

Genesis 3:16-19
Mark 12:1-2

Everyone has a cracking point. There comes a certain point in our relationships with others or in our feelings about ourselves when everything snaps. You and I are emotionally and physiologically structured so that we can withstand only so much. There is only so much garbage, so much heat we can take. Then, like the valve on a pressure cooker, we simply blow off. Perhaps the six most dramatic words in the human condition are these: "I just can't take it anymore."

Every person has a cracking point. It happens to even the most passive and sedate person. I'll never forget an incident from my childhood. It occurred when I was thirteen years old. My best friend's family used to gather on certain weekends in the fall at their "old home place" near Atlanta. They frequently included me on their trips.

We would all go to a college football game in Atlanta on Saturday. Then on Sunday after lunch all the aunts, uncles, brothers, sisters, and assorted friends like me would bid one another farewell. My friend's father, Mr. W., was one of the nicest, most even-tempered persons I have ever met. He seemed always to be in command of his emotions.

One Sunday, as we packed the car to return home, it started raining. All the relatives were gathered on the porch watching Mr. W. pack the trunk. His wife came out in the yard and stood there under her umbrella giving Mr. W. instructions. For ten minutes or more she kept up an incessant cadence of instructions: "Put this here; put that there." Finally, Mr. W. had had enough. He started flinging items out of the trunk and all over the yard. Mr. W. flung all the suitcases, garment bags, travel kits and everything. Clothes were everywhere: in the mud and on the hedges. Mrs. W. just stood there crying in the rain. I can still visualize her holding that umbrella and crying while all the relatives on the porch were laughing. One of them whispered in my ear, "Mr. W. just hit his cracking point."

Those points exist for everyone. A problem begins in loneliness, fear, anger, busted relationships, lack of communication, resentment, or stress and we reach a cracking point. Then, the debris from that moment is scattered all over the backyard of our horizon. Sometimes we, unlike Mr. W., don't have a lot of relatives and friends to come running off the back porch and start repacking life for us. Sometimes all we can do is stand in the rain and scream, "I just can't take it any more."

In a recent survey the American Medical Association asked several thousand general practitioners across the country, "What percentage of people that you see in a week have needs that you are qualified to treat with your medical skills?" The responses ranged from one percent to 25 percent. The average was ten percent. In other words, ninety percent of the people who see a general practitioner have no medically treatable problem. Most of the respondents said they prescribed tranquilizers. The patients are ill and suffering real pain. They may even die prematurely. But essentially a problem that begins when lifestyles and relationships reach a cracking point moves from one bodily system to another until it stops at some particular organ with nowhere else to go. Then it becomes defective and the doctor can practice "end organ medicine."[1]

Everybody has a cracking point. And God can identify with that. God, apparently, has a "cracking point," too. There have been times, if Scripture is correct, when God has reached God's cracking point. That point for God seems to come when humans attempt to forget their human condition, that they are tenants of this world and not owners.

It started with Adam and Eve. The Lord gave them everything. God put up with everything they did except one thing. The hunger of humans God put up with and even built a garden. The loneliness of mankind (Adam) beat God down so God created a companion (Eve — mother of all living). The dominance of humans gnawed at God so God let the humans name every living thing on the planet and have dominion over them. All God said was, "I don't want you to try to take over and become like me. Enjoy what I've given, but I couldn't take your trying to take over the knowledge of good and evil."

But an evil force came along and said, "God won't crack. Don't worry about it. You can do anything. You can have your eyes opened and be like God."

So they tried it. And that was God's cracking point. At the time of their greatest success, Adam and Eve ran into God's cracking point. Like a madman hurling baggage from the trunk of a car, God called out the debris God was going to leave all over the backyard of humankind. "I will greatly multiply your pain in childbirth; you will have to earn a living all the rest of the days of your life; you will sweat and toil; and when that's over, you will return to the ground from which you were taken; you are dust and to dust you shall return" (Genesis 3:16-19). Then God drove them out of the garden.

In reality, the response from God seems all out of proportion to the mistake — from our point of view. But not to God. Human arrogance is God's cracking point.

As we view the Bible, we can say God's cracking point is consistent, from the Tower of Babel, when humans tried to reach into the heavens and God busted them into different languages, to God's relationship with the Pharaoh, when Pharaoh tried to own something that wasn't his. The cracking point came when humans tried to be like God and take over.

The last parable Jesus ever told points to God's cracking point (Mark 12:1-12). After Jesus told this parable, his enemies finally ganged up on him. The biblical record states, "The scribes and chief priests tried to lay hands on him at that very hour." All the top-level Jewish brass were in agreement. This prophet from Nazareth had to be silenced forever.

The parable of the wicked tenants pictures a God dealing with humans who resent the fact that they are only humans. They want to be God. A man plants a vineyard, digs a pit for a wine press, rents it out to tenants, and leaves. When harvesttime arrives, this owner sends a servant to get some fruit from the tenants. They beat him up and run him off. Twice more the owner sends servants.

They beat one of them up and kill the other one. All the owner has left is a beloved son. So he sends him, saying, "They will respect my son." But the renters have become profiteers. They want to steal the property.

Under Jewish law, three years' undisputed possession of a piece of land enabled a person to claim ownership of that land over the holder of a deed. The tenants were elated when the son came. They got their hands on the heir. They killed the owner's son.

Jesus reported, "What will the owner do? He will come and destroy the tenants."

When the scribes and priests heard this, they exclaimed, "God forbid!"

Now, my friends, immediately following this parable, Jesus was asked, "Is it lawful to pay taxes to Caesar or not?" Jesus simply responded, "Give Caesar the things that Caesar owns and give God the things God owns."

Obviously, the meaning is clear — *woe be unto us if we try to give ourselves the things that God owns*. That's God's cracking point.

Most of our problems in life come when we turn over to ourselves things that don't belong to us. When we try to play God, we crack up. When we use other creatures to selfishly maintain our own high standard of living, we crack up. When our own ambition wildly leads us to covet things that are not ours, we crack up. When we sever relationships with other people and jealously try to steal for ourselves the integrity of those other people, we crack up.

But humans and God have in common more than the ability to reach the cracking point and shout into the rain, "I just can't take it anymore." We and God still live on after our cracking points. There's life beyond the cracking point. In fact, what we do with life beyond the cracking point is more important than what happens up to that moment. People do live beyond their cracking point. And we can look to God for an example of how to do that, as well. *When you get on the other side of your cracking-up point, that's when you have to return to your essential faith in a God of love.* That's when you have to get down to basics.

106

One spring day in Washington, D.C., an excursion boat was on the Potomac on its maiden run. A large number of Congressmen and Senators were invited. The day was a hot one. So a famous Senator removed his shoes and socks. He hung the socks on a railing in front of him. One of the members of the press noticed that someone ran by him and inadvertently brushed against one of the socks. It fell into the water and was gone. The Senator went over to the railing, picked up the remaining sock and threw it overboard. The columnist was impressed. He confessed that if it had been him he probably would have brought the remaining sock home. "I have a ... drawer full of single socks ..." he said. "That's my problem. My life is full of single socks. I've got to clean out these good for nothing things and get down to some new simple basics that work."[2]

Sometimes after our cracking points you and I carry around things we should throw away about ourselves and God. Things and beliefs sometimes get lost and need to be jettisoned so we can return to a new appreciation of what God did after reaching the cracking point. There is a tendency for us to go through life mesmerized by our past losses and hurts. We tend to forget what God has done for us. Instead of a firm belief in a loving God, we hold on to a drawer full of religious single socks. We forget that what God did in Jesus after his cracking point was the match to what he did to Adam and Eve and the wicked tenants in the vineyard. *The New Testament account of the cross is the matching sock to everything we fear about God.*

Perhaps the best dramatization of God's cracking point and afterwards was given by a man from Greensboro, North Carolina, named Marc Connelly. In 1929, Connelly, a black man, wrote a play called *The Green Pastures*.[3] It was an attempt to portray, in the language of uneducated blacks from the deep South, a vision of God and heaven. The play opened in New York in February of 1930 and ran for over a year and a half. In Connelly's view of heaven the angels hold some magnificent fish fries. The final scene revolves around just such a fish fry. A large kettle of hot fat has a fire going underneath it. A rustic table is piled high with piles of biscuits and cornbread, and the cooked fish are in huge dish pans.

There are two large churns of custard which looks like milk. There are glasses and a dipper beside the churns. The angels are milling around, flapping their wings. But God is seated in an armchair with his face in his hands. Every now and then he looks up and stares out toward earth and cries. The angel Gabriel walks in and comes up to the armchair.[4]

> *"You look worried, Lawd."*
> *God nods his head.*
> *"Here, have a cigar, Lawd."*
> *But God says, "No thanks, Gabriel; don't want no cigar."*
> *Gabriel goes over and gets a cup of custard. Then he returns. "You look awful, Lawd. You look awful. You been sittin' yere, lookin' dis way, an awful long time. Is it somethin' serious, Lawd?"*
> *God responds: "Very serious, Gabriel. Look at my chillun down there on earth. They's killing one another. Stealin' from and lying to each other. They's committin' adultery and runnin' after money. My heart's broken."*
> *Gabriel is awed by his tone. He knows the Lord just can't take it anymore. "Lawd, is de time come for me to blow de horn? Just say the word, Lawd. Just snap you finger and I'll blow de horn. We'll wipe 'em all out dead right now. Worse than Adam. Worse than Noah. Worse than Pharaoh. Say de word, Lawd, and I'll blow de horn."*
> *God waves Gabriel off. "Not yet, Gabriel; I've decided what I'm gonna do. Ain't but one thing left to do. I'm a gonna go down there myself. I'm gonna live among 'em. Eat among 'em. Love 'em. Help 'em. Even die among 'em if I have to."*
> *The Lawd gets up from his armchair and walks away from the fish fry. Gabriel goes over to the empty chair and he stares down at earth. All the heavenly beings come over and look down, too. And from the back a voice is heard: "Oh look at him! Look at him. Dey goin' to make him carry that cross up dat high hill! Dey goin' to nail him to it! Dey goin' to nail him to it! Oh dat's a terrible burden ..." But as the light fades, they see the Lawd down*

there smiling gently. And all the angels burst into song.
Cause they'd seen what the Lawd had done after he got
to his cracking point.

As we wander this earth as sojourners, struggling with our human condition, we affirm that God's grace is a *response* to that condition, not a reaction to it or a rejection of it.

---

1. See Bruce Larson, *There's A Lot More To Health Than Not Being Sick* (Waco, Texas: Word, Inc., 1981), p. 20.

2. *Ibid*, p. 132.

3. *The Green Pastures* was first produced at the Mansfield Theatre, New York City, by Laurence Rivers, Inc., on February 26, 1930 and closed on August 29, 1931. Marc Connelly's original play may be found in *Sixteen Famous American Plays*, edited by Bennett Cerf and Van H. Cartwell (Garden City, New York: Garden City Publishing Co., 1941). It was produced in many versions. I have used a combination of the original and later productions, trying to retain the meaning and purpose of the original while fitting some of the language into my sermon.

4. *Ibid*.

Giving And Receiving

2 Samuel 7:1-11, 16

The Scriptures from some of the prophets pointed toward Yahweh's choice of the family of David as the vehicle for God's divine gift to humankind. Yet the message from Samuel marked a transition in David's status. According to the passage, David wanted to build Yahweh a "house." He proposed to do what all self-serving rulers in that ancient world would have done. Much of Israel's worship life was well established at that point. The tent which housed the Ark of the Covenant was a recognized institution. A conviction began to emerge in ancient Israel that God dwelt within this tent in its Holy of Holies. King David wanted to build a divine residence of cedar which would contain the Holy of Holies.

Nathan, the prophet, originally blessed this idea. But God challenged the idea and offered a second opinion. The temple would be built by David's son, Solomon. Instead, Yahweh would make David himself the "house" of God by guaranteeing his embodiment concretely in this man's family and dynasty. What a transition. The achiever, the one who wanted to give the gift to God, became the receiver of God's gift.

One of the amazing aspects of the Bible is its honesty. The sordid aspects of the human condition are included with the positive aspects. Human failure and human triumph comprise the environment for God's revelation of grace. The guilty as well as the guiltless find their way into the pages of this chronicle of God's revelation to humankind.

The Scriptures use the example of David's desire to do something for God to teach us all a lesson about patience, waiting, and freedom. The changed mind after David's quick conclusion points to a particular character of the God of the Bible. This God is a come-and-go God whose dynamism cannot be settled or confined to one place. Unlike every other god, this God needs no house, wants no house, and has no house. At a deep level the housing project denial points toward David's love for God. Daniel Day Williams is correct: "Love always makes itself vulnerable by willing the freedom of the other."[1]

The love David displayed toward Yahweh and Yahweh's freedom was no small matter for that time and place.

In preliterate and simply-structured societies, religion played a unifying role in life. The village was a self-contained society in which all rituals and symbols were religious ones. "The religious" was not relegated to one aspect or activity of life, distinct from the other aspects. Speaking of the religious and the nonreligious or secular as two different dimensions of life would have been foreign to a preliterate society. To live at all was to live within a religious community with clearly defined rites of passage on the journey home. Every major event in life, from pregnancy and childbirth to the cutting of the first tooth, puberty, the first haircut, marriage, and vocation, carried religious rites of passage. These rites symbolized the human condition as it was understood by society.[2]

A wholeness of outlook characterized the civilization of David's time. The private and the social were not separated from one another. Religion tended to unify or support all elements of life, both social and individual. David's recognition that God needed no house was a fundamental aspect of his being allowed the honor of the "Davidic ideal" which ultimately produced the Christ child. Only as David was willing to "let go" of his desire to bring a gift to God and let God bring the gift to him was the revelation made complete. The text is more than a rhetorical inversion. It is a powerful message for today's Christian. We, too, are called to let go and let God bring God's gift to us.

Do you remember your first day of school? It was one of life's great separations. Perhaps your parent drove up the circular driveway of an elementary school. You, perhaps, clutched her hand as tightly as possible as you passed legions of strangers on their way to the classroom. You stood at the door and, perhaps, she literally had to push you in. The classroom probably appeared to be the most foreboding room you had ever entered.

Looking back, that time of "letting go" of mother's hand was a necessary step. It was indeed the time to "let go" and enter another experience. Life is essentially a series of separations. We let go of certain experiences in favor of other experiences. Friends are gained and then we are separated. Sometimes couples marry and at other times they separate. Sometimes our "letting go" involves places: we leave our hometowns; we leave our schools; we even leave our churches. Sometimes we let go of roles or patterns of relating. We let go of our roles as parents, as children, as students. Sometimes we even "let go" of attitudes and beliefs. In those moments of "letting go" we come to realize how intensely loyal we are to the people, the places, and the attitudes which have shaped us.

Letting go is a necessary part of life. The Bible is full of separations. Abraham and Lot separated so each could live and multiply. In the newly-found freedom as humans with a mind of their own, Adam and Eve had to separate from the Garden of Eden. In the book of Exodus, God told Israel: "I have separated you from all the people that are on the face of the earth" (33:16). David was told to let go of the idea that he controlled God's housing needs. Jesus himself was separated from his family and his family's business. In order for the early church to be more than four little families meeting together in upper rooms to remember Jesus, those people had to separate and trust God to come among them in God's own freedom.

God has given our human personality many weapons with which to encounter life and find the way home at the end of it. We possess fight and flight responses, administrative ability, anger, ego, temperament, grief reaction, and the like. These characteristics sometimes make it difficult for us simply to let go and wait for God to be God.

The Bible tells us that right after he was baptized, Jesus Christ faced the greatest temptation of his life. He had just realized that he was the Messiah. He was at the point of beginning his ministry. Satan tempted him to try to live his whole life in a moment's time. Satan promised him instant accomplishment of his ministry. Listen to the account: "The devil led him up to a high place and showed him in an instant all the kingdoms of the world. And he said to him, 'I will give you all their authority and splendor ... so if you worship me, it will all be yours' " (Luke 4:5-7). Just like that, promised the devil. Instant achievement. No waiting. No having to grasp the slow wisdom of the world. A shortcut, just for the taking, in an instant, was held forth. But who was deceiving whom? The devil was merely offering to Jesus in a shorter span of time what would ultimately be his anyway. God had promised Jesus that achievement from the very beginning at Bethlehem. The devil was merely offering Jesus something he was already promised. But the devil did offer it to him *in an instant*. That was the difference.

We moderns often find ourselves unable to let go of our need to be in charge and allow God to bring to us the gifts God wants to give. The late L.D. Johnson used to contend that one of the bizarre facts of life is this one. The more religious people become, the less patient and comfortable they become with the mystery and freedom of God. Those who consider themselves very religious tend to point their finger at us and claim God is this or God is that. The freedom of God is the heart of all religion. You'd think the closer you got to God the more overwhelmed you would be by the awesomeness and indescribable nature of God. You'd think the closer you got to God the less clear-cut would be your expression of God.[3]

David's ability to step back and let God provide him with the same gift he wanted to give God was an impetus of inversion that was reflected in the grand gift to come. No greater ruler ever commanded the Israelite people. David was depicted as God's personal choice to lead the chosen people. He unified the two nations of Israel and Judah. He was impetuous, aggressive, charismatic, manipulative, and, above all, a great administrator. He removed the last vestige of Canaanite power in the land.

But when David allowed the inversion to take place, when he allowed God to give him the gift, he established a process which foreshadowed the coming grace of God through Christ. Kings normally give gifts. They do not receive them, especially from God. Consider the images used by the descendant of David, Jesus the Christ, to provide this same wonderfully good news.

Jesus washed with water. Whether it was the smelly feet of the disciples or his own baptism, he showed that this image was definitely a change. He took a towel, wrapped it around himself, and washed the smelly feet of his disciples. That was, indeed, out of sync. Everyone knows that disciples wash their *master's* feet. The proper image is of a religious leader like our society's Pope in Rome sitting on an altar with a huge canopy of gilded bronze ringed in Renaissance splendor by the Swiss Guard in their scarlet and gold. That's image projection at its finest, is it not? Everyone knows that winning coaches have coliseums named after them, author books, do television commercials, and have swimming pools in the shape of their school's mascot. Messianic coaches do not go into the locker room after the game, take out towels and basins of water, and start washing the smelly feet of their players. Yet this crazy son of God would do just that. That's a powerful image, one must admit.

Secondly, Jesus gave suppers with bread and wine to show that his new life was a brotherhood or sisterhood. That, too, is an image that shocks us. Banquets are given in honor of great people; great people do not give banquets for the poor.

Jesus touched people with his hands — whether they were lepers or diseased or dead, like Lazarus. He touched people society would *not* touch. What a reverse image projection that was! Most of the societal projection of a great religious leader is the number of *important* people the leader touches — the winning coach, the Hollywood actor, Miss America, the converted infamous criminal, the bestselling authors. Not Jesus! His hands touched those that society would *not* touch.

This strange process of inversion which makes us the receiver of a gift from God is the essence of the biblical perspective on our human condition. It recognizes a transition in our status as worshippers of God. We are now the receivers of the ultimate gift: God in Christ comes to make us the house of God's dwelling. This notification is as heady for us as it once was for this precarious tribal chieftain named David. There is no greater joy that can be promised us.

---

1. Daniel Day Williams, "The Vulnerable and the Invulnerable God," *Union Seminary Quarterly Review*, Vol. 17, No. 3, p. 225.

2. Some of the material in this sermon has been previously published in Harold C. Warlick, Jr., *Homeward Bound* (Lima, Ohio: CSS Publishing Co., 1991) and is used by permission.

3. As quoted in L.D. Johnson, *Moments of Reflection* (Nashville: Broadman Press, 1980), p. 39.

IV. RESPONSIBILITY

Picking Ancestors

Psalm 16:3-6
1 Kings 3:5-12
Joshua 24:14-24

On a hot, dry June day I was riding on a bus with 33 other Americans through the mountain passes in southern Greece. We were headed to the ruins of ancient Mycenae. When the bus stopped I couldn't believe we had chosen that place to visit. Mycenae is actually a mountain of rocks with hundreds of steps, over 2,300 years old, leading to the top. Mycenae was a little kingdom ruled by an overlord who had built his fortress on this tremendous mountain. The gates of Mycenae contain the first coat of arms of Europe. Two lions stand facing one another with their front paws resting on two small, united altars. This coat of arms of the royal house of Mycenae is the oldest example of sculpture in Europe. It is also the oldest example of trying to preserve a family tree. The people of Mycenae were the first to whitewash their ancestors. You see, the last dynasty of Mycenae was a horrible one. They committed every crime in the book — slavery, incest, and cannibalism. You name it and they did it. Yet they persisted in using the beautiful lions as their coat of arms.

Genealogists amaze me. Virtually every family has a coat of arms on their wall today and an impressive family tree. I have both in my family. But, like everyone else, I have a number of people in my family tree about whom little is known. The late dean of Duke University, Harold Bosley, had a friend in Iowa who worked up his family tree. Like most of us, this man had a great time working up his family's coat of arms and the remarkable line of men and women of integrity and high community repute who emerged as he traced the family from Boston to Iowa over its hundred-year history. But then the genealogist did a no-no. He started tracing down a few of the forebears about whom little was known. On a trip to Vermont he decided to look up the grave of one of

119

these people. You can guess the rest: he found him in the section of the old cemetery reserved for bums![1]

One of the true facts of life is that history is written by the winners, or at least the survivors. The losers do not write much history. If you go to Gettysburg, Pennsylvania, you will see that, quite properly, the majority of the monuments there are to the Union soldiers.

Now, choosing ancestors is not all bad. In fact, the Psalmist said that we must pick and choose among our ancestors. It is true. You can tell a person or a people or a church not so much by their ancestors but by the ancestors they have selected to follow. The United States does not have one heritage. It has many. To say our heritage is all good would be untrue. We have made some of the most colossal and humiliating follies known to humankind. To say our heritage is a bad one would be equally untrue. We have a landscape that is dotted with some of the greatest successes humans have ever seen. We can say with the Psalmist, "Lord, you have made my lot secure. The boundary lines have fallen for me in pleasant places; surely I have a delightful inheritance" (Psalm 16:5-6).

I think it is good for us to remember our Western religious concepts of freedom and responsibility and focus on the importance of picking the right ancestors. The Bible is correct: a person is not compelled to see everything, try everything, and honor everyone. We have to make choices. We have to pick and choose. This was a message Jesus hammered home again and again. Jesus said that the eye is the seat of the body. He constantly emphasized the importance and the peril of seeing. There is such a thing as "a deliberate rationing of the intake of the eye."[2] There is much to see in this world, and our eyes are bombarded by the gentle people and the ruthless people. We live in a world of advertising and family trees. We are not forced to look at all of them. We have to practice an aristocracy of looking. We have television, but we do not have to look at everything. We have a world of sex and violence, but we do not have to keep staring at it. We may not be responsible for the things we see and for the things people give to us, but *we are responsible for the degree of attention we decide to give things*. We must pick and choose.

120

And if we, as part of our created human condition, must pick and choose, why not pick and choose the highest and the best instead of the lowest and the worst? Surely, we have ancestors buried in the sections of old cemeteries reserved for bums. We are not responsible for their being there. But *we are responsible for the degree of attention we give them and how much we emulate them.* The same is true of our great country. We have cast away in certain sections of our past the sordid legacies of mistreatment of the American Indians, Joseph McCarthy, slavery, segregation, Watergate, and a thousand other less than desirable events and people. I personally believe we are not responsible for their being there. But we are responsible for how much we emulate them.

The Western religions, Judaism, Christianity, and Islam, exalt individual freedom. Adam and Eve in the garden are faced with choices and limitations. Eastern religions, such as Hinduism, Buddhism, Confucianism, and Taoism, downgrade individual will. They tend to emphasize the Divine power as impersonal and inclusive. In fact, for an Easterner, God is oriented toward nature and humans are uncreated and eternal. Even time presents little urgency and demand for responsibility since it is circular, following the eternal cycle of nature's seasons. Western religions are oriented toward history, toward truth being expressed through particular persons, whether Moses, Jesus, or Muhammad, and toward a personal God for whom time is urgent. Even the Garden of Eden story recognizes this. The curses extended to strife between male and female, the harshness of human labor, and the snake having to crawl on its belly end with the statement "all the days of your life." But the injunction that the woman shall experience pain in childbirth omits this statement for obvious reasons: women cannot bear children all the days of life. Choices have to be made within a limited time frame. From the earliest biblical writings to the command of Jesus to his followers to "follow me," the Western heritage is clear: we make our history and finish our creation by the choices we make within the freedom of the will God has given us. To have choices is to pick and choose among them. Unlike the other created animals who live by instinct, the human animal lives by choice.

Such is to accept or refuse the created order of being a responsible being who makes and shapes his or her own history.

Rabbi Beryl Cohon once went to a dinner party with a friend who teaches history in high school. This friend proudly proclaimed that he tears things apart in his classes. He rips off the popular notions, the myths, and the legends. George Washington, by the time he is through with him, emerges a first-class bum. He contends that all the nonsense about his character, his integrity, and his dependability is for simple minds. Rabbi Cohon pulled him aside and asked, "After you have debunked and pulled apart and analyzed and exposed every bit of pretense and sham, what do you put together? What do you give your children that they may respect, and by which they may be guided decently?"[3]

It is a fair question. We teach ourselves to expose, to pull apart, to analyze. But *do we teach people to put things together?* The same is true for churches and religion. We also have ancestors. Every church I have pastored has, at some point, had a minister get a divorce. Every church I've ever known has had fights, and mistakes. Every church in the world has hypocrites. Every minister and every church member has moments of ill-temperament and folly. Every church building has a leak. Every program within a church has weaknesses. Likewise, every one of those entities holds up the Kingdom of God. It is the only institution that claims to have as its sole purpose the worship of God. It is a very easy institution to expose, pull apart, analyze, and debunk. We can do that. But can we teach people to put things together, so they may respect God and be guided decently in their efforts to be responsible human beings?

Every nation, every person, every people has to pick and choose whom they will serve and how much attention they will give to certain things they see and experience. This is an essential part of the human condition. One of the great moments in history is recorded in Joshua 24. Joshua knew that it was time for the twelve tribes of Israel, if they were ever to be united, to pick a god to worship and emulate from among all the gods of their ancestors. Consequently he assembled at Shechem all the descendants of Jacob (Israel). He said: "We've got three choices: 1) the gods our forefathers worshipped beyond the river in Mesopotamia; 2) the local gods here in Canaan; or 3) Yahweh, the one Lord who has led the house of Joseph." Joshua recounted how Yahweh had led Abraham, Isaac, and Moses; how he had led them out of slavery into the Promised Land; how he had led them over the citizens of Jericho. Then Joshua said, "Choose among the three choices. As for me and my house, we will serve the Lord."

This is much more than a story that is 3,000 years old dealing with choices that were 3,000 years in the past. You see, those three choices have to be made by each succeeding generation. You and I have to choose. We can worship the gods our forefathers worshipped beyond the Atlantic Ocean. The gods of Europe united church and state. If you did not worship the god of the Church of England, you didn't thrive in England. If you did not worship the Catholic Pope, you didn't thrive in Italy. If you did not worship Allah, you did not do well in the Middle East. If you did not worship where the Lutheran heads of state in Denmark and Germany worshipped, you did not thrive. You could not go to college, own property, or be treated civilly if you did not worship the gods of the government. Now, there are those who say we should choose to worship those gods from beyond the River. They say our founders didn't really mean to have separation of church and state, that we need to saturate their brand of Christian principles throughout our laws. They want to merge government with fundamentalist biblical ideas. We should be a religious republic with a moral majority and a partisan god, just as Prussia had a moral majority and a religious state. They even have political candidates right down to television evangelists who run for President. We can indeed choose to worship the gods our forefathers worshipped beyond the river in Mesopotamia.

Secondly, we can choose to worship the local gods in Canaan. This is our "promised land." All of our forebears were immigrants — people who searched for a new Israel, a new beginning, and freedom from tyranny. And, like the twelve tribes of Israel, we have prospered in our Canaan. We have local gods of prosperity and wealth that we can worship. The gods of prosperity are everywhere. All you have to do is call an 800 number and you can talk to them. The shiny car, the new house, the inflated importances of society — all these things are the new local gods of Canaan. We can worship them. We can totally lose consciousness of the ethical God and his demands to feed the hungry, visit the sick, and minister to the needy. This God that Joshua called "Yahweh" and Jesus called "Father" is indeed rivaled by the local gods in the promised land.

Or, we can choose to follow the God of Abraham, Moses, Isaac, Jacob, Joseph, and Jesus. The choice was there for our political founders. George Washington faced it when the people wanted to make him king. Abraham Lincoln faced the choice when he looked upon a land smoldering with division and lack of freedom. Thomas Jefferson faced the choices when the Library of Congress had burned and the Capitol was under siege. To remain in the world is to choose your gods: 1) the gods your forefathers worshipped across the water before you got to the promised land; 2) the local gods of prosperity; or 3) the Lord God who has led you to this point in your history.

At a critical juncture in his life, King Solomon had a dream. God appeared to him and said, "Ask for whatever you want me to give you." What an opportunity. What a choice. There were no exceptions. "Ask me anything and I will give it to you." Solomon did not ask for wealth and gold and silver. That was unusual because the ancient world put great stock in gold and silver. They covered their ceilings with gold, ate from golden plates, slept in golden couches, and quaffed wine from golden goblets. Yet, Solomon did not ask for gold.

Neither did he ask for vengeance on his enemies. That was also unusual. Ancient coronations began with the music of massacres. Neither did Solomon ask for victory in battles or world renown. He did not ask for a long life. A long life was just as treasured then as it is today.

This is what Solomon asked for that night: "Give your servant, O God, an understanding heart that I may discern between good and bad. Help me to make the right choices."

Today, you and I are very fortunate to be citizens of this great country. This is the Promised Land. We should thank God we are

Americans. We can say with the Psalmist, "Lord, you have made my lot secure. The boundary lines have fallen for me in a pleasant place; surely I have a delightful inheritance." But such an inheritance demands that we exercise its responsibilities. This recognition of the place of choice in our human condition places before us avenues of responsibility that are not always the richest, quickest, or easiest roads to travel. We are, in fact, called upon to pick the right God.

---

1. Harold A. Bosley, *Sermons on the Psalms*, p. 41.

2. William B. J. Martin, *Little Foxes That Spoil the Vines* (Nashville: Abingdon, 1968), p. 89.

3. Beryl Cohon, *Shielding the Flame* (New York: Bloch Publishing Co., 1972), p. 91.

The Long Way Around

Exodus 13:17-19
Matthew 12:43-45

Exodus is more than a word for an ancient journey. It is a permanent condition of every Christian this side of heaven. We are always being liberated from our slavery to certain ideas, stations in life, and people. Likewise we often find ourselves slipping from the freedom of controlling our life to the *slavery* of certain attitudes and preconceptions which only make us think and feel that we are free. Yes, we are always moving from bondage to freedom to bondage to freedom.

Life is full of people trying to make an exodus from what they consider to be a particular problem. One of the most amusing issues, of course, is our effort to deal with aging. All of us are aging and we are, in effect, in bondage to the aging process. Sonny Throckmorton has authored a song about a person who tries to get away from aging and find the promised land. The song is about a person called "Middle Age Crazy." Middle Age Crazy has just reached his fortieth birthday. He trades his Oldsmobile for a new Porsche car and his gray business suit for jeans and high-heeled boots with an embroidered star. Middle Age Crazy is bald on top and he's quite a sight to see. He had a wife he had loved for a long time, but the thrill is gone. He and his wife spent a while building up a business, but the long, uphill climb is now over and profits are high. So he dumps his wife. Forty years old going on twenty, he has a sweet young thing beside him that just melts in his hand. And she understands that he's Middle Age Crazy, trying to prove that he's still a man.

The story of Middle Age Crazy is a tragedy. An individual tries to become liberated from despair. Breaking free from the bondage of his past, he thinks he will find hope but instead falls victim to another form of bondage. His cure becomes worse than his disease.

All of us find ourselves in need of exodus. There are times when self-acceptance is hard to come by and we are tempted to try to leave that situation, lifestyle, or perspective. Sometimes, however, what we could *go to* is worse than what we *got out of*. A particular experience in my own life leaps into my consciousness. Shortly after arriving in Boston to begin my seminary career I was assigned a job as Assistant Minister in Park Avenue Congregational Church. Such an assignment pleased me. What more could you ask for than to work at the corner of Park Avenue and Paul Revere Road? All went well in the preliminary arrangements which lasted through the fall. New assignments were comfortably handled. Then came time for the church Christmas party. It was held in the parlor of a beautiful home and I ventured there with great anticipation. One of the church members was a professor in the New England Conservatory of Music. The entertainment for that evening consisted of that woman playing "Jingle Bells" on the piano in the style of various composers, with the church members trying to guess which composer would have written the song that way. For over an hour I sat there surrounded by people shouting out "Wagner, Beethoven, Bach, Mozart, Schubert," and so forth, while I just sat there and stared with my mouth open.

I returned to the dormitory that night totally deflated. It just would not work. If that was "class," I certainly did not have it. So I sat down and wrote out my letter of resignation. I reasoned that I would carry it to the chairman of the personnel committee. He was a "class" person and would understand when I told him I couldn't make the jump from the athletic fields of South Carolina to genuine musical sophistication in one year.

I went up to the floor of the building where this person worked. As I sat in the office, letter of resignation in hand, his secretary came out to tell me that Mr. Hanson was very busy. He hadn't slept much the night before and his phone had been ringing all morning. Finally, after what seemed to be an agonizing wait, Mr. Hanson, bleary-eyed and with his tie loosened, came into the lobby. "Come in, Mr. Warlick," he said. "Pardon my appearance, but a few church members rang my phone off the hook last night griping about the god-awful Christmas party. What a disaster. Nobody knew what was happening. We kept throwing out every composer's name we knew, hoping that every now and then we'd hit the target and get the blasted evening over with. Wasn't it awful?"

"Yes, it was," I responded. "Well?" he asked. "Well what?" I countered. "What did you come to see me about?" he quizzed. "Nothing. Nothing at all," I answered. "I was just passing by."

I began that day by taking little baby steps into getting acquainted with some of the dearest friends I would ever know. I shudder when I think that I almost made a quiet exodus from a minor discomfort into an even worse form of slavery, that of forever feeling rejected. The slavery of self-rejection is a great slavery. Through a minor misunderstanding I almost stereotyped an entire people.

All of us have those moments when we have to deal with the exodus desire. The exodus desire is part of our human condition. Most of us in our athletic endeavors, our student life, our business life, our family life, or our pleasure life face a time when we might be tempted to think we'd be better off quitting. The point is this: *Just escaping a perceived bondage does not always lead to freedom.* Whether it be the "Middle Age Crazy," my "Jingle Bells" experience, or a host of your situations in life, *how we effect freedom is more important than freedom itself.*

Jesus the Christ told a disturbing parable about an empty house. A house is in bondage to a problem, an unclean spirit. We are told the owner kicks the spirit out. *The owner has won. But a house cannot remain empty.* Since the owner does not replace the evil with good, the evil returns and seven other devils accompany it. Thus, the house is liberated from the bondage to one spirit in order to be free to be in bondage to eight spirits. Jesus is articulating a situation that happens when we seek freedom without replacing it *with responsibility.* Therefore, how one is freed and for what end are the crucial issues in liberation. None of us remains empty.

One of the disturbing aspects of the hopelessness in today's world is its contribution to fly-by-night religious hucksters. Many people are fleeing their perceived states of doubt and negativism about life straight into the arms of television evangelists and superficial hucksters who claim to put band-aids on their wounded hearts. At the same time they liberate their cash while promising genuine hope for the future. Such quick cure, fix-it religious entrepreneurs leave their victims in worse shape than before. Theirs is not a quiet journey from despair into a lasting hope.

One of the amazing facts of scripture is that Satan is very seldom pictured as ugly and hideous. In fact, most of the time, from the temptations of Jesus to the cross, *evil is presented as the most handsome and attractive way out of a mess.*

Perhaps this helps us understand the call of Israel out of Egypt and our call to be the people of God in our day. We are told that the Israelites made a courageous exodus from Egypt. God overcomes Pharaoh and they are delivered. But, amazingly enough, God does not lead the Israelites to the Promised Land by the shortest route. They do not go along the northern edge of the Suez and then along the coast of Gaza. That journey would have taken two weeks at the most. *Two weeks!* Here are people who had been in Egyptian slavery 215 years. They finally are freed and head for the land of promise only two weeks away. But God doesn't lead that direct way. The way God leads them takes *forty years! Why?*

Scripture says that the near path led through the land of the Philistines. The people might see war and run from it. But read the scripture again. *The people might see war and win and like it.* The Bible tells us that the children of Israel "went out of the land of Egypt equipped for battle." They were ready to fight. They had been caged up and downtrodden. They were now strong. They had their history with them and they even carried the bones of their original charter member, Joseph. They had been mighty enough to conquer Pharaoh. They were armed physically with military hardware, and armed psychologically with the bones of Joseph. They were liberated. They were like Middle Age Crazy. They had traded in their slave clothing for military armor and they had the bones of Joseph by their side. They were the children of Israel trying to prove they could be a man — trying to prove they could be mighty like the rest of the young nations at that time.

But freedom from bondage was not God's total intent with these people. *They were not freed because God needed successful, arrogant smart alecks.* The people were freed in order to bear witness to a God of love and service. Had the Israelites traveled the two-week path, win or lose, they would have escaped the bondage of one evil, Egypt, only to acquire bondage to even worse evils like arrogance, triumphalism, vanity, and greed. Yes, how a person is freed and for what end is crucial. *Those people were freed to witness effectively to a God who is morally and spiritually good and thereby change the attitudes of the world.*

That, too, is the meaning of our liberation in Jesus Christ from the bondage of despair. We embrace hope in God to bear witness to moral and spiritual goodness. Our marching orders always demand that we take the long way around. The exodus experience provides an interesting commentary on great accomplishments. Great achievements succeed only in steps of time and only in harmony with responsibility. Look at what happened to those people in over forty years. The impulse to hurt was transformed into the desire to bless. Savageness was channeled into commitment. The people began to move from the way of the tiger to the way of the lamb. Even the "eye for an eye and a tooth for a tooth" which seems so savage to us was an improvement for those people. Prior to that, if a tribe member put out the eye of a member of your tribe, you got your tribe and wiped out his tribe; men, women, and children slaughtered all for the sake of an eye. Yes, the way of the lamb had begun.

It takes strength to bear witness to a God of love.

To be certain, Israel did not totally live and move in the way of the lamb. Hostility, antagonism, and deceit filled many pages of the Old Testament. But her exodus was a beginning of the little baby steps of time. Out of her long history came a revelation that climaxed when Christ culminated the "Way of the Lamb."

You and I are always traveling from despair toward hope and back again. That movement seems to be a permanent condition of the human race. Always there are new freedoms to be obtained, new challenges to be met, and new lifestyles beckoning us. But how we succeed in that movement and to what end is crucial. We are called to take the long way around. That's harder. It means we must go the first hopeful mile before we can go the second. But the difficult way of service is the only way that gives lasting hope. That is the only way to responsibly bear witness to a God of loving-kindness.

The Shortest Distance

Matthew 8:5-13; 12:9-3

None of us relishes complications. We want issues to be simple. But eventually freshmen are no longer freshmen — they get four months under their belts in college. Rush week comes, so some join fraternities and sororities. Even the Chaplain isn't new to them anymore. Attendance patterns at the services in the university chapel and the reasons for them become more ambiguous. None of us relishes ambiguity — the state where things can have more than one meaning. We want issues to be clear — good or bad. We like the definite "yes" or the definite "no" — truth or lie. We've been at this knowledge game long enough to know there are a lot of "ifs" and "maybes" in life. I was present when a graduate student in history came back from Chapel Hill to Furman for homecoming. He verbally tore into his former history professor. "Before I came to this place and studied under you," he declared, "life was very clear and simple. I knew clearly what was right and wrong, good or bad, truth or falsehood. I came from a small family in a small town. I knew enough, I thought. But you made me complicated. You pointed out all these ambiguities and contradictions in history and religion. And I can't go back to being simple anymore."

Ambiguity is indeed a real problem in life. When a person moves beyond a certain plateau in life, ambiguity is there waiting.

Our parents taught us right and wrong as total absolutes. They had to do that. In childhood few of us could handle ambiguity. *Our teachers got us started in math by teaching us that the shortest distance between two points is a straight line.* We needed that data base at that time. We were hardly ready for calculus and Einstein in the fourth grade. Then we moved up to a different level of reality and discovered that because of the curvature of the earth, the shortest distance is a curved line, not a straight one.[1] No airplane would attempt to fly to Europe in a straight line. It would be too far. You

131

either take the circle route by Iceland and Northeastern Canada or you stay home.

The Apostle Paul spoke of this: "When I was a child, I spoke as a child; when I became an adult, I reached a new plane of thought." Before Paul became a Christian, his life was fairly simple. He knew, he thought, the clear right and the obvious wrong. Amazingly enough, after he gave his life to Christ things got more, not less, complicated. He encountered ambiguity. The farther he traveled the worse it became. He started saying things like, "We look through a clouded glass and only see things dimly. We are certain of Christ, but in the meantime, until he makes all things clear in his kingdom anew, we prophesy in part and speak in part. We just don't know everything."

There are, of course, certain religious statements which avoid ambiguity: "Jesus Christ, the same yesterday, today, and tomorrow!" No ambiguity in that. People pack auditoriums and television studios to hear charismatic leaders give clear answers about right and wrong. Religious empires are built. If a person can promise to separate life between what is real and false, right and wrong, the masses will give that person their money, their allegiance, and their devotion. It's a natural inclination. Can you imagine Paul standing in such a place and going out over the airwaves with: "I prophesy in part and I speak in part. I see the truth like a man looking through a foggy windowpane. I just don't know everything." Well, he would not be on the air very long. People want a straight line. That's the shortest distance to God, is it not?

What does it take to evoke a response from God? Does it take a gallon of faith? A pound? An ounce?

In the account of the healing of the centurion's servant, a *huge amount* of faith brings a healing. Jesus healed the servant long-distance because "... 'not even in Israel have I found such faith' " (Matthew 8:10). Here it would seem that the formula is one gallon of faith equals a cure.

But at another time, Jesus said that if we have faith the size of a mustard seed we can move mountains. Here it would seem that an ounce of faith is the magic ingredient in the formula.

132

Yet in other encounters, Jesus worked miracles when faith did not exist at all. A man in the synagogue had a withered hand (Matthew 12:9-13). Scripture doesn't tell us if the man had ever heard of Jesus or had any faith in him at all. Scripture maintains that the man never asked to be healed. Jesus simply healed the man. Here it would seem that no faith at all is required for Jesus' work.[2]

What is the magic formula? What determines when God shall act and when God shall not act? Certainly God is not whimsical or moody. There must be a better explanation.

I think Jesus and Paul evidenced to us that *ambiguity is part of the human condition and we do ourselves more harm by trying to avoid it than by embracing it.*

I don't like being complicated. I don't like ambiguity. I like my religion straight. But sometimes straight isn't the shortest distance to God and truth. I wish that God had just separated the sheep and goats on the earth instead of mixing them all in together until the afterlife. I wish God had simply given us a formula and said, "Apply this. These are from Satan and these are from God. Here is evil and here is good." Instead, God left us that parable about the wheat and the weeds growing together in the same field — good and evil both flourishing in the same ground. I wish it were like tonight's basketball game where the home team wears the white jerseys and the visiting team the colored jerseys. At least you'd know which side to cheer for. Instead, life's often like a scrimmage between the same team with the same color uniforms. You often have to run the play and set it in motion, then see who's coming to defend or advance.

Ambiguity is a reality in life. There is never a formula for God. The Old Testament records show that sometimes God waits to act until God sees our faith and sometimes God acts where we can observe no faith at all. God is God. We have difficulty squeezing God into a formula to write on a tract or religious blackboard and apply every time we have a problem. If there were a set formula as to prayer, daily readings, or particular appeals, then the early church would have left us a little pamphlet with that formula on it, instead of this Bible which is exactly 1,303 pages long.

133

Children have died whose parents prayed a great deal. The dead are strewn across the battlefields of a hundred wars, the dead for whom millions of parents and spouses wept. Mothers and fathers have died in a thousand different ways. Trouble, tragedy, and defeat move among us. One group will say that such is God's will. Another group calls it Satan. Another group says Divine power doesn't work.

The simple truth of all faith is that we are not God. We are humans. There are things we may not know for centuries. *Faith is not in what we know, but in what we do not know and yet believe.* There is ambiguity in the world and we cannot play at being God. Yet it does not make sense to turn from God's strength just because there is ambiguity in life. It takes more faith to trust God in the blackest midnight when there appears to be no answer at all than to fit God into a formula. Those who have genuine Christian character may be the most flexible of all humans.

Jesus has told us that God is a presence in life; that God has triumphed once and for all over evil. Good emerges and evil feeds upon it and destroys. Yet forces we do not understand make use of evil to bring good again. Trust experience. Jesus said, "My power and my presence I leave in this world. Trust your own experience. Trust the tradition of those who have given their lives for the faith." Let their lives shape your own character.

The great Danish theologian Soren Kierkegaard said, "Life can only be understood backwards, but it must be lived forwards." That's true. God reveals God's presence not merely in a word on the gilt-edged page of the Bible or in the flutter in some hopped-up religious heart. God is as much present in the curved line as in the straight line. God is a mysterious presence in time of absence. God does not demand order. God is revealed and present.

That is the history of the God of the Bible. The God of the Bible is different from any god known to humans. In Egypt the belief was in the status quo of the cosmic order. The Pharaoh was the divine head of this cosmic order, the sun god. Everything had a place, a royal line, a formula.

Mesopotamia was a chaotic place. The people there believed that men and women were created evil. So the king, the god, was the one who had the greatest power, the greatest numbers, and the most money. You simply learned your place in society and called on the king to help you. There was a formula, a given place for you.

God was made known in a regular pattern. In family life the inheritance was passed on to the oldest son. The most powerful, the most prayerful, the most successful figure was the representative for God. God's presence was there. One did not look for God in the darkest nights of the soul — in ambiguity and tragedy. Wherever God's presence was, it certainly wasn't there.

But look at our God. Abraham experiences a family tragedy. Ishmael is his firstborn son. Isaac is the younger half-brother. God promises Abraham that his family will be blessed as a great nation. Ishmael is the firstborn, the carrier of the family order. But Ishmael is thrown out into the wilderness at the insistence of Abraham's wife, Sarah. Abraham is crushed. Ambiguity settles over him. He doesn't know which way to lean. So God reminds Abraham in this out-of-the-ordinary crisis that his presence will be with both children. God reveals Godself right in the midst of something Abraham cannot avoid. Then Isaac marries Rebekah and has twins. Esau is the oldest and, as the one who was birthed first by a few seconds, is supposed to get the blessing and wealth of Isaac. But Jacob, the younger twin, tricks old blind Isaac and snatches his brother's rightful life. Where is God when the formula is broken? Right there. Right there to carry on the promise and bring about an ultimate reconciliation of the twins. Then Jacob is confronted with an ambiguous situation. He works seven years to marry Rachel and is tricked into marrying Leah, the older sister of Rachel. The formula, if there was one, is broken to pieces. Jacob finally gets on track with Rachel, but by then he's had ten sons by Leah. Rachel finally gives him Joseph but dies in the birth of Benjamin. The death of his wife almost breaks Jacob. Two little boys without their mother. Surely this Joseph and Benjamin will have it rough. The pattern is broken, the order is disturbed, the formula crushed and eradicated beyond recovery. The straight line, short distance to God is snapped. So Rachel, dearly beloved wife of Jacob, is buried in the cemetery beside the road outside a little one-horse town which later was given the name of Bethlehem.

And the one who was born there of her lineage placed his followers in the midst of ambiguity. But he said, "Look for me. I will be there. Do not avoid the complexity of life. I will be revealed and present in it."

A little child stands in front of a gumball machine. It is filled with gum. There are at least seven different colors. He has the dime it takes to operate the machine. He wants a green ball of gum. He trustingly places the dime in the slot and pulls the lever. Out comes a red ball. He did everything right. He had enough money and he believed. The machine let him down. He can't understand. He is angry at the machine. He shakes it violently. He kicks it. He speaks harsh words to it. In tears, he declares that's the last time he'll trust a gumball machine. What he wants doesn't always come rolling out even if he has the correct faith and pulls the proper lever. He gets the red ball because the machine does not have his welfare at heart.[3]

If Jesus taught us anything it should be that God is not a gumball machine. God has our welfare at heart. God is not mindless and impersonal. God is present in the midst of ambiguity. And God loves us too much to expect us to carry the whole load by ourselves. That is why God in Christ came to our kind of existence and took the burden off our back and placed it on Jesus.

Sometimes we have to stand in our pulpits and point to this presence. Sometimes we have to have the courage to embrace this mysterious presence in ambiguity. We don't have the demand or the opportunity, much less the courage, to do it often. But true preaching is not therapy. True preaching is not church management or a reinterpretation of the Bible.[4] True preaching is scary! It is scary, just as life is scary, because there is not a magic formula to preach. There is not even a regular pattern to be handed down. *There is only a presence to be felt, a hand to be placed in our hand, which shapes our character in the direction of forgiveness.*

---

1. Thomas Conley, "Some Cooked Fish and a Blessing: Reality in Religion," The Pulpit of Northside Drive Baptist Church, Atlanta, Georgia, April 17, 1988.

2. Arnold Prater, *How Much Faith Does It Take?* (Nashville: Thomas Nelson Publishers, 1982).

3. Will Oursler, *The Road to Faith* (New York: Rinehart & Co., Inc., 1960).

4. David Buttrick, "Preaching in an Unbrave New World." *The Spire*, Vol. 13, No. 1 (Summer/Fall 1988).

Forgiveness

Luke 7:36-50

The subject of forgiveness concerns much more than a desired character trait. In fact, forgiveness is a necessary ingredient in understanding the human condition. *People who do not learn how to forgive do not enjoy life.* The world hands us many irritating people. Some of them frustrate us to no end. If we embrace resentment instead of forgiveness, our relationships and our careers don't get very far. If you want to be a success in the world — major in forgiveness.

A newspaper carried the story of a man who bought a new Cadillac. Every time the car hit a slight bump there was an awful thumping. Twice he took the car to be examined. But they never could find the cause. Always there was the thumping. Finally, the servicemen narrowed the problem to one door of the car. When they took the door apart, they found a coke bottle inside. In the bottle was a note which read: "So you finally found me, you wealthy _____ _____ _____ _____ (blankety-blank)." You see, a worker was so filled with resentment he thought he could destroy the satisfaction of the person who had enough money to buy a Cadillac. Actually, the worker's grudges and resentments had infested his own mind and his everyday job. The satisfaction being destroyed was his own.[1] Thus he made his work-life a slave to his perceived enemies.

Our greatest danger in resentment lies not in the wrong done to us but in the wrong we can do to ourselves if we let ourselves become inwardly hardened. Can you imagine having to work in a job which stirs up a vindictive response in you? Who has the reward? You or your enemy? These polar opposites in character development, resentment and forgiveness, are central to understanding the biblical perspective.

How impossible Jesus' ideal seems at first — "love your enemies and pray for them that persecute you." But it is not

138

impossible. In fact, on second glance it seems to be the most practical and rational rule for daily living that could be laid down. The only rewards in life come through working through relationships. There is no reward in having a small circle of like-minded friends.

Doris Donnelly, in her incisive book *Learning to Forgive*,[2] tells about a family she knew. They were very proficient in the use of resentment. They couldn't forgive anyone. Nothing was ever their fault. The family consisted of two parents and their three daughters. The friends of each family member were under constant scrutiny to determine whether or not they belonged to their group. The family socialized together, sat together in church, and participated in the community, all as a small group. Failing to include the three sisters in a birthday celebration, or not greeting a member of the group with beaming smiles and deferential courtesy, resulted in ostracism. The family lived to be stroked by others. One year the parents gave the same Christmas gift to each of the daughters' teachers, to the pastor of the church, and to the principal of the school. Anyone who did not respond immediately with profuse gratitude was eliminated from the list for the next time. The family took every delay as a personal slap in the face. And everyone scissored out of their lives knew there was little hope of being sewn into their lives again.

The mother of the family died suddenly. The father and the daughters naturally expected large crowds to gather for the final farewells. They enlisted the aid of the local police to handle traffic on the morning of the funeral. Phone calls were made to neighbors and to their "friends." Announcements were sent to people who had moved away. The local motels were alerted to save a few rooms for out-of-town guests who might appear at the last minute and need accommodations. Exactly ten people showed up for the funeral. The husband, the daughters, their husbands, one grandchild and two members of their small circle of friends were the only people who attended the services. It was truly embarrassing. The town laughed about it for years afterward.

People who scissor others from relationships think they are cutting people out of their lives. In reality they are cutting themselves out of the larger human family. They not only die alone, but whether they know it or not, they live alone as well.

It is a fact of existence that small circles of mutual resentments are not easily broken. You can take out to a lake a group of goldfish that have been swimming for their lifetime in a small fish bowl. You can turn them loose in the lake, but they will continue to swim in small circles, the dimension of their former bowl, for quite a while without accepting the massive freedom awaiting them. Jesus called the phenomenon "saluting only your brethren." And he told it straight — "What reward is there in that?" It creates an attitude of smallness which is destructive to career, family, and self.

During the ministry in the villages of Galilee, Jesus preached passionately about forgiveness. It was a strange doctrine to most of the disciples. Peter wanted to be legal and statistical about it. But Jesus stated there is no limit to forgiveness. It's a matter of forgiveness becoming a part of the essential character of your life. You can't forgive people 490 times without it becoming a permanent character trait. You cannot serve two masters. Either you will bow before the altar of revenge and scissor people out of your life; or you will bow before the altar of forgiveness and sew yourself to the wider fabric of humanity, as imperfect and impulsive as it sometimes is.

Peter had not realized the greatness of forgiveness. You cannot forgive someone and pray for him, even if he persecutes you, without becoming a person of love. Forgiveness creates a loving spirit. Jesus told Peter, "You must forgive from your heart." The key word is *kardia,* which is translated "heart." But the Greek word means more than the organ of the body. It means the seat of the inner person. Forgiveness is more than an act we do; it is an expression of who we are.

Look at how it worked in the lives of those around Jesus. In the example of the woman who received forgiveness from Jesus, the main object of the teaching is Simon (Luke 7:36-50). Simon, a Pharisee, was not a loving person to begin with. Jesus contrasts the conduct of the woman with that of Simon. The woman was loving and kind. She loved Jesus very much. And she had many sins to be forgiven for. But her actions, her deeds, indicated that she had become a new person. Simon was, of course, quite satisfied with his righteousness. He had experienced no forgiveness which might have made real for him the personal mercy of God. In his personal relationship with people, then, he exhibited little or no love. Simon didn't even extend the little customary courtesies to Jesus when he entered Simon's house. So Jesus blatantly stated, "The person who is forgiven little, who is self-righteous and proud, scissors out those who are less righteous, and loves little."

Apparently, though, Jesus' life of forgiveness wore off on his disciple Peter. Perhaps it was Jesus' forgiveness in Peter's presence of the soldier who came to arrest Jesus and experienced Peter's cutting his ear off. Perhaps it was the frightful experience of hearing those words of forgiveness uttered by Jesus toward his enemies as he painfully died on the cross. Whatever precipitated it, Peter apparently grasped the greatness of forgiveness. Following Christ's death, Peter wrote a letter to Christians in the northern part of Asia Minor. We know it as the Book of First Peter. Peter began the second chapter with these words: "... strip away all malice and all guile and insincerity and envy and all slander ... for you have tasted the kindness of the Lord" (1 Peter 2:1, 3).

What an incredible power forgiveness turns loose. It is an expansive spirit. A person who has done his or her best and seen others walk off with what he wanted, who has planned and missed, aspired and failed, but can still walk through life with an unenvious and forgiving heart, being happy in his own best self, is a person who has won a great victory. That person is a slave to no one. Life itself becomes his or her ally instead of enemy.

The central thesis in Jesus' assertion about the kingdom of God was that small circles of people would become increasingly larger circles of people through winning over and including their perceived enemies. That is the acid test of Christianity. *Virtually every other group in society can do everything else Christians can do.*

Christians have programs. So does every other group. Christians recite creeds — so do sororities, fraternities, and thousands of other groups. Christians sing songs. So do other groups, from "99 Bottles of Beer on the Wall" to "The National Anthem." Christians raise money. So does everyone else.

Frankly, friends, our Christian character is revealed mainly by the way we forgive other people, especially our enemies.

The greatness of Christianity lies not in its development of small pockets of congenial intimacies. The greatness of Christianity is in its expansive spirit that overthrows resentments, takes in enemies, embraces rivals and seeks the good in all sorts of people across all the barriers that class and race can erect.

What can you as an individual do that really evidences your Christian character? The answer is simple — forgiveness.

---

1. See *His Hands: Resources for Lent and Easter*, ed. Jon L. Joyce (Lima, Ohio: CSS Publishing Co., 1977), p. 64.

2. Doris Donnelly, *Learning to Forgive* (New York: Macmillan, 1979), pp. 24-25.

Return To The Pit

Genesis 50:12-21

The older one gets, the harder it is to find a place to hide. It's a simple fact of life, but it possesses a host of ramifications for human behavior. Have you ever tried to find a child who did not want to be found? A small child can squeeze under any bed, behind any cabinet, and behind any bush. As he grows older, the number of places he can hide will rapidly diminish. There won't be as many physical objects to hide beside, under, or behind. In like manner, I think pastoring and belonging to a small or medium-sized church is a phenomenon all its own. With increased intimacy come fewer opportunities to hide — to hide personalities, perspectives, and opinions. When I pastored a 2,600-member church, there were people out there on those back pews that came for years without my knowing their name. And they certainly did not know me. In fact, that's why some of them came — to melt rather anonymously into that maze of a public.

But one of the elements in life which catches up to every one of us is the fact that we can seldom outrun and hide from bad experiences. Bad experiences have been part of our human condition from the beginning of recorded history. As Adam (humankind) found in the Garden of Eden, you eventually run out of running room. Somehow, sometime, somewhere, you must face the experience and decide whether or not you are going to rise above the misery of those memories.

Usually we all have to go back to a place where we were hurt, back to a place where we felt indignity, back to a person with whom we suffered what, at the moment, we considered to be a personal defeat. Sometimes we cannot scurry for cover. Sometimes we just run out of running room.

The Bible contains an amazing story about a manipulative, arrogant, tattletaling little twit named Joseph. The little brat was the apple of his father's eye, the favorite son. He was the paragon of

143

Oscar Wilde's saying that "wealth is somehow the negation of childhood." To say that Joseph grated on the nerves of his brothers would be an understatement. Joseph's father gave him special presents that he did not give the other children. And the seventeen-year-old brat loved to parade his clothes and toys and Daddy's money before the other brothers. He kept an eye on the older boys and whenever they did anything he ran to bring an ill report to Daddy, who also took it literally and sided with little Joseph. Joseph was always daydreaming about his future. One day he went out to the fields and gathered his brothers around him. He said, "I've just had a dream. We were all binding sheaves in the fields when, guess what? My sheaf arose and stood up, while your sheaves gathered around mine and bowed down to it."

That was really too much. The brothers were steaming inside. But shortly after that, Joseph returned to the fields. He couldn't wait to tell the brothers another dream he had had. "Here we go again," muttered his brothers. "Guess what?" asked Joseph. "I had another dream. The sun, the moon, and the eleven stars were bowing down to me."

Can you imagine how such a pompous, spoiled person would grate on your nerves? What would you do if you had a brother like that? Joseph's brothers were so angry they made up their minds to kill him and throw him in a pit. But Reuben, one of the brothers, the oldest in fact, got squeamish. He persuaded them not to kill Joseph but to throw him into one of the pits. The brothers thought this wise, so they grabbed Joseph, stripped off his precious robe, and threw him into the pit.

At that moment a passing caravan stopped. The brothers got even a better idea. Let us sell the little rascal. So they did. The caravan packed Joseph off to Egypt.

Then the little rascal experienced a tremendous rise and fall and rise in Egypt, culminating in vast power and wealth. Eventually his original homeland became devastated by famine. The process came full circle and those brothers who had tried to kill him had to come to him for food. Talk about having to stare a bad memory in the face! But Joseph was forgiving, and besides, his father was still alive, so the whole scene was one of joy.

Eventually the father, Jacob, passed away. Joseph and his brothers carried out the promise they had made to their father relative to his funeral. All the dignitaries of Egypt went with them as they returned to the homeland. The Bible said: "It was a very large company." They went to the large family burial place, the Cave of Machpelah, and there they laid Jacob to rest.

As the huge caravan of mourners returned to Egypt, they had but one route to travel — the caravan route. They had to pass the very pit into which Joseph's brothers had once cast him. It must have been a traumatic moment for the brothers. All promises to the father had been kept. Joseph was then free to do anything he wanted to do. He was then middle-aged, as were his brothers. Joseph had returned to the pit. As he stared into that pit, he must have remembered the indignity he had suffered at the hands of his brothers. At that point he said nothing and just returned to Egypt.

The brothers were worried. "What if Joseph holds a grudge and pays us back for all the wrongs we did to him?" they asked. They sent a message to Joseph, asking for forgiveness. Then they threw themselves down before him and said, "We are your slaves!" They knew Joseph had returned to the pit. And their father was no longer alive to protect them.

But Joseph said to them, "Am I in the place of God?" *"Am I in the place of God?"* In other words, when you go after revenge, when you set yourself up as judge and jury of a personal wrong, you put yourself in the place of God. Think about it. Joseph went on to say, "You intended to harm me but God worked it out for good."

He was able to move from being an arrogant young man who had tormented his loved ones to a person of forgiveness. *No one can forgive who cannot put personal tragedy into its proper perspective.*

I am personally convinced that the biggest crisis that accompanies middle-age is the fact that that's when we have returned to the pit. We run out of running room. Our parents are infirmed or deceased. Our career covers are tightened. Our reputations are established. The uphill run of childbearing and marital adjustments has ended. We start turning around and making the journey back home. Chapters of our lives that we thought were closed decades ago are suddenly reopened. Our character is not truly tested until we return to the pit. We begin to wonder if we viewed our parents as a convenient necessity when we were young and an inconvenient nuisance when we got older. Consequently we wonder how our children will view us. Questions about the meaning of life begin to resurface. We used to think we would live forever. In fact, we were positive we couldn't die. But we start worrying. We sense that we are mortal. We have more to lose now. Career questions, long ago put to bed, get out of bed and stare us in the face. There's not that much room to hide and move around in anymore. We have to pass by the pit again. And, my friends, when you look into the pit there are only two choices you can make — *are you going to spend the remainder of your life forgiving, or trying to get even?* That may be the most critical question you ever have to ask about your career, your marriage, your children, your church, your family, your community, and even yourself. Am I going to spend the rest of my life forgiving and loving, or trying to get revenge?

Joseph looked into the pit and he asked the pivotal question: *Am I in the place of God?* The more powerful a person is, the greater the impulse to say "yes."

Secondly, Joseph came to the conclusion that no matter how bad the experience, when you put it in a proper perspective, *nothing* is without *some* value. There is a spark of God in the human soul, perhaps almost extinguished, that is never quite dead. Consequently forgiveness is probably the only response that makes us truly human. If you cannot forgive yourself for your own shortcomings, you are standing in the place of God. If God can send his only son to be crucified for your sins and can forgive you for the bad mistakes you made in parenting, family, relationships, marriage, your job, and your church, for you *not* to forgive yourself would be blasphemy. *The first person Joseph had to forgive when he looked into the pit was himself.* He forgave himself for having been an arrogant, manipulative teenager. If he had not, out of his own guilt he would have tried to get even.

Finally, Joseph had to face life's storms instead of trying to run away from them. So did the brothers. They could no longer drift

146

with the wind, trying to keep away from the things they were afraid of. No one can outrun fear. Trying to get even in life is actually a way to run away from fearsome difficulties. Revenge is a method of avoidance.

An old cowboy once conveyed a profound lesson of life. When this country was first settled, a number of Easterners moved to the prairies with their cattle. They took with them various types of cows. Unlike in the East, freezing rains and bitter winds cut across the prairies. Snow piled into enormous drifts. Temperatures could drop quickly to below zero degrees. Flying ice would cut into the flesh. Most cattle would turn their backs to the icy blasts and slowly drift downwind, mile upon mile. Finally, they would run out of room and would come upon barbed wire and boundary fences. They would pile up against the barriers and die by the scores.

But the Hereford cattle acted differently. Cattle of this breed would instinctively head into the wind. They would stand there, facing the blast of the storm, heads down against the fury, as if they were literally forgiving the wind for cutting into them. Almost all the Herefords survived.

After Joseph looked into the pit, turned around, faced the wind, and said, "I am not God," he became one of the greatest personalities in human history. Prior to that moment he had been simply a powerful and rich man who had overcome teenage adversity and made the social register. He spent the rest of his life forgiving and loving. The rest of his contemporary dignitaries followed the winds of monetary and political drift, personal vendettas, career opportunism, and family and personal convenience. They finally piled up against the barriers of their society and died by the scores, still hoping to get even.

When you return to the pit, and you will if you haven't already, look into it. It will be your ultimate test of character. You will have to decide whether you will spend the rest of your life loving and forgiving, or trying to get even.

Doubt And Human Will

Psalm 8:3-8
2 Corinthians 2:17—3:3

Ministers do not like to deal with doubts. We traffic in truths, eternal certainties, and faith. The word "doubt" is often relegated to a preacher's verbal doghouse. We don't preach sermons asking you to doubt something. Preachers fear doubters. Thank goodness we have removed the part from the wedding ceremony where the pastor used to ask "if there is anyone here who knows of any reasons or has any doubts that this ceremony should take place, let him speak now or forever keep his peace." For generations pastors feared that someone would speak up and doubt that the couple should get married.

One of the great anxieties of life is that someone might stand up in the face of one of your certainties about life and say, "I doubt that! I just doubt if that's right."

Doubt is a genuine possibility in Western religion. In the West we view human beings as God's creation and hold to an exalted view of human will. Western and Eastern religious views contain distinctively different perspectives on the human will. In the East, human beings are viewed as simply one species among many natural beings. For example, the religious art of the East takes nature as its primary subject. Such landscape paintings suggest vastness, solitude, and continuous movement. Mountain and water contain the two ends of the natural religious spectrum. The place of human beings in that vastness is small. In fact, humans are so small that we have to look closely for them in the paintings if we find them at all. Eastern artists paint figures occasionally, but not so much as we do in the West. Humans are viewed as no higher in the scale of things than any other kind of matter that comes into being. As such, the religions of the East downgrade individual will.[1] We in the West, on the other hand, exalt the individual will. Few religious

148

writings depict this exalted will better than does a selection from the Psalmist of the Old Testament:

> *When I look at Thy heavens, the work of Thy fingers, the moon and the stars which Thou hast established; what is man that Thou art mindful of him, and the son of man that Thou dost care for him?*
>
> *Yet Thou hast made him little less than God, and dost crown him with glory and honor. Thou has given him dominion over the works of Thy hands; Thou hast put all things under his feet, all sheep and oxen, and also the beasts of the field, the birds of the air, and the fish of the sea, whatever passes along the paths of the sea.*
>
> Psalm 8:3-8 (RSV)

Our Western emphasis on the human will, coupled with the realities of murder and violence in a fast-paced secular society, have helped sustain alternatives to religious belief systems. We encounter philosophies that are atheistic, human-centered, and this-worldly. Humanism, often a negative philosophy, begins with an explicit rejection of belief in God. Atheistic humanists believe that scientific evidence and rational analyses of human experience do not warrant belief in a God who directs human destiny and who loves and cares for his creation. Christian humanism, through a union of Marxist-Socialist commitments and Christian theology, plays a significant role in some contemporary liberation movements.

When confronted with these alternative systems in a very unequal and unjust secular world, many Christians find certain traditional beliefs laboring under increasing doubts. Such doubt often causes the once bright and familiar lights of the home toward which we march to glow exceedingly dim.

It is of great comfort, therefore, to learn that the child of Bethlehem who points the way home through the darkness is also a doubter. The central force of our faith is the birth in Bethlehem of the world's greatest religious doubter. Yes, Jesus was a doubter. Think about it. We are saved by Jesus' faith, and sometimes I think we are also saved by Jesus' daring doubts. Jesus is, in fact, a Savior for doubters. He was born into a world of universally accepted falsehoods and dared to stand up and cry: "I doubt that."

"An eye for an eye and a tooth for a tooth" was the true law. "I doubt that!" said Jesus.

People trusted in long prayers, rigid laws, and Sabbath rules as essential to true religion. "I doubt that!" said Jesus.

The popular idea was that Samaritans were an inferior people. "I doubt that!" said Jesus. "A good Samaritan is better than a bad Jew."

It was destined that way from his birth. You see, people believed that shepherds and lepers were unclean. Shepherds roamed the hillsides, keeping watch over their flocks. They could not always wash their hands or be careful about how they prepared food. They could not keep to the dietary laws of Judaism. "Shepherds are unclean and inferior" was the great truth of the established religion. In actuality, the words "for you a Savior is born," as they were spoken to the shepherds, amounted to a great first century "I doubt that!"

"To you is born this day in the city of David a Savior." That is extremely important. You see, in a way, we are all doubters. Not only is doubt a part of the human condition, but, in a strange way, it is a Christian character trait indispensable to a vital faith. We live with skepticism, questions about God and humankind, and uncertainties about life. Tell me Jesus is only the Savior of the true believers, the one who points the way toward home only for the great people of faith, and more often than not, I am left without a Savior.

Tell me Jesus is a fellow doubter, a Savior come to lift me out of my doubts, to empty himself that I might be exalted and find my way home, and his story then is a story that is enacted with me and for me.

We are all doubters. We believe yet we possess unbelief. We may, even after all these years, doubt the Christian story, although none of us would dare admit it.

There are human reactions to the Christian story which are rather unconscious ways of doubting the story. What goes through your mind when you hear about Caesar Augustus, about Joseph and Mary, about the shepherds in the fields, and about the multitude of the heavenly host, praising God and singing?

Perhaps some of us do not listen very carefully, and that happens to me quite often.

Perhaps the story of this Christ seems like a nice fairy tale being told, far removed from the realities of life.

Perhaps, also, some of you, when you hear the story of his birth, life, and death, are reminded of the days of your youth long since gone by. As the late Karl Barth said on Christmas, it makes you think of when you "were told this story for the first time, of the Christmas tree, of the presents and the candies, of how beautiful things were, but are no longer and never will be again."[2]

These are some of our human reactions to the Christmas story. We are doubters even though our faith, our belief system, and our hope propel us into a church while others choose to stay home.

That's why the angels must come again. If we are to receive the Savior for honest doubters, the angel of the Lord must pass through the streets, the homes, and the churches. It is not enough simply to peddle the story. Something must be revealed to us and in us. The angel of the Lord must come to honest doubters like you and me, and point the way home again.

Peddling the story simply will not work. There's too much doubt, too much questioning, too much skepticism in us for that.

Harry Emerson Fosdick told of a family he knew who always observed Shakespeare's birthday. "Every year on Shakespeare's date of birth, the father of the family, who was a poet, would light candles, call in a circle of congenial friends, and celebrate the evening with a great party. They would keep the birthday through giving gifts and reading Shakespeare's poetry to each other."[3]

That's nice, isn't it? It's memorable, noteworthy, and quite a way to mark the passage of time.

The story of Christ is, hopefully, more than that. But it is more than that only if the Christ spirit comes to us through our doubts and skepticisms and lets something be born anew in us. The angel must pass through our homes and our churches each year or, at some point, our honest doubts will come to the surface and overwhelm the story.

One of the amazing recognitions of the early Christian church was that the peddling of a great story, even that of the resurrection or the babe in Bethlehem, would not be enough for a world of honest doubters to find their way home.

The Apostle Paul wrote a letter to the Corinthian church in which he said, "We are not, like so many, peddlers of God's word; we are sincere ... do not believe us because we peddle a story ... you yourselves are our letters of recommendation ... written not with ink but with the spirit of God, not on tablets of stone but on tablets of human hearts" (2 Corinthians 2:17—3:3).

Paul knew the Corinthians were, like us, too smooth, too scientific, too cautious, too doubting to be taken in by peddlers of stories. Apparently the peddler in the Mediterranean world had a reputation for cheating. The peddler took his message casually. His chief concern was: "How can I twist it a bit to make it appeal to an unconcerned audience so that they will buy it, and I will make a profit?"

There have always been religious peddlers in the world who have no experience with God's truth and who do not even believe all the hype they are saying but make a tremendous profit for themselves.

Paul said, "We are not peddling stories. There are plenty of people who can do that. We are asking you to accept the reality of God in your hearts. You, not the stories, will be God's letters of recommendation in the world. God doesn't need miraculous stories; God doesn't need a lot of ink; God needs you — your life — your expressions, to make the angels' truth heard again."

We should doubt the peddlers of wild stories, but we must never deny the reality of the spirit of God that is written in human hearts.

The angels of God must continuously pass through the streets, the homes, and the churches of our fast-paced Western society each year. We must hear the voices of something that is a current reality if the home lights are to shine for us.

I see these angels all the time. And each time I encounter one, those faint lights of home start to glow brighter. One afternoon I saw an angel as I sat in my office scribbling away on a legal pad. I looked up and out of the window of the office I saw Sallie Memory slowly shuffling toward the sanctuary. Now, Sallie Memory was a member of our church who resided in Evergreens Nursing Home in High Point. On the day in question she was more than 94 years old. My initial thought was, "My goodness, what's she doing away from the nursing home? She might fall down."

Well, Sallie had arranged for someone to bring her by the church because she had heard we had cushions in the pews and she wanted to sit on one and look at the Christmas decorations. She had also read in our newsletter where we were a little behind in the budget, so she had someone take her to the bank where she withdrew $100 in cash. She brought that over to "help us."

It took Sallie two little rest periods to walk the distance from the parking lot to the sanctuary. Finally, she got in there and sat down on the first pew. Her eyesight was too poor to see the poinsettias, but she could see the Chrismon tree. And she loved being there. She loved the cushions and the tree and what that place represented in her life. She and I just sat in there for a few minutes and somehow the place looked different. It looked better.

That kind of faith and expression of worth, evidenced in a 94-year-old lady getting out of her bed in the nursing home and coming over to the church with her frail body and money from her savings account, should say more to us about there being some truth to this Bethlehem event than any story we could ever peddle.

Doubt as part of the human condition must find its theories made flesh. Doubt and human freedom mean that the only kind of theology worth pursuing is applied theology. Only the persistent presence of faithful visionaries can provide evidence in a world of doubt. Frankly, most of us must, at times, depend on the vision of others to point the way for us when our own doubting eyesight begins to see only flickers of the lights of home. In this strange way, our doubts become the vehicles not only for God's spirit but for human solidarity as well.

----

1. Robert C. Monk, Walter C. Hofheinz, Kenneth T. Laurence, Joseph D. Stamey, Bert Affleck, and Tetsunao Yamamori, *Exploring Religious Meaning*, Third Edition (Englewood Cliffs, N.J.: Prentice-Hall, 1987), pp. 158-159.

2. Karl Barth, "Christmas 1954," in *Deliverance to the Captives*, trans. Marguerite Wieser (New York: Harper & Row, 1961), p. 21.

3. Harry Emerson Fosdick, *What Is Vital In Religion: Sermons on Contemporary Christian Problems* (New York: Harper & Brothers, 1955), p. 37.

V. CHARACTER

Dependability

Mark 5:1-17

Certain events in life occur that are both odd and dangerous. One such event happened to me upon returning from the state capital this year. I was driving up Interstate 26 from Columbia to Greenville, South Carolina when my eyes beheld a strange and frightening sight. An automobile was coming down the right-hand side of the interstate in the wrong direction. Apparently its driver, in wanting to head east, had gotten confused, missed a ramp, and entered the westbound flow of traffic. The immediate reaction of the cars heading in the proper direction was to slam on brakes and stop. We expected the driver of the approaching car to pull over to the side of the road and ease into the westward flow of traffic until a ramp off was reached which would allow him to enter the eastbound side of the highway. Much to our surprise, the driver of the car panicked and tried to cut across the huge grass gully which divides the two sections of the highway. It took but a few seconds for the car to get stuck in the soft mud and grass. There it sat, stuck at the bottom of the deep chasm between the two sections of the highway. As I watched the car rock back and forth with its wheels spinning, I thought of the profound truth of life: When you try to head in two directions at once you actually wind up going nowhere fast.

Today's world is a world of different lifestyles, people flowing in two different directions. As we look through the window of life, we who call ourselves Christians see an excellent way in which to travel. We see a lifestyle of service, marital fidelity, compassion, and a relationship with a personal God as the ultimate meaning of our existence. On the other hand, there exists a lifestyle which resembles a "herd of cattle" approach to life. Marital fidelity is scorned; the church is seen as worthless; drugs and other intoxicants are viewed as the "in thing"; God is seen as irrelevant; and accumulation of money and possessions is seen as the ultimate meaning of our existence.

Now most, if not all, of us at some point in our lives get headed down the wrong direction. In our God-given freedom we occasionally go down the wrong ramp in life. Would that we would pull over to the side and ease into the lifestyle for a period, seeking some chance to change direction. But, alas, most human beings are like the driver of the automobile in the illustration. Instead of turning around, we try to cut across the traffic barriers in life. Correspondingly, we wind up somewhere in the middle, with our wheels spinning.

Would that evil were merely a force that we could pull out of people and by doing so make certain they never head in the wrong direction again. In the illustration of the driver in the ditch, would that the problem could be solved by merely pulling the car out. But you and I know that the problem was not with the car, but with the driver. Somehow the driver's whole approach to driving has to be examined and dealt with. The same is true with people, even ourselves, who are headed in the wrong direction in life.

For long decades those who studied ethics focused on the dominance of utilitarianism as a proper way to make decisions. The principle of the greatest good for the greatest number dominated politics as the way to attack social problems and educational needs. This outcomes approach to decision-making focused on contextual or situational ethics. An action was determined to be right or wrong based on its results. Now, the dominant utilitarianism of the past may be dying in favor of an emphasis on character. We are realizing that moral principles do not stand up without assessing the moral qualities of the people involved. Good people tend to make good decisions. Certainly Jesus did not give blanket speeches nor did Paul write open letters. They spoke and wrote from communities where character was cultivated.

I'm sure that many of us in looking at children, teenagers, spouses, and friends who are heading in a wrong direction wish that we could just pay someone to pull the evil out of them. Unfortunately evil is not something that occupies a space in us and can be extracted like an abscessed tooth. There is a movie, titled *The Exorcist*, which has made a lot of money from exploiting the concept of evil. The movie is based on a reported case of exorcism in

Maryland in 1949, at which time a Catholic priest received permission required by church law to perform a specific ritual pulling evil out of a person. We, as Christians, know that dealing with evil is not this simple. Evil in life is a mystery. It is a mystery that haunts our human condition. In our God-created freedom, evil is a choice before us, a direction on the highway, not a *thing* which possesses innocent people. Evil must be addressed as much by character as by principles and programs.

Given, then, the fact that evil is a possible choice for every man, woman, and child, how do we get people to choose something better? In a world in which 8,000 American men and women, most of them under 25 years of age, go to jail *each day*, how do we get people to change their direction? In a world of drugs, intoxicants, sexual confusion, divorce, and parent-child problems, how can we encourage people to change their lifestyles? People constantly ask me, "Preacher, how can we get so and so to change?"

Initially, let me say that I have never seen anyone change his lifestyle simply because someone lectured him about how bad he was. When we, as Christians, attempt to create changes in lifestyle among people we do so not by lecturing them but by letting them experience our *dependability*. People look at the church, at its teachers, committee members, leadership, and membership and ask not "What do they say?" but "Are they dependable?" Unfortunately there is very little dependability in today's world. Churches are armed with flashy individuals, critics, exhibitionists, and sharp talkers. Yet people searching for a new lifestyle would much rather see a few people that you can *depend on for support*.

You see, we cannot teach truth, we can only awaken it in people. Do you remember how we acquired trust in the Christian lifestyle? It was not through explanations of our parents or other people. No verbal attempts to preach goodness really got through to us. In like manner, we make a mistake in the church when we try to preach the gospel of Christ by means of assurances and explanations alone.

Reuel Howe, in his book *Man's Need And God's Action*, (Greenwich, Conn., Seabury Press, 1953), notes that the church in carrying on its teaching function has put too much faith in the use of words and used too little the "language of relationship." Indeed,

159

Jesus himself engaged in very few religious "arguments"; he simply related his lifestyle to individuals in need of a change.

We can learn much about helping people change the direction of their lives through examining Jesus' method of "relating" himself to others. The fifth chapter of Mark contains an account of an unusual experience. Jesus encountered an extremely hostile person one day. This man was so hostile in behavior that his neighbors claimed he was possessed by demons. When Jesus asked the man for his name, the reply was "legion, for we are many." Now in the Roman army a legion was organized as a body of 6,000 men. The man responded to Jesus with a number instead of a name. He was explaining to Jesus that the reason for his madness was the fact that he was a divided personality. "You ask who am I; we are many."

Here existed a man who somewhere along the road of life had driven his mind into a ditch. As he had struggled to get out, he had traveled in one direction after another. Finally it dawned on him that he was more like 6,000 people instead of one. In characteristic fashion Jesus related to him as one single human being who needed to put himself together. "Let the herd run off the cliff, if they want," was Jesus' response. "You can't be all things at once. Be cured and become one again."

What transpired next is of extreme importance to us. *Jesus wanted the man to witness in the area where he was known.* The man begged Jesus to let him go with him. But Jesus refused him and said, "Go home to your friends, and tell them how much the Lord has done for you, and how he has had mercy on you."

So often we want to run off in all directions in a personal crusade against immorality. Yet Jesus came down hard on this wish to boast to others. Jesus said, "The best way you can help me is to go home to your friends." Again, the issue of dependability leaps at us. Jesus knew the tremendous impact on others that a faithful, dependable person can have among his own friends. He also knew that often people's wishes to rush off on their religious high horse comes from the attempts to cover up the fact that no one — their church, friends, family, or neighbors — can depend on them. So Jesus perceptively stated, "Go home to your friends and tell them ..."

Perhaps the most salient method Jesus possessed for relating to people was his bringing *the healing love of God instead of wrath.* This characteristic should speak directly to us Christians. Jesus confronted a Samaritan woman one day. He went out to her instead of waiting for her to realize her mistakes and come to the temple. He knew that if he waited for people to find their own way to the temple, he would wait a long time. If we as a church wait on young people and adults to find their own way into church from the suburban manors, the pool halls, the shanties, the bars, the family squabbles, and the hospitals, we will be waiting a long, long time! If we do nothing else, we must be there simply to relate to them.

Notice also that the first thing this Samaritan woman did was try to get Jesus in a religious argument *to keep from talking about her lifestyle.* One of the first things a minister learns in life is that people who are always arguing about the Bible and splitting hairs about religion are really trying to divert attention away from their own lifestyle! They are trying to keep attention focused on religious issues so no one will ask them personal questions!

Jesus looked the woman straight in the eye when she started spouting off about religion. After she had quizzed and questioned him for a few minutes, he finally said: "Woman, let's talk about something other than religion and Scripture. Where is your husband?"

Jesus knew a lot about religion and Scripture. He could have debated with her for hours. He also knew that this woman had had five husbands and was then living with another man. Jesus could have pointed the finger at her and said the Old Testament says, "Thou shalt not this and thou shalt not that." He then could have told her where she was going. But he simply said, "Let's talk about something other than religion or Scripture. Where is your husband?"

I imagine that the Samaritan woman returned home that day with something wonderful awakened in her. I doubt that she said, "I met a really great person today who knew a lot about the Bible and showed me how my lifestyle was wrong." I doubt that she said, "Here is a man who helped me get my theology straight and really knew all the answers about the questions of the Old Testament." Instead, I imagine that she declared, "I met an amazing man today. He told me that God loves me just as I am. And he helped me to understand myself. Truly this must be the Messiah!"

How can we help people avoid the ditches of life? How can we help people change their lifestyles? Initially we can become dependable. We can show to others that our church, our family, and our friends can depend on us for support. Then we can start making the love of God more important than our own religious hang-ups — even scriptural hang-ups.

Our whole person will become involved in our deeds. As we act dependably, we will be shaping ourselves along dependable lines. Our character will be the cause and the consequence of what we do. Old dogs will learn new tricks. Instead of living by principles we will begin to live by our convictions. Our convictions about the God whose world this is will enable us to have living convictions that will shape actual lives instead of propositions to be juggled. A dependable character that is convinced that truth is more valuable than money, or that none should go without food or shelter for lack of a job, will drive the vehicle we call the self much more genuinely and lastingly than principles like justice and mercy. Instead of the greatest good for the greatest number, our particularity of character will not allow our principles about how to treat the neighbor to be separated from the essential question, "Who is my neighbor?"

Courage

Judges 6:25-31
Romans 12:1-2

I harbor few illusions that people take to heart messages about character development. Yet later in life we just might look back and remember certain experiences which shaped us more than we could have imagined. W. T. Leitze taught me that very early in life. W. T. Leitze was one of the kindest, most trusting individuals who ever lived. Mr. Leitze, a 60-year-old bachelor who weighed at least 300 pounds, was my ninth grade algebra teacher. Mr. Leitze's whole life was centered around his students. His lectures always interwove basic algebraic principles with Christian morals. He had abiding faith in his students and could move a class of 15-year-old boys and girls to tears as he voiced his dreams for the contributions that class could make to society.

Well, one Friday morning Mr. Leitze walked into the algebra class a little late. As he stood by his desk and glanced around the room, he raised his eyebrows in surprise. The bottom part of the huge pencil sharpener, the part that catches the shavings, was gone. Mr. Leitze told everyone to look at the pencil sharpener, and all eyes turned to the side of the big wooden cabinet where the main body of the sharpener was bolted. "It seems that someone has forgotten to return the bottom part of the sharpener to its rightful place," he began. "Knowing this fine, upstanding, honest group of young people as I do," he continued, "I know that it is just a matter of forgetfulness."

Then Mr. Leitze went on: "We don't want to embarrass that person, who I know wants to return it, so here's what we'll do. Each person, beginning with me, will place his and her head down on the desk and close their eyes. No one will look. I forbid it. And the person who forgot to return it can get out of his seat and take it back."

When Mr. Leitze spoke, one did as he instructed. Mr. Leitze placed his big old head down on his massive arms and closed his eyes. The rest of the class did the same. After a few seconds, a pair of feet hit the floor and we could hear them shuffling back toward the wooden cabinet. I smiled to myself at the honesty of a classmate. It wasn't one of the three most logical candidates, three football players, because Mr. Leitze seated everyone in alphabetical order and the shuffling came from a different part of the room from where Warlick, Wiggins, and Zier were seated.

Presently, we heard some rattling and noise from the area of the pencil sharpener. Then the same shuffling feet returned to the area from which they had come, and all was silent. Mr. Leitze broke the silence. "All right, children, I'm proud of you," he boomed. Almost in unison Mr. Leitze and thirty pairs of eyes looked up and turned to the wooden cabinet. The whole sharpener was gone! Someone had taken the rest of the mechanism. There were four holes in the cabinet and the outline of where the pencil sharpener had been.

The whole room was mesmerized. Mr. Leitze put his head down on the desk and started crying. When he did not stop, one of the girls ran and got the principal. The principal came rushing into the room. "For God's sake, Leitze, what did you expect them to do?" he roared.

I'm more realistic than W. T. Leitze. I don't expect massive changes in character. I do, however, possess hope that our highly intelligent and principled world can summon the courage to act on its convictions as well as its theories.

It's been said that the degree, B.A., stands for bachelor of abilities. To some degree it might. I know that whenever rationale is summoned for questionable behavior, the first line of defense is the alibi, "but everybody is doing it." In fact, talk to some people and you get the opinion that everyone is drinking to excess; everyone is sexually active; everyone is cheating; everyone is bending the rules.

I've often wondered about that. If it's so wonderful and indeed, everyone is doing it, why do they have to pressure me into doing it? Did you ever think of that? If everybody is really doing it, why do they need you and me to do it?

In our world, if you have to live by one rule, live by this one: respect the customs of others but not at the expense of your own values.

One of the most poignant passages of Scripture is the twelfth chapter of Paul's letter to the church in Rome. J. B. Phillips translates it in these words: *"Don't let the world around you squeeze you into its mold.* Renew your own mind and do that which is good and perfect." In other words, we may have to live in a crowd, but we do not have to live like the crowd. That is hard to do in an age of conformity, isn't it? It is difficult to stand as a minority with different values, different use of money, and a different language in our world. Such is perhaps the biggest problem a young person faces in growing to adulthood in a world of casual sex, easy drugs, and infatuation with economic and material success. It is easy to be brave when everyone agrees with you; but the difficulty comes when you have to stand out, one among many, remembering your obligations as a child of God. It is just as difficult for adults. It takes some real effort to live a good life in today's world. More people are selfish than are generous. More people stay home tonight than come to worship services. More people have shaky marriages than strong ones. More people spend less time with their children than in personal pursuits. Ah, but it is difficult not to let the world squeeze you into its mold. It is difficult being in the minority. And it doesn't get any easier the older you get. It gets harder because you have more to lose.

For most of my life, the one Scripture verse that had the most practical application was Romans 12:2 — "Don't let the world squeeze you into its mold, but renew your own mind and do that which is good." I memorized that as a teenager and I have had to hold to that in many situations in life. Frankly, I used to go to my dormitory room in college and read that in the Bible many a night. I must have underlined it in a dozen different colors of ink. You see, I played football in college, and even way back then college athletics was something else. The majority of college football players did not go to the library every night and study. And there was always the man who came by after a victory with ten $20 bills rolled up in his fist and said, "Nice game," as he stuck one in your pocket. The majority did not say, "No, thank you. We're not allowed to take that." There was always the restaurant owner who knew all the players and winked as he said, "Drink all you want; the tab's on me." The majority did not say, "No, thank you" or "One is enough." And drugs were becoming prevalent even in my college days. Even then, we had six or seven guys who could have opened a pharmacy. The fraternities were mild in comparison to today's, but even then at our parties, it was still the minority posture to say, "No, thank you" to many things.

When you hear or read about a decision handed down by our Supreme Court, the name is announced of the justice who wrote the minority report. Interestingly enough, if you wish to view most of what is now majority law or majority action in our country, you could go through the past four decades of decisions and read the minority reports. Most of the good causes in our way of life began with a minority and grew until they reached a majority. In fact, when our country began, only one-third of the people really wanted independence. The "best" two-thirds in the colonies said, "You are crazy to try to fight Great Britain with a few amateurs." They were a crazy minority, indeed.

One of the craziest minority reports in history is chronicled in the sixth chapter of Judges. It seems that the majority of the people in that culture worshipped a strange god named Baal. Baal was the pagan fertility god, so the people had erected a huge altar to him. Well, an angel of the Lord God came to Gideon and told Gideon to make a minority report. Gideon was to take his father's strongest bull, one that was seven years old, and hitch it up to the altar of Baal and pull it down. And while he was at it, he might as well cut down the sacred pole the people worshipped, and burn it. So, Gideon took ten men and one night they sneaked out and hitched up the bull and pulled down the altar to Baal, and burned the sacred pole. You can just imagine the furor that took place the next morning. Everyone in town woke up and knew what had happened. It didn't take them long to find out that Gideon had done it. The whole town came marching down to Gideon's house with blood in their eyes.

Gideon's father, Joash, went to the front door. The crowd yelled, "Bring out your son that he may die. He has pulled down the altar of Baal and burned the sacred trees next to it."

Joash stood before the crowd and said, "Wait a minute, let me get this straight. You are having to defend your god against one little man. Your god is so weak he needs you to protect him from one little man? You have to plead for the god of the majority of the people? Let Baal take care of himself. If he is so great, let him plead for himself because one little minority person has pulled down his altar."

That seemed to make sense to the people. From that day on they called Gideon, Jerubbaal, which means, "Let Baal take care of himself if he can."

I repeat: If everybody's doing it, and it's so great and powerful, why can't it take care of itself? Why do they try to pressure you and me into doing it? Is it so superficial, so weak, and so fake that it has to pressure someone into doing it, too?

Finally, consider this. There are some things that are so destructive that the only way you can be successful is to possess the courage not to engage in them at all.

In the movie *War Games*, a scientist built a marvelous computer named Joshua. Into this computer were placed all the responses and counter-responses the American defense system could make in a nuclear war. A child accidentally gained access to Joshua and started playing thermonuclear global war. Joshua, of course, did not know it was just a game. Joshua assumed total control over military weapons. Even the generals and scientists could not shut him down. Fortunately the builder of Joshua had created him with the capacity to learn from the consequences and moves of the game. Joshua began to accelerate his responses, projecting deaths on both sides from nuclear missiles and fall-out until the computer rapidly tallied up the losses for each side. Finally, Joshua shut itself off with the statement — *"Strange game; the only way to win is not to play."*

There are some strange games we play in life. The only way for an alcoholic to win at the game of drinking is to possess the courage not to play the game. The only way for a gambler to win at gambling is to have the courage not to play the game. The only way for a married person to win at the game of having an affair is to summon the courage not to have one. The only way for a teenage girl and boy to win at the game of going to the beach with a six-pack and a blanket is to practice the courage not to play the game. The only way for a father to win at the game of concurrently seeking undue wealth, vengeance on his enemies, personal gratification, and accomplished parenthood is to have the courage not to play that game.

From personal experience I can tell you that the only surefire way to quit smoking is not to smoke in the first place.

All of us have to learn what not to do in life. Then, having learned what not to do, we have to stand apart from the crowd and rely on the courage within us to help shape our character.

Strength

1 Corinthians 1:25-27
Matthew 5:1-8

In our fast-paced and advertisement-oriented world, it is easy to get trapped. In fact, there are people who specialize in trapping the public.

The invitation comes in the mail. You are invited to visit a new condominium complex at some beach, lake, or mountain setting. The advertisers will give you gas money to drive there. They'll provide you with free lodging and free meals. Why, you even have guaranteed prizes waiting on you, perhaps a new Oldsmobile or a color television. Of course, you could also wind up with a cheap transistor radio or a quartz watch instead. All you have to commit to is a thirty-minute tour and a short sales pitch. You are free to say "no"; there will be no hard feelings.

How can these companies afford to do this? Well, it's easy. The odds have been figured to the fifth decimal point. Seven and a half percent of visitors will buy because they like what they see. Another 28 percent will start to give in before they leave. "They've been so good to me! I owe them something. So what if I don't want the property. I should have thought of that before I came."[1]

After two or three days of plush living, you can hardly say "no" without feeling like a slob, an ingrate, or a rip-off artist. The figures have been researched and they are accurate. In our society, *36 percent* of the people will buy something at first sight or start to give in if they are made to feel like an ingrate or a rip-off artist. It takes real strength to say "no." The figures don't lie. There's a 36 percent chance you and I will give in to anything. That's why major companies now send you magazines or books and simply tell you, "Send it back if you don't want it." No obligation. They know that 36 percent of the people would rather buy something forced on them that they don't really want or need than send it back. I mean, the psychiatrists and the marketing people have got the percentages

169

down to the fifth decimal. *Exactly 36 percent of us will grab something at first sight or give in to feelings of being a slob, an ingrate or a rip-off artist. It's so hard to say "no."*

There is almost a fifty percent chance of divorce in today's world. We cringe at that statistic. But I suspect we are looking at the wrong end of the issue. If the data holds true, then 36 percent of married folk probably never wanted to be married in the first place. They didn't have the strength to say "no." They got trapped. The invitations had been mailed and the caterer was planning to come. What would the preacher have thought? How could you have returned the gifts? Besides, if you didn't want to marry Susie, you should have thought of that before you did all that other stuff and went that far. It was too late to say "no."

Thirty-six percent of the people co-habitating together outside of marriage probably didn't want to do that in the first place. They got trapped by circumstances. Thirty-six percent of the people who have had sex before marriage probably didn't want to do it in the first place. They got trapped. Thirty-six percent of the people who smoke probably never wanted to smoke in the first place. They got trapped by peer pressure. Thirty-six percent of the people who cheat, commit adultery, or live an amoral lifestyle did not want to do that in the first place. They got trapped by their emotions. People get trapped in jobs they really didn't want in the first place, but someone pays their travel, is nice to them, promises them the moon, and they feel like an ingrate if they say "no." So they move their families and start over somewhere else.

I may be wrong — completely wrong — but I think most of us parents do not fear that our child will grow up to purposefully take drugs, drink too much, join the wrong crowd, or be sexually irresponsible. *What we really fear is that our child could become one of the 36 percent of the people who get trapped by life.* If that is true, and there is a good chance that you and I will give in to anything, then maybe we should view the Bible and its teachings in a new light. The Bible is not a book of rules. It is not a literal history or even a precise compilation of biographies. The Bible is essentially a compilation of people who have interacted with God and found a conscience that helps them understand those experiences and realities in life that are beyond human understanding. *The Bible is a book to help us understand, avoid, and move beyond getting trapped by our inability to say "no."*

Dickens said, *"I wear the chains I forged in life."* Is not the pivotal and age-old sin the human belief that we have advanced ourselves to the position where we consider ourselves beyond being trapped? We posit to ourselves that we are too smart, too experienced, too rich, to fall for certain temptations. Is that not the very fabric of the Bible, from Adam and Eve getting trapped by the serpent and the fruit to the righteous, religious folks who were trapped into crucifying Jesus and releasing Barabbas? It takes real strength not to get trapped!

In the realm of personal morality and private morals, we are faced today with some of the saddest demonstrations of decadence in the history of this country. It isn't enough to say, "I was trapped," or, "We have a nosy press." Morals are such a big issue because we do wear the chains we forge in life. Jesus is right: "He who is unfaithful with little will be unfaithful with much." If there is sexual freedom before marriage, and people violate their principles before marriage, it's hard to avoid trouble after marriage. The person who cheats before he or she attains a responsible position in the company will face many more temptations to cheat after a responsible position has been reached. The farther you travel in life, the more opportunities, not fewer, you have for wrongdoing. You think it's easy to lose your moral fiber at 18? Wait until you're 38 or 48 or 58.

How does a person find real strength in life? How do we keep from getting trapped, from leaping at the first thing we see or from feeling like an ingrate, a slob, or a rip-off artist if we say "no"? Essentially, whether we practice them or not, I think we all come to realize the truth in Jesus' teachings. We do live in a moral universe. None of us is free. A mother went into pain and labor so that we could be here. We all carry the name of our father. A Savior hung on a cross, bleeding to death, like a slab of meat, for six to ten hours so we could gather here with some knowledge of a forgiving and loving God. Born free? None of us is born free. This same Savior promised that if we would learn afresh each day what God wanted for us, his mind could be in us to keep us from getting trapped. He also articulated some strange ideas about real strength and real happiness in life. Happy and strong are the pure in heart. Happy and strong are they that mourn and cry. Happy and strong are the meek, not the smart-alecks or wiseguys. Happy and strong are the peacemakers. Happy and strong are those people who go two miles when asked to go one. Happy and strong are those who do not commit adultery but keep themselves under control. Happy and strong are the people who not only love their friends but also love and pray for their enemies. Such people do not leap at everything. Nor do they feel guilty or unpopular when they say "no" to something or someone. They realize that ultimately we all have to live longest with ourselves. It's the sure shots, not the hot shots, who really make it.

Former Major League Baseball Commissioner Peter V. Ueberroth was asked to speak about the finest and strongest athlete he had ever seen. Ueberroth should be a good person to comment on athletics and strength. He directed the 1984 Olympic Games in Los Angeles. He saw Carl Lewis, the wrestlers, the weightlifters, all of them. As commissioner of baseball, he worked with all three major television networks. He has seen Jose Canseco, Roger Clemens, Mark McGwire, Mickey Mantle, Willie Mays, Hank Aaron, and hundreds of other successful athletes. He ought to know real strength if anyone does.

Peter Ueberroth stood in Kenan Stadium in Chapel Hill, North Carolina, and gave his answer to thousands of people. The finest and strongest athlete he ever saw was quite clear. He encountered this athlete a month before the Olympic Games. The Olympic torch was being run across America by relay. Every runner, in order to run, had to donate $3,000 to a charity in his or her hometown. That's how you got to run. Donate $3,000 and you could run the torch a kilometer, about six-tenths of a mile, and pass it to someone else who had also donated $3,000. People would stand five or six deep along the roadside to watch and cheer these runners.

At one point in the relay, a female runner finished her run with the torch with a strong stride. When her kilometer was up, she bent over to light the torch of the next runner.

And this next runner had to hold the torch with two hands. She was a little nine-year-old girl. Everyone could see that she was severely crippled. Obviously, she could not run a kilometer. But they lit her torch anyway. There was a policeman there with a big white plastic helmet on, gunning his motorcycle engine impatiently. He started ahead, waiting for her to take a step. She tried to take one halting step after another. Finally, she was able to limp with a little cadence, going hesitating step after hesitating step.

She had trained for a year with a ten-pound hammer because the torch weighed nine pounds — but it was still obvious that she wasn't going to make a kilometer.

Everyone learned later that the little crippled girl and her mother raised the $3,000 by bake sales and garage sales to donate to charity in her little town in New Mexico.

This little girl had a huge smile on her face as she limped along. She kept going, with the huge torch wobbling in her two hands. She became wringing wet with perspiration and slowed almost to a stop several times. As she walked, a strange thing happened. Instead of being five deep along the roadside, the crowd became ten deep and twenty deep and thirty deep. They had banners saying, "Run Amy Run. Run Amy Run." And people started to cheer. Her whole school turned out. She was exhausted, but this beautiful smile was still on her face. The little athlete made her kilometer. She lit the flame of the next runner who was off like a shot. There was a special look of triumph on her face as she stood there. She had achieved something very, very special. And on the side of the road was a motorcycle policeman. He had his plastic helmet up and a huge white handkerchief wiping his eyes.

Peter Ueberroth states flatly: *"This young lady ... was the finest and strongest athlete that I ever saw."* [2]

It takes real strength not to get trapped by your body, weak or strong. It takes real strength not to get trapped by your anger or your emotions. It takes real strength to deny yourself in order to contribute to others. It takes real strength to go out in public when all might laugh at you. It takes real strength to labor over and over again to reach a mighty and lofty goal. It takes real strength to triumph over life and not become trapped by it.

In our diverse and fast-paced world, you and I do not need different circumstances. We need better character. We need real strength. And that's exactly what Jesus tried to tell us.

1. Data furnished in Art Greer, *The Sacred Cows Are Dying* (New York: Hawthorn, 1978).

2. Peter V. Ueberroth told the story in his commencement speech at The University of North Carolina, May 10, 1987, Chapel Hill, North Carolina.

Humility

Luke 10:25-37

When Jesus of Nazareth walked this earth, he continually met people trying to justify themselves. These people tried to show themselves to be righteous and acceptable for God. One particular lawyer, evidently a man who had done much good, put Jesus to a test, saying, "Teacher, what shall I do to inherit eternal life?" Jesus answered him with the poignant and lasting parable of the Good Samaritan.

I read the parable of the Samaritan many times before I grasped its full significance. The Samaritan performed good deeds. Yet he performed them in an almost anonymous way. In fact, Jesus did not even bother to give him a name. I have often wondered what the Good Samaritan's name was. This man who used his wealth, his possessions, and his managerial ability for a fallen comrade — what was his name? Apparently his name was not important. He did not show off his good works like an egomaniac. He was a model of humility. Consequently Jesus used his example to show us that doing good is not enough. We can do good in a gentle, humble, Christian way. Or we can shout it from the rooftops, and expect people to grovel at our feet.

Let's give the Good Samaritan a name. Let's call him John Samaritan. Now let's thrust him into our world. Can't you envision the historical marker: on this spot, in the year A.D. 31, John Samaritan made his now famous act of compassion toward a wounded man! And certainly the inn where the wounded man resided would be named "John Samaritan Inn." I can even visualize a huge sign standing in the woods next to a hospital — future site of John Samaritan Home for Beaten Travelers; this project built through a donation from the John Q. Samaritan endowment trust. Of course, there would be a John Samaritan commemorative medal. And I can see the bumper stickers now: "Come and hear John Samaritan, the Chaplain of Jericho Street." Afterwards, the audience could

175

purchase the latest book by John Samaritan, *I'm God's Great Gift to Humankind,* telling, once again, the true story of how John Samaritan personally saved a beaten, bedraggled traveler.

Perhaps a beautifully engraved invitation will come in the mail one day. The invitation will read: "You are cordially invited to attend the 10th anniversary of John Q. Samaritan, Ph.D., Th.D., D.D, as helper of beaten travelers." The reception probably would be held at the Willie Leper room in the Samaritan Inn, named after the one out of ten healed lepers who came back and thanked Jesus.

Such frivolity is sheer fantasy, of course. Those people in life who truly deserve monuments do not need them. The true fact is that the Good Samaritan did not leave his name. Likewise, Jesus exhorted those he healed to remain silent about his activities.

If there is a need in our world today, it is for human beings to roll up their sleeves and, seeking no personal aggrandizement, minister to their neighbors. Henry Ward Beecher put it this way: "Religion means work; religion means work in a dirty world; religion means peril; blows given, blows taken as well ... The world is to be cleaned by somebody; and you are not a child of God if you are ashamed to scour and scrub."

As Jesus told the lawyer that day, one can only be a "professing" Christian by living the life of a Christian. Jesus came not to answer questions, but to ask them. He did not come to save people from their problems, but to save them from their indolence. He did not come to ask us to do good, but to call us to a finer way of doing good, to a deeper devotion to others and less to ourselves.

So often we *over-promise* what life with Christ will be like. Our theme has been "Christ is the answer." Christ is the answer to the extent that he is the greatest resource in the world. Christ is not the answer if by "answer" we mean deliverance out of the struggle of life altogether and peace right here and now. Even after Palm Sunday and Easter, no neat solutions for life dropped from the sky. Consequently when Jesus was arrested and crucified, many people departed Christianity forever, the way a dissatisfied customer reacts to a product that does not live up to its advance billing.

Yes, there will always exist a need for Good Samaritans. The Christian calling today is for dedicated men and women to perform acts of kindness without leaving their name. Many people in our world feel that God has forsaken them, that God hears not the words of their groaning.

Today two percent of the nation's population controls 33 percent of the nation's wealth, while one-half of the families in America have less than $500.00 in savings. One out of every five American families has no savings at all — none!

Women today are taught to yell "fire" instead of "help" when attacked, because the former brings more volunteer assistance.

Even telephone companies are now teaching small children not to say, "Jones residence, Bill Jones speaking," but to say, "Hello," because people play so many dirty games over the phone and criminals try to find out if parents are not at home.

Yes, Good Samaritans are very much needed in our world. We know this. But we remain inactive. Why? Because it takes a risk to be a volunteer. The law in our country holds a volunteer accountable for any error he makes, even when helping a victim. Were our Good Samaritan to come upon a beaten traveler with broken legs on North First Street and, in trying to move him to a hospital, accidentally snap his spinal cord, he would be sued and convicted of negligence. So men and women hold back from daily acts such as these. While this is regrettable, so is our refusal to act like men and women in those small opportunities for service that are thrust upon us each day. Without proper recognition, few people will do anything of service to their neighbor.

But the progress of civilization has come from just such a thing: men and women, whose names we cannot remember, have performed acts of kindness at great sacrifice to themselves. The Christian is the person who gives his or her time, money, and managerial ability unselfishly to others. The Christian humbly looks around each day of life for someone to help.

There have always been men and women who have appeared in heartbreaking situations and through sheer courage brought hope and light to others. They are symbolized by a plant called Rosebay willow herb or "fireweed." This plant, like Good Samaritans, grows in the most unlikely places. Its flowers can be seen among the ruins of a building blackened by fire or along the walls of a neglected house. It gives a cheerful color among debris and death. During the Second World War, "fireweed" served as a symbol of the renewal of life among the rubble, debris, and wilderness that followed the bombing and air raids.

In my humble opinion, "fireweed" is the unifying symbolic expression of the Christian. The Christian is there. Although the name may not be remembered or even left, the Christian's time, money, and abilities are there amid the suffering of the world.

When asked to explain the reasons behind UCLA's phenomenal record of eight basketball championships in nine years, Coach John Wooden replied, "It is amazing how much can be accomplished if no one cares who gets the credit."

It is, indeed, amazing how much can be done when we focus on the task at hand instead of our own recognition. It is amazing how much a church can accomplish if none of its members cares who gets credit for the church's ministry.

The Good Samaritan — I wonder what his name was? Oh well, it really doesn't matter, does it?

Friendship

John 15:9-17
Hebrews 12:1-2

All of us purchase, erect, and decorate a Christmas tree. This little ritual evokes some of the most beautiful memories we possess. When I was a child, our family placed an angel on top of our Christmas tree. After all the lights, ornaments, and icicles had been hung and wound around the tree, I got to climb up on a chair and place the angel on the top. That was always my job. I am now four decades older than I was the first time I put the angel on the tree. But I am still the one who places the angel on the top of the tree. Actually, I guess I would become upset if they didn't let me do that. You see, that little ritual enables me to participate in memories of my childhood.

The Christian faith relies heavily on memories. Its communities of faith carry a common memory that has been passed on from generation to generation. You and I can draw from this memory as we try to understand the human condition. The author of Hebrews had this in mind when he or she wrote: "We are surrounded by so great a cloud of witnesses ... Jesus Christ the same yesterday, and today, and forever."

As the adopted children of an impartial God, you and I must focus in a new way on our adopted kinships and friendships as we march toward death. When society becomes complex and stressful, human beings have to pay more attention to their networks which aid success and happiness. For example, in 1975 there were only six organizations in the Manhattan phonebook that had names beginning with "Networking." By 1985 the Manhattan phone book had over forty organizations beginning with "Networking." Now the title appears in hundreds of corporations. Peter Stark, the president of one of the largest public relations firms in the country, says: "Networking is the most powerful success tool to get you where you want to go."[1]

Networks are important for Christians also. Essentially, the writer of Hebrews is saying that you and I have a religious network that we cannot do without. In fact, this network is composed of people who have been dead for generations, as well as the people who currently sit around us in the pews. All of us are part of a religious memory that can lift our visions, fire our hearts, and encourage us about humankind. It is vitally important to hold on, even in the face of death, to the important symbols and rituals that have been passed on from generation to generation. The writer of Hebrews laid out a picture of all the Jewish heroes — Abraham and Isaac, Moses and Gideon, Samson and David. "Look at them," the writer urged. "Look at them. From generation to generation they conquered kingdoms, stopped the mouths of lions, roamed the hills in animal skins, and died — all for their faith. They are your kin." And then the writer came to the ultimate hero. "All these people have carried the baton until now. But now they are witnesses from past generations. Now it is your turn. You must run the race now. Look to Jesus. Remember your leaders, the ones who have passed you the baton, and run the race now yourself. You are part of the network."

Whatever else we need for living, you and I must have a family and a church community. In his profound work *Understanding Prayer*, Edgar Jackson relates that a group of scientists did experiments with rats to determine what gave them a will to live. In one of the experiments they placed healthy rats in vats of water to see how long they could float or swim before they gave up the struggle for life, and drowned. The rats swam from sixty to eighty hours before they gave up. A similar group of rats, just as healthy, were placed in similar vats, with one major difference — they had their whiskers cut off. Rats' whiskers, of course, serve as their chief contact with the world about them. They provide sensory clues to the object and spatial relationship between rats and their world. These rats exhibited quite different behavior. Within ten minutes some of them were dead. None of them showed half the will to live of the first group.[2] The will to live in all living creatures is lessened when its relationships to memory and space and objects are broken off. You and I have to be surrounded by clouds of witnesses; we have to be placed in a community that cares about us; we have to have some assurances that from generation to generation we have carried forward stories and acts of love that will be part of the ongoing human understanding of life and God. These rituals and relationships within the church — these are our whiskers. These are the things which give us clues as to how we relate to our world and find our way home at the end of life. Cut them off and our will to live is reduced.

The cards of Christmas, the story of the young pregnant woman going to Bethlehem with her husband, the lighting of the Advent candles, the birth of a Messiah, the giving and receiving of gifts — these are not mere excuses for increased commercial activity or backdrops for family reunions and college bowl games. They are our whiskers as to life and its destination. These help provide religious socialization. Cut them off and our will to live is reduced.

One fall, I had one of the most enjoyable visits in my life. I went to see a fifty-year-old man named Don Terry. Don was the chairman of the pulpit committee of the first church I pastored. But more than that, he was a friend with whom I had enjoyed golf, college athletic endeavors, and many a Christmas season. Don and I had always secured the trees that the church placed in its sanctuary at Christmastime. The year of my visit, Don was diagnosed as having cancer. He had only a few more months, at most, to live. I walked into his den and there he lay in a hospital bed, barely able to peek above the sheets. His frail body weighed less than 95 pounds. He could no longer walk and talk with his children, swing a golf club, or watch television. A huge smile covered his face and he whispered, "We had some real good times, didn't we, Hal?" I responded, "Yes, we did. We sure did." And he proceeded to recall for me incidents I had long since forgotten — times we had played, lived, loved, and laughed. And most of all, he recalled the members of the church congregation, some of them long since deceased. He talked of Christmas and the worship services and the things we had done together. The cloud of witnesses was in the room hovering around his bed when, for one last time, he smiled and said, "We had some real good times, didn't we, Hal?"

As I walked out of that den, past some obviously downcast and heartbroken relatives of his, I did not feel remorseful. In fact, I felt somewhat heartened. Sure, the baton would soon pass from his hands into others. But the man had memory. He had history. He had had the knowledge of church and Advent and Christmas. He was happy. He was on his way home to be a witness to surround, from generation to generation, all those who would worship in that church. He had had community and now he would be forever a part of the memory of someone else who would use his story as a guidepost home. When his money accounted for nothing, when he reached the point he could no longer walk or even breathe on his own, he had memory and he belonged to a community that would outlive his own life. He had not cut off his whiskers at an early age. He had filled his reservoir with Christian witnesses, memories, symbols, and worship. The cloud of witnesses called him home only three days after I left his home. He moved from the community of the living to the community of saints.

You see, that is all a church can do for you and me. The most striking feature of the early church was not its doctrine, its growth, or its leadership. Its most striking feature was that it was a community where people loved each other, grew together in their common experiences in life, and lived their lives in joy. It was from generation to generation an adopted spiritual family, moving toward an eternal home.

Advent and Christmas are more than just a movement of services, particular and peculiar to the year in which they take place. We light the candles, for me, in the church of particular people with their own history and identity, and in the presence of many others who have worshipped there long before them.

Some of your memories of kin and congregation are much longer than mine. Some of you have memories of a spiritual family that are much shorter. But your whiskers will grow with each passing season. And one day the next generation will have you for their cloud of witnesses as they sing the carols, hear the words, light the candles, and carry forward the memory and the power of Mary, Joseph, and the Christ-child.

Many people have heard me preach time after time, month after month, year after year. They are familiar with my manner and my message. Some of them will, in time, learn every gesture, every eccentricity of delivery, even the distinguishing marks of my vocabulary; and I will have very little to say to them that is new. Over and over again they will hear my ideas, the attitudes I have toward truth, and the causes that are most on my heart.

But they will come — just as I have come into the walls of a church from year to year. They come not for me or out of habit. They come because they are a part of the adopted family of God. We are kin. Our Christian family started generations before us and it will outlive our own lives on earth. We come together because networking is, indeed, the most powerful tool to get us where we want to go, which is beyond the state of aloneness in our march toward home.

The fact that we have been adopted by a mothering God into a world family heading toward the home of an impartial God creates incredible opportunities for friendship. It means that friendships will not be limited to this earth's boundaries of time and space.

Perhaps it is strange to use an illustration with which you disagree. But I do that. Dennis Campbell, the former Dean of Duke Divinity School, is a friend of mine. He is a person I respect. Dennis has served as a pastor. He recounts the first time he was called to the home of a church member who had died. When the call came to his study, Dennis was talking with a physician whose father and brother were preachers. "Remember," the physician said, "what they want is not a friend. They have plenty of those. They want a pastor. What matters is not who he is in his individuality when he arrives at the house. What matters is that he is the pastor. They need a representative figure, one who represents God and God's community. What they want is not a friend. They have plenty of those."[3]

Through the years, I have come to almost totally disagree with that statement. Most people do not have plenty of friends. In fact, some of the craziest and most desperate acts in our society are carried out by people trying to win someone's friendship. A person can know a million people and still have only a few friends.

Almost a decade ago, I wrote a book on loneliness. Anytime you write a book you get letters from people who find something in it that rings true with their experience. I imagined receiving letters from lonely, friendless widows in nursing homes; abandoned children; people whose lives were involved in drudgery on an assembly line and crying out for friends. The first letter that was sent to me was from the wife of Billy Graham. The second letter came from then presidential candidate John Anderson, who was carrying the book along on his campaign trips. I am not certain that most people have plenty of friends. In fact, I think it is easier to find a pastor than to find a friend.

Jesus Christ articulated in John 15 a powerful model of ministry. He said to his disciples, "No longer do I call you servants ... but I have called you friends, for all that I have heard from my Father I have made known to you" (John 15:15). He said this to people who had called him "teacher," "Lord," "King," and "priest."

The great theologian Jurgen Moltmann interpreted this to mean that in the fellowship of Jesus the disciples became friends of God. They no longer experienced God as Lord, nor only as Father; they came to experience him "in his innermost nature as Friend." Consequently friendship became their vocation in a society dominated by masters and servants, parents and children, teachers and pupils, superiors and subordinates.[4]

This vocation was an extension of the Old Testament idea spoken between Naomi and Ruth: "One true friend is worth more than fourteen relatives." And it's true: Your family is given to you but you get to choose your friends. In essence, Jesus' words were saying, "One God who is your friend is worth twelve gods on Mount Olympus or 100 gods from the Greek mystery religions."

The issue of friendship is especially critical in our kind of world. Several studies suggest that our society is losing the capacity to make friends. Most of us no longer belong to permanent, lifelong personal communities where everyone is linked by a continuous tradition of reciprocity.[5] It is possible to be surrounded by "friends" one day, and deserted the next.

All of us need expressive emotional relations with all kinds of people. Someone has said that people do not make friends. Instead, they recognize friends. Having friends is such a critical thing because friends furnish us with proof that in a world of betrayals and pain and death there are reasons for trust. In a world of solitude, there are some relationships that need protecting, touching, and greeting. None of us can carry all our burdens alone. And when we triumph there is little worse than having no one to delight in it with us. People want to have friends and they want to be a friend.

Virtually the entire Bible, from Genesis to Revelation, is about love, friendship, and death. The Bible asserts that close, loving friendships are as basic a need as food and shelter. All the great people of the Bible revolved their lives around significant friendships. And when our Lord returned from his tomb he appeared not to the crowd on the hillside or the scores of people he had healed or preached before; he appeared to his earthly friends.

There is no greater story of friendship in literature than the intense friendship between Jonathan and David. Scripture says, "The soul of Jonathan was knit with the soul of David," and Jonathan loved David as his own soul. David returned that love, based on a complete mutual understanding and limitless admiration. Jonathan even placed his friend's interests over those of his father. The friendship of these two Israelites overrode political loyalties; Jonathan even accepted the idea that David might become King instead of him. Between these two friends there were no secrets. The friendship between the two even involved David's agreeing to look after Jonathan's children if he were to die. This intense friendship, lasting until death, depended on the willingness of each to forego self-interest and convert their separate identities into togetherness.

Even the birth of Jesus Christ depended on a friendship. One of the most moving passages of Scripture is the meeting of Elizabeth and Mary. Both women were pregnant. And there is something special about friends waiting together in hope, and sometimes fear, for some anticipated event. Elizabeth and Mary came together and enabled each other to wait for events they could not fully understand. They affirmed for each other that something was happening that was worth waiting for. The visit of Elizabeth and Mary is a beautiful expression of what it means to be together, gathered around a promise, affirming that something is really happening that is beyond human control. And from the cross, our Lord and Savior looked into the eyes of his beloved disciple, John, and uttered, "My friend, please take care of my mother."

The best thing about genuine friendship is that it is not destroyed by mistakes or wrecked by occasional failures. Friendship, thank God, is stronger than our weaknesses. Friendship is what enables us to make it through life together as we march toward a common death and a common home.

If we can characterize friendship, I think it is the willingness to do something specific for another person instead of stating a general position. A friend is someone who picks a specific thing and does it.

Several years ago, a memorable article on friendship was written by a woman named Madge Harrah. Madge had received a phone call from Missouri saying her brother and her sister and her sister's two children had been killed in an automobile accident. She began making arrangements to travel to the funeral. Her mind, quite naturally, was so numbed that she could not think. She was moving in a fog. The doorbell rang. A neighbor, Emerson King, stood there. "I've come to clean your shoes," he said. Puzzled, she asked him to repeat what he had said. "I've come to clean your shoes," he said. Then he explained. When his father had died, he had a difficult time getting the children's shoes cleaned for the funeral. So he had come to take that chore off her hands. "Give me all your shoes," he said, "not just your good shoes, but all your shoes."

Madge realized that the children's shoes were indeed muddy. She collected them and located the shoe polish. Emerson got a knife and sponge and settled on the kitchen floor with some newspapers. He worked and worked until he had all the shoes cleaned. He even scrubbed the soles so they could be laid in the suitcase.

The presence of this friend on the kitchen floor, methodically and quietly doing this chore, gave Madge the strength she needed to do the things she had to do. The experience changed her. Now, whenever she hears of anyone who has had a loss, she doesn't say, "If there is anything I can do just let me know." She picks a specific thing and does it.[6]

A friend is someone who doesn't come up to you and say, "If there's anything I can do, let me know." A friend does something. I thought of this incident one weekend when I was in South Carolina. I also thought of Joseph of Arimathea, the secret disciple who gave Jesus a costly funeral. The Scriptures say: "Joseph of Arimathea, being a disciple of Jesus, but secretly for fear of the Jews, sought out Pilate that he might take away the body of Jesus" (John 19:38). Joseph was a prominent and wealthy man. But he was a silent man with respect to following Jesus. He had done well for himself and he did not want to blow it by becoming an open friend of this Jesus of Nazareth. In that horrible spectacle of the cross he remained silent. Afterward he felt guilty, so he tried to "say it with flowers." He bathed the corpse of Jesus in the most precious of perfumes and wrapped it in the finest of linens. He gave Jesus a funeral that was the finest culture and money could purchase.

Poor Joseph. To remain silent and secret while a friend is alive is an awful thing. Flowers and perfume and linen are nice, but a single act of kindness to the living is worth more than a spray of flowers to the dead.

One of my dearest friends in life was a lady named Ruth Babb. She at one time was an astute businesswoman who married a widower who happened to be a Baptist minister. He had pastored First Baptist, Laurinburg, North Carolina; and First Baptist, Seneca, South Carolina. When her husband died, she faced a quandary. She did not feel comfortable remaining in the church where her husband had pastored, so she joined our church and sought a place to work. And work she did. She built a ladies Sunday school class from four members to more than forty members. She was kind, wise, and gracious. They even named the class after her. But her hearing failed her, so she had to resort to reading lips. Even in that state she was still the best advice-giver I ever knew. She was a minister to ministers. In a strange yet real way, she was Mother Confessor to the clergy of the city. Her small, white frame house was both a sanctuary for the weary and a temple for those seeking understanding of God. She trained me and she trained more ministers than any seminary professor.

Even after I left her church, she wrote beautiful prosaic letters of encouragement and wisdom to me no matter where I lived. Ultimately her eyesight became almost as poor as her hearing. She moved into a home with her sister. Finally, her health deteriorated to the point that she was placed in the Baptist Home in Laurens, South Carolina. She subscribed to our church sermons for months, until one day she wrote that she had better be removed from the list because she could not see well enough to read them.

Our secretary, Jennie Herndon, on her own, found a way to enlarge the print four times its normal size. Jennie sent every sermon to her in the nursing home. One day Ruth typed Jennie a beautiful letter of thanks. Jennie came into my office and said, "Who is this woman? I've never known anyone who could express herself so beautifully."

Finally, word came to us from the home to cease the correspondence. The woman had lapsed into a semi-comatose condition and hardly knew anyone anymore. She would never again get out of bed on her own.

When we were in South Carolina one weekend, I saw her sister, Alice. I thought of all the times I had said, "If there is anything I can do for Ruth, just let me know."

Diane and I decided that we should go by that nursing home and see Ruth. We got the directions. It was eighty miles out of the way on our return trip to High Point. That day at lunch everyone tried to talk Diane and me out of seeing her. "She doesn't know anyone anymore. She won't know you are there. Remember her as she used to be. You won't even recognize her. Your two boys will be tired and it won't be worth it. Send flowers to the funeral."

We decided to go anyway. At least we would know we had been there. It was, indeed, a long, out-of-the-way trip. When I entered the room, I did not recognize the still figure in the bed. Her arms were restrained. She could not have weighed more than sixty pounds. I stood for five minutes, with no hint of life coming from the person in the bed. So I turned to leave. My eyes caught a yellow pad on the table. The nurses had been writing on it in huge letters four inches high. Things like "Time for your bath. It is September. Alice called."

I took the pad and flipped it to a blank page. In letters four inches high, I wrote "Harold Warlick" and held it in front of her face. The eyes squinted. Finally, the lips moved and said, "Harold Warlick, he was the best friend I ever had." I pointed to myself. Her lips moved again: "Is this a dream?" I wrote on the pad, "No, this is not a dream." I reached over and pinched her hand. She smiled and said, "Good. This is reality. How is Diane?"

I wrote back, "She's outside with the boys. I will get her." Diane walked into the room and stood up close to her face. Ruth squinted and said, "You look so pretty."

We wrote some more general conversations on the pad. And when we left she said, "I will pray for your church." Then she lapsed into the condition in which I had initially found her.

The next day I called a friend back in South Carolina to tell him of my visit to her. But he interrupted me. "She didn't know you, did she?"

"More than that," I responded. "She knows a better me than even I know." That's what a friend is. A friend knows a better you than even you yourself recognize. In this complex and difficult world, I commend to us two things: 1) Never say, "If there is anything I can do just let me know." You just pick out a specific thing and do it; and 2) Remember that a single act of kindness to the living is worth more than a spray of flowers to the dead.

When we realize our adopted state, we move with friends and kin toward an eternal orphanage. There is no other way. The sheer magnitude of the destination evokes from our earthly lips not a triumphal shout of righteousness but a humble prayer:

Almighty God,
Be with us in these days of our living
Before our frail bodies they bury,
To help us find a little of what you gave,
To Jonathan and David, and Elizabeth and Mary.
And when before you and your hosts we stand,
To be judged for our faith and our sins,
Grant us the sheer grace and joy,
Of living in eternity with a few of our old friends.
Amen.

1. Peter B. Stark in a speech, "Networking," delivered before the County of San Diego Department of Social Services, San Diego, California, August 8, 1985.

2. Edgar N. Jackson, *Understanding Prayer* (New York: World Publishing Company, 1968), pp. 177-178.

3. Dennis M. Campbell, "The Ordained Ministry As A Profession," *Quarterly Review*, Vol. 3, No. 2, Summer 1983, p. 28.

4. Jurgen Moltmann, *The Passion For Life*, trans. M. Douglas Meeks (Philadelphia: Fortress Press, 1978), p. 57.

5. See Robert Bain, *Friends and Lovers* (New York: Basic Books, 1976), pp. 256-257, and Eugene Kennedy, *On Being A Friend* (New York: Continuum, 1982), pp. 20-21.

6. John Killinger told this story when he was Senior Minister, First Congregational Church, Los Angeles, California, on June 21, 1987.

Tolerance

Psalm 18:28-36
Luke 2:1-20

One of the most difficult things in the world is to give up to a greater good something which you have created or found. Most of us are familiar with what physicians call postpartum depression. Here is a mother who has carried a little child in her womb for nine months. The child has been part of her body. Her nutritional system has supplied its needs. The tiny heart has been beating in rhythm to the mother's own heart. But if that child is to live and flourish there comes the time of delivery. The child is born. It is given up for other hands to touch, other eyes to behold, and other systems to nourish. Giving up something you have created and nourished is very difficult to do. That's why we sometimes want to keep our knowledge of the way home at life's end to ourselves.

I have experienced the phenomenon each time I have published a book. Alone in the recesses of your mind, you create ideas and movements of thought. Then you commit them to paper. Next, you work on expressing that creation to a congregation in a sermon. It's your creation, your artistry, your entity. It belongs to your moment, your time with the good people of your church. It's your child. Then a publisher puts it between two covers and makes your little creation available to thousands of people. Suddenly, a minister in Tennessee and another one in California are preaching, to a good effect, your brainchild, your creation. In fact, it is no longer yours. Like the ripping open of a feather pillow in the teeth of a strong wind, your little creation is scattered and gone. Sometimes you are tempted to regret that. You tend to want to keep your creation within the personal range of your own activity. "It's mine. I'll hug it to me to my grave before I let it enter upon its own independent history."

Yet the path the Christian faith has chosen to take in its final journey home is based on the ability of those who find it only to give it up. This process cuts against the grain of human nature. If I discover a direction signal toward home, is it for my tribe, my kin only? How open-ended is my possession of faith in God and its attendant belief system?

From the very beginning of the Judeo-Christian heritage, it appears that faith in God has been a very fluid and tolerant pilgrimage. To choose the heritage of the child who points the way is to choose a very tolerant system. The tolerance of the Christ-child begins in the story of Jochebed, the mother of Moses. The first two chapters of the book of Exodus refer to one of the big events of human history. If all the decisive military battles of the world were taken together they would not be of greater importance than this event that took place on the banks of the Nile River. The event took place 3,330 years ago. A mother named Jochebed had to suppress her own maternal love in favor of a larger purpose for her creation. The Pharaoh at that time had issued an edict to kill all Hebrew male children. For three months Jochebed hid her little boy. But she knew she could no longer take the risk of hiding him. If she kept him to herself, he would die. So Jochebed got down on her hands and knees. She wove by hand a little ark out of the long stems of the papyrus plant. Then, with her own hands, she plastered it inside with clay to make it smooth, and outside with a sealer to make it watertight. She remembered that Pharaoh's daughter was accustomed to come down and bathe at a particular spot. So Jochebed took her little boy, this infant that she had created, this blood of her blood that she had carried for nine months, this child she had rocked to sleep night after night, this child that she had invested all of her time and resources in, and she laid him in the basket and pushed him out into the river to be found, educated, and adopted by other people.

Then, she stepped back and became the nurse, not the mother, of the child she had given birth to. She went to Pharaoh's household every day until the child was seven years old, pouring great things into his mind and heart during those most formative years of his life. It was she who instilled in him a belief in God. It was she who imparted to him the sacred traditions of Israel and who told him of the divine promise to Abraham. Then, when little Moses was seven years old, Pharaoh's daughter adopted him and gave him an Egyptian education.

What an education it was. You see, the Egyptian educational system had conceived of a very important idea called monotheism: that there was only one God instead of many gods. Moses had an opportunity to become exposed to that concept.

Jochebed stepped back and became the nurse, not the mother, of the child she had given birth to. And 3,330 years later you and I know that sun (that there is but one God) is still rising.

One of the amazing things about life is that when one observes a painting it is impossible to distinguish a rising sun from a setting sun. The painter himself or herself paints a rising sun in exactly the same manner in which a setting sun is painted. If you took a famous painter into an art gallery and showed him a painting of a landscape, that painter could not tell you whether the sun was rising or setting. You would have to ask the artist who began and completed the painting himself what his intention had been.

Religions have risen and fallen on the landscape that we call human history. Geronimo and his tribe believed that they were living in a "home" the great god Usen had given them. Apparently that belief was a setting sun. The ancient Greeks pointed toward Mount Olympus as the "home" of the gods. In a very direct way that sun began to set before the first human being ever climbed to the top of the sacred mountain. So it was for Artemis, goddess of the Ephesians, and the Mikado of Japan.

What about the child of Bethlehem who points the way toward this home called heaven? Do we indeed know 3,330 years after Moses that that sun is still rising?

If we do purport to cling to a rising belief, it lies precisely in its ability to lop off circumscribed ideals of God. The child who points the way toward home must be a liberating child whose views are as broad as life itself.

One of the telling aspects of the human race is that it invented the wall long before it invented the wheel. The human race invented the wall first, to keep certain people and things on one side and other people and things on the other side. Then the human race got around to inventing the wheel to enable it to move beyond its walls.

Walls are necessary. A little child first learns that he cannot get out of a crib. It's for the child's protection. Then an expandable gate is placed at the top of the stairs to keep the infant from falling down them. The wall or the fence keeps an animal from running loose. Two years ago, we placed too small a wall in front of our family dog. He leaped the wall and was last seen headed at full run up the hill toward a shopping mall.

There is something endemic to the human condition that wants us to build a wall of protection for ourselves before we venture out into the wilds beyond. There is also something in our condition that resists a wall and entices us to try to jump over it. Tell the human race that there's a wall around the tree of knowledge of good and evil and it will leap over that wall, pluck the fruit, and eat it. Tell the human race that there's a wall called the sound barrier and it will build a plane fast enough to leap that wall. Tell the human race there's a wall out there that keeps us from traveling around the world without refueling and we will build a funny-looking plane and two people will battle the elements for nine days and leap over that wall. In a strange way, walls were meant to be scaled.

My junior year in high school was a pivotal year in my life. I had grown up in a relatively small town. Like many high schoolers, I had not experienced the mobility I thought I should have experienced. But that summer our basketball team spent two weeks in the biggest city I had ever stayed in, a place called Raleigh, North Carolina. The late Everette Case ran a camp at North Carolina State University. Mr. Case divided his summer groups into three leagues. The championship league was an amalgamation of three teams — ours, one from Clemson, South Carolina, and one from Andrews, North Carolina. Our group lived together in a dormitory on the North Carolina State campus. Now, placing together a group of high school boys from three small towns was really asking for trouble. The night lights of Raleigh seemed to be pointing their fingers directly at us and pleading, "Come on, boys, this is what you're really here for." After two nights of chasing us all over town, Mr. Case moved us to another dormitory. This dormitory had a huge hedge and a wall behind it. The windows were high off the ground. Mr. Case got one of his tallest players to sleep in the room by the locked front door, and figured that we would have our wanderlust significantly curbed.

Like a strong west wind, the word would come flying through the corridors, "The counselor's asleep. The counselor's asleep." Out the window would fly the homemade rope ladder. In rapid succession fifteen boys would descend. Like a well trained group of Marines, we would round up several trash cans, stack them against the wall, and over the top we would go into a strange, new, wonderful world. Obviously, these furtive nighttime flights over the wall affected our physical performance the next day. But in a strange way, they were worth it. Once we had gone over the wall the first time, the sheltered, regimented, austere life was impossible to return to.

In a strange way, in the most prosaic fashion imaginable, something like that took place in the birth of Jesus Christ. In the eighteenth Psalm, the writer makes an amazing claim ... "by my God I have leaped over a wall." To be certain, there is a dimension of religious freedom in God, and especially in Christ, that you and I must never forget. That freedom must become a part of our character.

In the child born in Bethlehem, human religious awareness leaped some formidable walls. As such, the event was more than a few wise men bringing presents; more than a report of angels singing in the sky; more than the birth of a royal king to a few chosen people.

The child was one who leaped completely over the wall of narrow-minded human religion. His pathway toward home became as broad as life itself.

Human beings had built a great wall around God. They said, "You can't get close to God unless you eat the right food. And you've got to wash your hands in the right way. Then you've got to have the food blessed by a rabbi." Well, that left many people shut off from God. Rabbis were hard to find in some remote places. It was most difficult for shepherds to eat the right kinds of food, much less round up a rabbi to bless it. Heck, most shepherds were lucky if they got to take one bath a month, much less wash their hands before praying to God.

195

So what did God do? One night some shepherds were tending watch over their flock. The heavens opened. God leaped over the wall. A loud voice rang clear and true: "Shepherds, unto you is born this day in the city of David a Savior." God leaped over the wall of dietary religious requirements and the race has never headed back there.

Human beings had built a great wall of holiness around God. God was unapproachable except through angels and miracles. If a person touched the ark of God in the Old Testament, he or she had to die. Surely God worked through legions of angels. This God was thought to be rather ghastly and far removed from human experience. In fact, the Old Testament speaks of a holy God or of holy, separate places 161 times.

But suddenly a young teenage girl who was doing her chores and taking care of the younger children around the house received word that she was pregnant. What's more, she was pregnant with God's child. Her husband was just an ordinary carpenter. They had little money and even less education. They were so common that they couldn't pull any strings and get a motel reservation. They had to deliver their baby, the son of God, in an animal barn. God leaped over the wall of human magic and superstition and right into the very essence of human life. And the world of religion was never the same again. Whereas the Old Testament speaks of God as the holy one or the separate one 161 times, the New Testament speaks of God as the holy or separate one only four times. God leaped over our wall and came to us.

Finally, we humans had built a great wall of human officials behind which we thought God lived. If you wanted to be religious, you had to see a rabbi or a priest or a king. God worked through channels, so to speak. Religious work was defined as prayer, fasting, and worship. There really wasn't much in the way of ethics. You never had to bring God into the workplace. You did your job and became religious when you went into the temple or synagogue. There you would communicate through priests who would hold their pastoral staffs of office, offer sacrifices, and carry out baptisms and scriptural readings. The temple was where the holy matters were conducted, and your job site was just your job site. One was holy and the other was worldly. God, of course, lived within those high walls of the holy places.

But look at what happened in the response of the child of Bethlehem. Luke tells it best: "And the shepherds returned, glorifying and praising God for all they had heard and seen."

The shepherds returned to the Judean hills and their flocks. They saw Jesus and they returned to the exact type of work they were doing before. They returned to their sheep. They did not shave their heads. They did not devote their lives to praying in the desert. They did not build a shrine in Bethlehem. They did not fast. They did not put on robes. They did not become priests. They took up their jobs again, and no bishop had finer office than they did. They took God back with them, glorifying and praising him for what they had seen.

Their work became religious work. And religious work became as broad as all of life. Think deeply about this. When those shepherds returned to their shepherding after having knelt at the manger crib, God leaped forever over the walls of the temple, the synagogue, and the church. Those shepherds became priests every bit as much as the royal priests in the temple. They returned to their work and lived by the light of Christ and transmitted that light to others.

Whatever your job is in life — furniture executive, salesman, politician, waitress, teacher, homemaker, middle management, physician, nurse — your work is just as holy as mine. You are a priest, too. You are on public display just as much as the minister of a church. There is no more church and world, holy and ordinary. If you cheat someone in your work, you cheat God. If you honor someone in your work, you honor God. The appropriate response to the vision in Bethlehem is not to abandon the world, or only to come to church in honor of its memory. The proper response to the vision is to go back to work and take it with you.

God leaped over the wall at Bethlehem and the old order passed away. The birth of this child was an act of religious freedom. It is a sacrilege to build a wall around God after the birth of Christ. When people use the Bible and their interpretation of it to build a wall between themselves and another group of people, it is a sacrilege.

197

When people use baptism of the Holy Spirit to build a wall between themselves and others, it is a sacrilege. When people fall into arguing about the interpretations of Jesus' writings and fall into building walls over creeds and church governments and denominations, it is a sacrilege. When we want the gospel to become what we want it to be instead of what it wants to be, we have lost grace. We have then lost the God of Bethlehem and returned to our own sacred cows.

God leaped the human wall, in order that the whole world might know the way home. God so loved the world that he gave the whole world his only begotten son, that whosoever should believe in him might be saved.

For centuries human beings had built a wall of prejudice, piety, status, magic, and holiness. This huge wall stretched throughout every land. One night a star shone down on the wall. And to the top God climbed. When God got to the top, a little baby was flung right into the midst of human frailty. The baby grew and pulled aside a dozen followers. They laid down their lives and formed a ladder from Jerusalem to Judea to Asia Minor to High Point. "Come," said the Christ, "believe in me. And if you believe in me, you must follow me. You must follow me right over the top of the wall into a way of life that is as strange as it is wonderful."

Permit me a confession, if you will. I accepted Christ as my Savior many years ago. But I grew up in a world of walls — whites and blacks, with a wall between them; Baptist and Catholic, with a wall between them; American and non-American, with a wall between them; rich on one side of a wall and poor on the other; the educated and the uneducated, with a wall between; religious walls and irreverent walls; male and female, with a wall between; Southern walls and Yankee walls; sophisticated and unsophisticated walls; country club and commoner walls. My salvation means nothing if I cannot one day say with the Psalmist, "With your help I can run through a barricade, with my God I can scale a wall — the wall of my own prejudice."

If there is a pathway through the human condition, then the initial assertion must be the final assertion: based on the Western tradition we have inherited, tolerance may be the most critical aspect of Christian character. The early Church certainly thought this to be true. As it formed its ethical principles it took over and used the valued principles of the Greek and Roman world — wisdom, temperance, justice, and benevolence. But these values were limited to the rich and powerful. Poor people and slaves could not be ethical or virtuous, in the Greek and Roman sense. Poor people could not receive an education, so wisdom was excluded from their grasp. Slaves could not vote or exercise political power, so justice remained beyond their grasp. In like manner, benevolence was reserved as a virtue for those who possessed something they could give away. Finally, temperance, or moderation, was excluded from those who had little of substance with which to face the temptation to excess. Consequently, the early Church added three values of its own: faith, hope, and love. This opened the door for people of all genders, races, and stations in life to be considered part of God's elect and society's virtuous citizens. This process of **tolerance** became the hallmark of Christianity's ministry to the world.

To be without tolerance is to be without character from the Christian perspective.

VI. WHOLENESS

Balance: Idealism And Realism

Luke 14:27-35
Romans 10:2

One of the hardest things to do in life is to live on the cutting edge between realism and optimism. Trying to balance these opposites, or at least hold them together in a living blend, is difficult. Idealists are not usually realistic. And the realists are not usually idealistic. Yet Christianity is a religion of balance. From the very beginning, the star and the stable were both part of the Christian story. Life is not all star. And those wild-eyed optimists who followed the star in the heavens at some point had to give up that idealism to deal with the reality of a baby in an animal barn. But life is not all stable, either. At some point those realists who faced head-on the little baby had to invest themselves enthusiastically in the hope of the Kingdom of God being ushered in.

Have you ever stopped to think how the Christian faith is actually a belief in God's ability to work through incredible opposites? The star and the stable. The wise men and the shepherds. The Rich Man and Lazarus. Peter and Judas. Paul the persecutor and Stephen the Stoned. The cross and the resurrection. Heaven and hell! The Jews and the Samaritans. The God strong enough to surround us with justice yet gentle enough to embrace us with grace. Incredible opposites. Jesus told his disciples they must simultaneously possess the characteristics of the serpent and the dove. "Be wise as serpents, and harmless as doves." Here, in the presence of Christ, the Old Testament concepts of the suffering servant and the messiah come together in the reality of a messiah who suffers.

It's as if Jesus is saying, "In order to determine the 'real thing' in life you must reconcile the kind of opposite extremes that infest and infect the human condition." Consequently, *every Christian must act for God out of a balance between emotion and knowledge, idealism and realism, optimism and pessimism.*

I think it's harder to hold these opposites in tension today than ever. Look at the confusion on television. Some of the preachers throw out a lot of heat but not much light. Emotionalism abounds.

But other prophets of doom emphasize special knowledge. All the esoteric philosophies and forecasts of reality really get us down.

How does one become wise like the serpent but harmless like the dove? How can we balance emotion and knowledge so as to live a hopeful life?

For much of my early life I lived on emotion and enthusiasm. Most of my teachers, coaches, and preachers thought emotion was the central essence of experience. It was drilled into my head that nothing significant is ever achieved without enthusiasm. In particular I remember our highly successful high school football coach, a motivation expert *par excellence*. In terms of backslapping, jumping around, and thinking positive thoughts, we out-enthused everyone we played. We had tremendous camaraderie. An especially successful gimmick involved having the ball carriers growl just as soon as they touched the ball. This got the adrenaline flowing. And that same approach worked wonders in our churches. We had some youth revivals which compressed a lifetime of decision making into a long Saturday night. You were afraid of being left out if you didn't get the zeal for Christ. Those forms of experiences that make you tingle and get goosebumps inside were everywhere.

But one day in college I had another revelation. It was my privilege to continue with athletics. For most of the month of August my first year our freshman team had been preparing for its initial scrimmage against the varsity. Since the varsity's first game was with Clemson University, all we had learned were Clemson's plays. We were an eager group, bringing with us the enthusiastic traditions of many high schools. We grouped together, screaming and charged-up. On the very first play our quarterback, with great confidence, took the snap from center and gave me the ball. I took the handoff and ran off tackle, growling as I had done in high school. Now in high school we usually just ran to the open area. So I never learned to pay attention to the defensive alignment or the quarterback's call of the defense. A huge, well-disciplined linebacker filled the hole. He slammed me in the chest, knocked my helmet off, and gave me a cut above the eye that took five stitches to close. As he helped me up, he said, "Kid, you better quit growling and learn how to run the ball." As I wobbled back to the huddle, I was painfully aware of a truism: While nothing significant is achieved without enthusiasm, *you are in real trouble if enthusiasm is all you have.* Nothing is achieved if all you have is well-intended idealism.

Jesus of Nazareth knew this. He knew it would take insight as well as enthusiasm to walk with God. Such was the meaning behind his parables of the tower builder and of the king preparing for war. Jesus issued a warning against any light-hearted assumptions. Jesus possessed some caution. Enthusiasm without realism can hurt you. Jesus encouraged His followers to know what they were getting into. They were to count the long-term costs. If they were to lay a foundation for something that they could not finish, they would open themselves up to ridicule.

Jesus wasn't appealing to fear of failure. He was not appealing for low achievement. But he apparently was afraid of mere emotion and idealism. Jesus recognized that life and its battles are long and hard. He stated that compulsive involvement is not the only human capacity needed for effective living.

Paul wrote to the church in Rome, "I bear them witness that they have a zeal for God, but it is not enlightened." Paul knew from his own life as an enthusiastic persecutor of Christianity that emotion focused on improper ends is a horrible disease. *When religion becomes exclusively emotional and has no interest in knowing anything, it ceases to be a religion. It becomes a manic-depressive cycle.*

But God has given us feelings as part of the human condition. And those feelings are an important part of Christianity. No great church was ever built on mere knowledge, spit, and tradition. At some point enthusiastic people, fired by a vision, have to want to share their life in Christ with others. In order to stay alive in Christ, you have not only to receive the good news of Christ but also to pass it on. Faith beckons one to share a God whose message is one of victory and growth.

Most people who are members of a church are there because someone invited them. Religion without enthusiasm becomes cold and abstract and isolated from anything anyone would want to join. Religion without idealism is dead. It becomes afraid to plan. It knows too much knowledge to plan, to risk, to visualize. Instead of becoming wild-eyed "fools" for Christ or mustard seeds on the grow, we can become well-informed, non-risking, coolly-calculated, "indifferent" realists. Jesus said, "When you try to save your life, when you play it safe, that's when you actually lose it."

The story is told[1] of a stranger who stopped for a drink of water at a farmhouse. He wanted to be sociable to the old barefooted farmer on the porch of the tumbledown shack. So he said, "How is your cotton coming?"

"Ain't got none. Afraid of boll weevils," said the farmer.

"How is your corn?" said the stranger.

"Didn't plant none. Afraid it wouldn't rain," replied the farmer.

"Well, how about your potatoes?"

"Ain't got none. Powerful lot of potato bugs in these parts."

"Well, what did you plant?" asked the bewildered stranger.

"Nothin'," replied the farmer. "I'm just playin' it safe."

Jesus put it in terms of some people who were given different amounts of talents to work with. You'll remember that one man buried his in the ground, afraid he would lose it. I'll guarantee you, like the farmer in the tumbledown shack, any Christian and any church can find a hundred valid reasons not to venture anything. Enthusiasm is a part of the collective need of a church. Jesus said that if we do not possess it we become like "whitened tombs, which indeed appear beautiful outward, but are within full of dead men's bones."

But what about knowledge? Who wants to belong solely to a community of religious specialists? For example, there were people in the church at Corinth who felt the *knowing* aspect of Christianity was what really mattered. They were "up" on the latest details of religious theories or "down" on those people who did not believe exactly as they did. Apparently they became excited about subjects like bodily resurrection and what heaven is like.

Paul rather quickly let these people know that love is not boastful or rude. Love does not insist on its own way. After all, Jesus said, "People will know you by your love for each other." He did not say, "People will know you by your knowledge of esoteric doctrines." One certainly does not need a doctorate in theology to read, appreciate, and understand the Bible.

But Jesus the Christ understood full well the importance of knowledge. He called us to love God with our mind as well. He warned against those who would come and lead people astray by false teaching. In fact, Jesus asserted that an act of loving cannot be fully realized without a high regard for the mind. Our Scriptures were set in a particular culture. All Scriptures are interpreted to us by someone. And there are plenty of people in today's world willing to interpret the Scriptures for us — very eager to tell us what they know. We have to be careful to whom we listen.

John Claypool relates the delightful story of the famous Mexican bank robber, Jorge Rodriguez.[2] Jorge kept slipping across the Texas border and robbing banks. He got so bad the Texas Rangers deployed a whole posse to stop Jorge. One afternoon a Ranger spotted Jorge slipping across the Rio Grande and proceeded to trail him to his hometown.

Jorge went into the cantina to relax. The Ranger slipped in, put a revolver to Jorge's head, and said: "I know who you are, Jorge Rodriguez, and unless you give me all the money you have stolen from the Texas banks, I am going to blow your brains out."

But Jorge did not understand English, and the Texas Ranger did not speak Spanish. About that time a little Mexican walked up and said, "I'm bilingual. I'll translate for you. " He put the Ranger's proposition in language Jorge could understand. Jorge answered, "Tell the big policeman that I have not spent the money. If he will go to the town well, face north, and count down five stones, he will find the money behind that stone." The little Mexican turned with a smile and said to the Ranger, in English, "Jorge Rodriguez is a brave man. He says he is ready to die!"

What you don't know can hurt you! Adolf Hitler knew that. In *Mein Kampf* he asserted:

By means of shrewd lies, unremittingly repeated, it is pos-
sible to make people believe that heaven is hell and hell,
heaven. The greater the lie, the more readily will it be
believed."

Yes, idealism and emotion must always stand before the judgments of realism and truth. Within the human being God has brought
together in a powerful marriage the forces of emotion and knowledge, idealism and realism. In our life with Christ we must never
pull asunder what God has joined together.

When we try to hold together enthusiasm for Christianity and
sound knowledge about Christianity, we can live by covenant instead of conflict. We can be wise as serpents and harmless as doves.

---

1. As told by Barbara Brokhoff, *Making Angels Sing* (Lima, Ohio: CSS Publishing Company, 1982), p. 74.

2. John Claypool in his sermon,"Authentic Christianity."

Covenants And Broken Promises

Hebrews 8:8-13
Romans 15:1-4

William Brown is a world-class tenor. He was the first performer to sing in concert before an integrated audience in South Africa, an audience which he insisted upon. He has twice performed in Carnegie Hall in New York. *Ebony* magazine listed him among the prominent voices of a decade. But William Brown is as important to many for his lifestyle, which radiates hope in God, as he is as a world-renowned tenor.

Perhaps the best way to indicate his approach to life is to recount for you a story. Many remember all too well the total chaos that existed in this country in the late 1960s and early 1970s. Values were in conflict, national conscience was pricked, and lifestyles were in confusion. Cities were rocked with demonstrations and ugly violence. Confrontations were everywhere.

In the 1968-69 concert season, the then young 31-year-old William Brown was scheduled to perform on the campus of Howard University in Washington, DC. The concert was sold out. But two days before the concert, Washington became a city under siege. Picket lines were all over the place. Riots and vandalism erupted with the slightest provocation. People were afraid to be out on the streets. On top of that, it began to rain on the evening of the concert. All music critics scheduled to attend the concert canceled their appearance. They, like others, were afraid to venture out into the dangerous environment.

At the time the concert was to begin, *there were only five people*, four women and one elderly gentleman, sitting as the audience in the concert hall which held 1,800 people. Five people in a place that seated 1,800! You can, perhaps, imagine the depressing setting.

The pianist who was to accompany Mr. Brown said, "Surely you're not going to go out there and give a concert performance! There are only five people out there. Let's go home."

Mr. Brown's response was clear. "Of cours, I'm going to sing. Those people braved bad weather and picket lines to get here. I have a contract, a covenant, with them. One thing my father taught me is to always do your best when you have an obligation to fulfill."

And perform he did. It was a part of his covenant with life to perform. One wintry morning William Brown was to sing in my church in North Carolina. The roads were almost impassable with ice and snow. I lamented the conditions to him but he imparted his philosophy to me: "I am here and I am in covenant. If only one person comes on Sunday we will make that person feel glad he or she came, for we will give our best." As it turned out, we had a packed house. But the size of the audience really didn't matter to the performer.

That's quite a perspective, to live life according to a covenant to serve rather than reacting to external circumstances. Imagine how strong a church would be if it so embraced a covenant with God to serve those who came that everyone, regardless of attendance, was always made to feel that he was especially welcomed. *I firmly believe there are higher loyalties beyond visible factors and finances.* If one has entered into covenant with God to live life in service of the Kingdom of God, one puts the same energy, the same pride, and the same time into one's work whether the crowd is large or small.

The history of the Christian faith, of course, is a history of promises, or covenants; a history of promises kept and promises broken. The term "covenant" in our Scriptures means a solemn promise made binding by an oath which may be verbal or symbolic. What is true in Scripture stands unchallenged in the affairs of humankind: *The vast majority of human problems arise because individuals fail to keep their promises.*

It is impossible for us to understand our faith without visualizing it as a history of promises between humans and God. The covenant of Moses contained promises people made to do certain things for God in appreciation for what God had already done for them. In typical human fashion, no sooner were the promises made than those same people began to break them. Consequently, great emphasis had to be placed upon the divine forgiveness, and that became the foundation of the New Covenant predicted by Jeremiah. Jesus spoke of himself as the New Promise, poured out in his blood, to cover all the past *broken* promises between people and God.

Jesus entered into an agreement with us. He said, "I'll give you eternal life. Life forever. Something beyond this earthly existence. There is a place where all misery is wiped out, all pain dissipated, all despair thwarted — *forever*. A place with many houses for you to live in — *forever*."

"All you have to do to keep your end of the contract is to live a life of service to your fellow men and women." That's the agreement, service to humankind instead of *conflict* with humankind. No one can doubt what is laid upon us for our end of the bargain. Consider the parable of the Good Samaritan or that more solemn utterance, where the dead stand before the throne of God dependent on whether they have fed the hungry, clothed the naked, given drink to the thirsty, and visited the imprisoned and the sick. "He that is greatest among you shall be your servant." That's a pretty straightforward assessment, isn't it?

Those who are in covenant with God live a life of service. It doesn't matter if you're given the opportunity to serve one or one thousand — you serve that one or that thousand to your utmost.

The statement is obvious: *no one individual possesses enough resources to cope with all of life by himself or herself.* Mutual hope is the process from the very beginning. Hope is not an isolated affair. Without mutuality we die; we are unfulfilled, not whole. Covenant is not a disembodied ideal. *Mutual service and involvement of persons create covenants.*

The Apostle Paul seems to sum up tersely the spirit of the whole New Testament in these words: "We that are strong ought to bear the infirmities of the weak, and not to please ourselves" (Romans 15:1).

On some terms you must make a pact, a covenant, with God, to live your life serving others and letting them serve you. This is the only way to become a whole person. Otherwise your life will be one of continually resolving matters by conflict. *Why?* Why is a marriage not based on mutual self-giving in trouble? Why is a life that has not been given over to service a life in jeopardy? *Why must you and I live in service?*

It's simple: popular interpretations of the Declaration of Independence to the contrary notwithstanding, human beings are *not* born completely equal in every respect. Partners in a marriage, members of a church, members of a family, neighbors on a street, employees in an office are not equal in *every* way. *All* are powerful in some respects and *all* are weak in other respects. A covenant of service is the only way the weak and the strong elements can live together on this earth. Without the ability to trust other people to fill in the gaps in our personalities, you and I are incredibly impotent.

Consider the obvious state of affairs. People are not equal in practical ability. Some can operate with a great deal of practical efficiency while some of us are better at creativity and planning. People are not equal in intellectual capacity. Some people possess innate and learned wisdom about many things while others among us are contented, and rightly so, with not venturing into those uncharted waters. People are not equal in spiritual capacity. While all of us have in us the power to open up our lives to the Spirit of God through meditation and prayer, some of us are thimbles and others among us are oceans in comparative capacity. People are not equal in their understanding of social issues. Some of us relate religion to the great social needs of the time, while others among us view religion primarily as saving our own spiritual hide.

We need to covenant with humankind rather than have conflict with humankind because *the greatest tragedy in life is not death. It is what we allow to die within us while we still live. It is the loss of hope.*

We rise or fall on the basis of our "covenants," our promises to serve one another. We live in a church because we have covenanted to help each other adjust our loads in life and carry them in the easiest manner. God calls us to live with certain burdens. We can't take these burdens off our shoulders, place them in a pile at the front of the church, and walk out of there leaving them behind forever. I wish we could, but we can't. Nor can we completely swap burdens with one another. We have to shoulder most of them ourselves. But we can form a "covenant" community in the service of God and others. Individually we are impotent, even to deal with ourselves. But in community there is every resource needed to adjust everyone's load to make it easier for all to carry on with their living.

A covenant to serve each other instead of conflict with each other is the secret of productivity in any realm. William Rainey Harper is correct: *"The question before us is how to become one spirit, not necessarily one in opinion."* Opinions change over the years according to external pressures and circumstances. *If all we develop are common opinions we are in trouble.* But a unity of spirit is an incredible achievement of lasting promise.

If we can make everyone around us feel welcomed, regardless of their opinions; if we can make our neighbors feel glad they know us and always put out our best effort at service as our end of the bargain for what God has done for us in Jesus Christ, wholeness, not conflict, will result. People of various opinions who now wander in doubt searching for light will find an anchor and a rock and a resting place in our hope in Christ. People who feel bitter and angry at seemingly unfair differences of society will begin to regard the world in a gentler, more humble, and more tender spirit. Their hope in the God of the mutual responsibility will be awakened.

In Christianity we safely dispense with many things. But the covenant between God and humankind, which affirms that the highest strength should be put at the service of the lowest weakness, is the central pillar of the gospel. The true test of our hope is the point below which it allows the weaknesses and frailties of our neighbors to fall.

Life is lived by covenant. Without that, there is little hope. Living within the covenant God makes with us enables us to reach for wholeness as we live in a shattered world.

New Eyesight

Luke 10:38-42
Mark 8:14-21

Each morning I try to eat breakfast with a small group of friends in the same restaurant. We usually sit in the same booth and repeat many of the jokes and stories we have told and heard dozens of times. One morning an elderly woman walked up to the booth and stood there, her face all aglow. "Notice anything different about me?" she asked. I made the customary observances — was it a new hairdo? A new dress? What?

"My eyes," she said. "I've got new eyes. I'm so proud of them, I just wanted to show them off to someone. For 65 years I lived with old eyes. Now I can see things I've never seen before. How do you like my new eyes?"

My friend had had a new type of eye surgery. For years she had labored with blurred vision, waiting on medical technology to catch up with her need. Seldom have I seen anyone as happy as she appeared to be that morning. New eyes are quite an addition to one's life.

Jesus was concerned with what humans see. He lamented the fact that so many have only a partial view of reality and do not see the wholeness of life. He called the eye "the lamp of the body." He uttered, "Blessed are the poor in spirit for they shall see God." Once he fussed at his disciples because they saw only an absence of something to eat when they had a chance to be alone with the Son of God. Their vision was defective. His words are clear, "Why do you discuss the fact that you have no bread? Do you not yet perceive or understand?" (Mark 8:17). Apparently a limited perception leads to a fragmented view of understanding what life was meant to be.

We are what we see. The eye is indeed the lamp of the body. When I first began my career as a minister, I kept a daily journal in my office. Each afternoon I would "write up" incidents from the day's experiences which seemed to me to be illustrative of some great religious truth. My wife correctly accused me of viewing life as a series of sermon illustrations. Even when I took trips to extraordinary places and met fascinating people, some of the experiences went right past my limited perception. Instead of "drinking in" life and being fully present to everyone and everything, I was looking at life as fodder for sermon material. I tended to view everything from the perception of a minister.

It happens to all of us. We miss much because of our limited and fragmented perceptions. Tom Downing of Chapel Hill, North Carolina, tells of a group of American tourists who had been given a splendid tour of the Louvre in Paris. It was question and answer time. From the back of the group came a question, "Could you kindly tell me what you put on these floors to make them so shiny?" The questioner was a chemical salesman. He saw the floors but missed the Louvre.

I went to a tennis tournament with a hosiery executive at beautiful Hilton Head Island. While live television captured tennis stars walking around, he was in the pro shop examining the socks to see which brands were being carried.

I journeyed to the mountains with the owner of a lumber company and he never commented on the beautiful Blue Ridge sunsets. But he told me what the lumber would come to a running foot if it were trimmed, dressed, and planed.

I traveled to Jamaica with my wife, Diane. We ate lunch one day at a table near the ocean. I looked out on the white sands with the crystal clear water lapping at the beach and the rugged mountains forming a peaceful background. The pressure of ministry was way north of Cuba and it seemed so remote and far away. "Just look at that," I blissfully said as I gestured toward the gentle beauty of the setting. "Yes," she replied. "That poor woman sitting over there trying to eat with those two crying children all over her, and her lazy husband who has finished eating hasn't even lifted a finger to help." We are what we see. And we see what we are!

The story about Martha (Luke 10:38-42) is one people like us need to hear over and over again. She had the Lord of life in her home and she couldn't stop working long enough to enjoy him. There is a little bit of Martha in all of us.

Jesus tried to tell Martha the real score in life. "Martha," he said, "You are anxious and troubled about many things in life, but only one thing is really important. Recognize the holy when you are in its presence. Stop knocking yourself out and enjoy what God is doing in your life."

We are what we see. Much of life has passed us by because we did not see it in its entirety. We saw only partial reality. How many times has God visited our communities of faith and we have not seen God because of the crowded mind that covered the vision? I confess that I often have to fight the impulse to rise on Sunday morning and say, "Wonder how many of them will show up to-day?" instead of anticipating in sheer delight, "Wonder where God is going to break in on us today and show us the road toward home that lies beyond death?" It's the difference between worship as a spectator sport and worship as an event.

Years ago, the Harvard Business School class of 1951 decided that they wanted to hold a worship service in the historic Old North Church to celebrate a reunion of their class. They had their heavyweights put pressure on the rector of Old North Church, and he reluctantly agreed to turn his Sunday morning service over to the class for their purposes. So what did they do? They booted the poor rector out of his pulpit that Sunday and asked *me* to preach. They took over the lay reader functions from Old North Church's lay reader and inserted their own class agents as readers. And they confiscated the main section of the sanctuary, relegating the regular attenders to the cramped balcony. They even changed the time of the service, moving it back thirty minutes so they could sleep a little later after the Saturday night bash and still get there. Well, it was quite a show — quite a show. The only item they had not anticipated was the fact that pushing the service back thirty minutes conflicted with the time the Gray Line tours of the church started.

About two minutes into my sermon the buses started rolling up. They unloaded hundreds of people in front of the church. The sextons kept to their posts and kept the doors locked. Well, Old

North Church has huge, beautiful clear windows. Naturally, the people came around to look through the window panes. They climbed up on one another and pressed their noses to the glass. It was eerie. Finally, one dear soul apparently thought this was the "real McCoy" as far as historic worship was concerned, so she took her instamatic camera, complete with flash, and started flashing away through the windows. That set them off. Out came scores of cameras with flash attachments. They started popping off the flashes like strobe lights through the windows. I looked down from that pulpit, trying to keep some semblance of a sermon going, and I saw the strained face of the president of the class mouthing the words up at me — "they are ruining our service. They are ruining our service."

By this time the sextons had had enough. They started trying to clear the crowd away from the windows. They did not have much success. The crowd pushed back. And I kept droning on with the sermon right to the very end. That was worship. Fortunately the two crowds never met because the Class of '51 hurriedly went out the rear of the church to Quincy Market to sip their Bloody Marys and eat their eggs Benedict, and the surly mob with the cameras came in the front door to buy the postcards and see where Paul Revere had gone to church. Where was God that Sunday? Goodness, we were all too busy and too engrossed to stop for God. Our fragmented and partial concerns closed the door on any majesty available inside or outside the church.

Sometimes that is worship, is it not? We attend the Saturday night bash and still manage to get part of the self into the building. If the pleasure buses aren't at the beach, the mountains, the ball games, or the relatives, they drop us off at church. The cacophony of sounds from outside rush in upon us. Through the windows peer the snarling faces of the kids who were hard to get dressed; the boss that we hate; the memories of funerals in that place; the children who used to be with us but now are gone; the mother or father who drove us crazy Friday and Saturday; the illness that claws at our perception like a never-ending shadow; the thin veneer of sophistication which covers our fear of our own death; the anxiety of listlessness and insecurity that clouds our days; the concern that one of our family members doesn't think going to church, or at least to this particular church, is the greatest thing since sliced bread. We hover at our little windows of life while the preacher counts the noses, hoping that there are more to count than there were in the years before he or she came. The ushers take up the offering, and we leave through the doors and hurriedly make our way to the restaurants, the country club, the tennis courts, the golf course, or the couch in the den.

Where was God? Who could have seen God?

Jesus spoke to all of us Marthas: "You are anxious and troubled about many things in life, but only one thing is important. Recognize the Holy when you are in its presence. Enjoy what God is doing in your life." Not only was Jesus correct, but we humans have found that that is the only way to see the whole of life.

Whole persons can see meaning where fragmented people cannot see meaning. The Gospels tell us that. Read the Gospels and take out the miracles and the crucifixion. What do you have left? Basically a lot of ordinary stuff. A woman who had been divorced five times and had a live-in. Lilies in the field; birds in the air; fish in the sea. An old woman with a bleeding ulcer. A farmer planting seed. People concerned about their inheritance. A boy blowing his father's hard-earned money. A pompous preacher on a street corner. An angry, hurt, and frustrated disciple swinging a sword at someone. Wedding banquets. Rude dinner guests. Lost and found animals. A hotel in Bethlehem with no vacancy. Guilt and grace. Success and failure. Ordinary things.

But Jesus' perception was different. He saw the majestic in the ordinary. He saw the permanent in the passing. If in the ordinary we can perceive God, we have a certain sense of meaning and purpose that is ours for the taking.

What kind of vision do we humans possess? Whole or partial? When we see a crying baby in a nursery, do we see a wet diaper needing to be changed, or do we see a little person trying to grow up and find the way home? When an older woman climbs the steps to come into her place of worship, do we see a decaying body striving for balance or a grand old ship trying to get into the home

218

port one more time to have her sails sewn together, her ballast adjusted and her faith strengthened for the passage through death?

Do we see only part of life or do we see it in its entirety?

Sanctuary

Revelation 21:1-5

One day, the beloved disciple John lay down inside his cave on the Island of Patmos and placed his head on a rock. He was in exile. In fact, he stayed on that tiny island eighteen years. John's secretary stood beside a shelf made of natural rock, writing down John's thoughts about his deceased friend, Jesus.

Exile is a horrible thing. Truly the place you have left has entirely disappeared and the place where you are going is not yet clear. But John saw something. He saw a new hometown. There was a holy city, coming down from God out of heaven, prepared as a bride adorned for her husband. In this city, God was wiping away all tears from the eyes of people; there was no more death, nor sorrow, nor crying, nor pain. All things were new there. And the city was pure gold. The city had no need of the sun, neither of the moon for light. A pure river was flowing, clear as crystal. And John heard the words, "Behold, this is the end of the line for those that keep the commandments of Christ. They may enter and eat again of the tree of life."

The human race, put out of Eden, surges aimlessly forward for thousands of years. But one winter's night, in a place so lowly, the cry of a newborn child breaks the stillness of night. The heavens open and the angels sing. And into every mailbox in the world the Lord God puts an invitation. It is an invitation to attend an open house, to come home to a place older than Eden and taller than Rome. There is plenty to eat, says the invitation. Pure gold all around. No tears, only laughter. You can socialize with the saints, the family members, and all the friends gone before you. What's more, you can meet millions of wonderful people you never knew had lived at all. Presents will be handed out. Those who received much on earth will receive fewer presents than those who received little on earth. It is a wonderful place. And you can even have a room for yourself, with your name on it, and stay here forever. It can become your permanent hometown. There is the obligation of an RSVP. You respond by following teachings of Jesus Christ to love God and your neighbor.

The vision of John of Patmos points toward a future action of God. The righteous will be gathered in a New Jerusalem, where humans can once again live in the presence of God. The horror of those last days, with their war, pestilence, and death, is to be closed by a final mighty struggle between good and evil, according to apocalyptic literature, the method of John's writing. Such writings center not only on the ultimate fate of individuals but also on the ultimate destiny of the whole human race.

Yet the writings of John of Patmos do not provide a complete vision for me. I did not witness the Old Jerusalem, so how can I recognize the New Jerusalem? I did not live in a country or time which persecuted the Christian church. The symbols of the Revelation, which point to the vindication of the righteous, are not the symbols of my world. While such an understanding is familiar in Christian, Jewish, and Islamic traditions, I must begin with something more immediate in my search for wholeness. I must begin with the basic human need to find sanctuary in a world of shelters.

Our world has long recognized the human need for food, clothing, and shelter. We have to eat, to dress, and to find a cave, a roof, or a shelter in times of bad weather. Our physical needs have to be met. Where would our world be without its homes, apartments, and condos? We even try to construct shelters for the homeless. We should.

In a bygone generation many a nervous young man sat in the parlor, den, or living room asking his prospective father-in-law for permission to marry his daughter. The stock response was this one: "Sir, I can promise you this — we may not have everything in the world, but your daughter will always have food on the table, clothes on her back, and a roof over her head." Most of the time that was sufficient.

I suppose we all conjure up fantasy images of the ideal life. Some of these ideas emerge out of the experiences and needs of our childhood. I've never really been enamored with clothes. That's somewhat unfortunate. Thank goodness my wife is conscious of

221

appearance or I would be even worse. Clothes have always had a functional purpose for me. Perhaps my childhood revolved so much around sports that my outfit for the season was established as a particular jersey, pants, and pair of shoes. Fortunately, our worship services have a certain uniformity and dignity due to the wearing of robes. Aside from the symbolism involved, it is easier and safer to cover me in a robe than to submit the congregation to my consideration of haberdashery. No, I have not lived in a world of clothes.

And food has always been food. We never went out to dine as a family when I was growing up. I ate whatever was being served at home or in the school cafeteria. My early life afforded me no menu selection. Food was food.

But shelter was another matter. I've always had some strong convictions about shelter. I have always wanted to live in a two-story brick home. Somehow a totally-brick home was a status symbol. Many a Sunday afternoon our family would exit our small, white frame house and pile into the family automobile. We would embark on that event which created the absolute in boredom for my sister and me: the Sunday afternoon drive. For what seemed like an eternity, we would slowly drive past these nice brick homes, just to look.

In that respect, we were a part of the dominant American consciousness. For many, your status is determined by the shelter you live in. After all, is not a person's shelter the best he can construct and afford out of his human possessions? We live in a world of shelters.

As important as a shelter is, there is another kind of protection people need in life. People also need a place of "sanctuary." A sanctuary is a shelter of the soul which gives a person a reason for living.

Jesus said to his disciples, "My peace I give unto you; not as the world gives do I give unto you" (John 14:27). One of our critical needs as we realize our human condition is to find that kind of peace in a world of shelters. If we humans are to remain sane, we must have both a shelter and a sanctuary. Humans need sanctuary more than they need shelter.

A sanctuary is quite different from a worldly shelter. It symbolizes a place where the values differ from the values of the world. The word "sanctuary" comes from the Greeks. Important cities like Delphi and Ephesus existed under the shadow of a sanctuary to a particular god or goddess. The "sanctuary" was a temple whose laws were in contradiction to the laws of society. As a Roman province, Ephesus practiced slavery. But if a slave made it to the sanctuary of Artemis, he or she was given protection and could not be arrested there. Onesimus, the slave of Philemon, made his way there before going to Rome and encountering Paul.

Out of those Greek sanctuaries to pagan gods came the first codes of ethics in the world. From the oracle in the sanctuary of Apollo in Delphi came the laws that stated that prisoners of war should not be killed but exchanged, that slaves had the right to a trial, and that it was unethical to poison the water supply of an enemy city under siege. A sanctuary was indeed a place where people put aside the storms of life and thought of peace and refuge.

Small wonder, then, that the early Christians began to call their great places of worship sanctuaries. Indeed, the kind of peace and love they found in this Christ completely turned the world upside down. There was a peace given that was unlike anything the world had to offer. The "sanctuary" came to symbolize a great shelter of the soul. Into those sanctuaries were placed the labors of a lifetime — great art, carvings, frescoes, and paintings. There was an acceptance there that passed everything the world knew of division, status, and turmoil. As men and women have built their worldly shelters they have also longed for wholeness, for sanctuary.

A sanctuary differs from a shelter in the manner of acceptance. The peace given by Christ is different from the world's peace in that it is unconditional. Your shelter is usually an indication of how much you have financially placed into it. A great deal of money constructs a very elaborate shelter. Those with little money to spend usually find that posture reflected in the quality and size of their shelter. It even takes money to keep your shelter. Most of us speak of owning "our own home." Yet, if we do not pay our taxes someone will come and take our shelter. That is the uneasy, partial peace of the world.

223

But a sanctuary is different. It symbolizes a kind of peace that the world does not yet understand. The European cathedral offered protection to the whole town from an invader. The huge doors were large enough to accept whole wagons loaded with provisions. Everyone from the town peasants to the government officials could find sanctuary within.

Today, the phenomenon is still one of acceptance. The sanctuary is yours. Regardless of age, contribution or lack thereof, or attendance, the sanctuary is yours. Regardless of your success or failure in the eyes of the world, you have a sanctuary. It's available for you just as you are. Though the words may sound lachrymose to many, they still convey a sense of comfort and assurance: "Just as I am ... without one plea, but that thy blood was shed for me." Acceptable here in this place just as I am? No improvements needed, no alterations required before I can enter the presence of the Most High? That is incredibly good news.

Open Gates Of Love

John 1:1-13
James 2:19-25

I accepted an invitation to be the preacher for a Good Friday service sponsored by the downtown churches of Knoxville, Tennessee. The service was held in a huge Episcopal church. So on the appointed day I flew into Knoxville, Tennessee, and had my brother-in-law meet me at the airport. He drove me to the church. I called the host minister to inform him of my arrival and received directions to the robing room. Since I still had a full thirty minutes before the service began, I stood out on a street corner a few blocks from the church, talking with some fellow clergy and watching at a distance as people walked into the church for the service.

Suddenly a young woman in great agitation came running down the street toward us. "Mr. Warlick," she screamed, "where have you been?"

This puzzled me. "Right here," I responded. "There's still plenty of time before the service."

"Didn't anyone tell you the service is televised live?"

I shook my head.

"The make-up man is beside himself. There's nothing he can do now but a few brush-ons."

So, I followed this woman, listened to the heavy cursing of her station's make-up man, and finally put on my robe. At precisely twelve noon they led me to a seat beneath an elevated pulpit with a staircase leading up to it. Surrounding the pulpit in a semi-circle was a battery of television spotlights. And hanging down from the ceiling above where the congregation sat was another row of powerful spotlights. I could not see three feet past my nose. When I stepped into that pulpit I stared into an ocean of bright lights. I could not see the face of a single person in the congregation. Instead of speaking to faces, I felt as if my words were falling over the edge of the pulpit and down to the floor. There were no faces to remind me of the loyalties, lifestyles, and struggles which compose human existence.

Then, as soon as the sermon ended and the last hymn had begun, someone from the television station led me through a back door for a cup of coffee and that was that. For all I knew I could have been preaching to an audience of nudists. Now, amazingly enough, I received a number of letters following the event from people telling me what a marvelous service it was. They *adored* the sermon. I think we probably did a fairly good job of admiring Jesus and his death on the cross.

But I could not experience true worship just being an admirer of Jesus. Worship is possible when you are united with people with whom you are bound together in ways of trust, hope, and shared loyalty. Somehow I felt less than whole.

Christian hope is much more than admiring Jesus. To be a whole Christian involves more than expressing how attached we are to the memory of Jesus. Jesus points to a *living* God. Therein is our wholeness. Tell me Jesus is only a god of bright lights to be adored and worshipped, and most of the hope for my life is gone. But tell me Jesus has opened the door to a power that can come into my life and take my many selves and unite them, and my human condition has been meaningfully restored to wholeness.

Jesus came to open the gates to a new age and to deal with real people. *He shunned the worship and the admiration of his followers.* Instead, he wanted us to walk through the gates that he had opened for us. He refused to accept titles of greatness, even to the point of asking, "Why do you call me great?" He satirized those who wore fancy robes and processed in kingly fashion in parades. He told his disciples they would do even mightier works than he had done. He also stated that the lowest member of heaven was as great as John the Baptist. In John's Gospel it was articulated that this light in the darkness, this Jesus who dwelt with God, would give everyone the power to become children of God.

Why did Jesus shun the admiration of his followers?

Let me share with you an illustration of what can happen when a pioneer becomes worshipped and admired rather than believed in and worked with.[1] For generations, perhaps centuries, human beings tried to run a timed mile in four minutes. But none ever did. The magic four-minute mark stood as the ultimate goal. As long as distances had been measured and clocked, no one ever ran that fast. Then, one day a man named Roger Bannister put forth a tremendous effort. With unbelievable courage, extraordinary drive, abiding hope, and immense personal power, he cracked that magic barrier. He ran a mile in less than four minutes. It made Bannister's name a household word. But amazingly, *within six months after Bannister's epic run, at least four other individuals ran the mile in less than four minutes.*

Why should it be that for as long as humans had attempted the clocked mile, over 75 years, no one had ever run a four-minute mile — yet when a person finally achieved it, so many made the same achievement within six months? The answer is obvious. Humankind had placed a psychological ceiling on what the mile could be run in. One person raised that ceiling, expanded hope, and ushered in a new age. Within six months at least four other people walked through the gates he opened. Today a mile run is not considered a good race unless several of the competitors break four minutes.

Let's conjecture a change in the course of history. Suppose that when Bannister clocked his four-minute mile, athletes proclaimed him a once-in-a-lifetime runner. "No one can hope to be like Bannister. He was perfect. It's blasphemy to try to be like him." Suppose they built a shrine out of the track where that "once-in-eternity" event took place and little shrines popped up all over the country where people could come and read accounts of how Bannister ran the epic mile. Suppose young athletes, instead of catching his spirit and training hard to do what he had done, became content to quote verses from Bannister's biography. Suppose people quit trying to stretch through the gates he had opened and instead put their effort into keeping his admiration at a high pitch. We know what would have happened. Bannister would have been the *only* person to have ever run a four-minute mile. Instead of a pioneer opening a new age, we would have a god being *adored* by millions, studied by scholars, and supported by a few track fans making small pledges of money to keep his memory alive.

Do we fully understand the implications of God sending God's only son to be the pioneer of a new age in which all men and women were invited to participate? You see, *humans had placed a psychological ceiling on God's love for and presence with God's people.* Their hope was at a low ebb. The legalism of Judaism, the ethical deterioration in the promised land, and the ugliness of human prejudice had created a psychological ceiling concerning how close a person could hope to get to God. So God opened the gates to a new era. God sent God's son to love and to relate to men and women as never before. God lifted the ceiling on love. God, through Jesus Christ, stated that all of us could run the race of life, live it more abundantly, and become sons and daughters of God. Jesus raised the ceiling and thousands walked in under it. The gates were flung wide open to the kingdom of God. The pioneer intended we should break some bread and drink some wine or grape juice, remembering what he had done, and share in the power and hope he had turned loose on the world.

But alas, after but short decades, men and women began slowly to close those gates Jesus had flung open. The ceiling was lowered again. People began to admire Jesus and adore his memory. They memorized his life instead of looking for *his power* in their own life. They began to say, "No one can hope to be like him. It's blasphemy to try." They embraced little visions and set small goals for themselves. They made salvation copyright and wrapped it up in stained glass. They even set Jesus' life to music. They made him the most *admired instead of emulated leader in the world. He became an absolute to be idolized instead of a power and a hope to be daily reckoned with.*

It's obvious that Jesus feared this. Jesus lived in a world and among a people who put great store by holy writings. Some Saturday nights when I'm working at the church, I stand in the parking lot and watch the Jewish people in the synagogue across the street. The procession of the Torah, the holy writings, is an inspiring sight. The Jewish people have always put great store in their holy writings. Now isn't it curious that Jesus, as God's son, never wrote anything?

228

Jeremiah, the Old Testament prophet, recorded God's words. He even had a secretary to jot them down so he could have them. Paul wrote dozens of long epistles to churches. But Jesus apparently never took care to write anything down. Nothing autobiographical. Not even a personal note. On one occasion he scribbled in the sand, when the adulterous woman was brought to him. But he wiped that out before anyone could see what he had written.

Apparently Jesus did not want to leave anything written down that people could idolize instead of catching his spirit and hope after he was gone! Jesus viewed his life as a liberating force and not as a graven image to worship. Perhaps the most critical issue facing us as individuals and as a people is this: can we walk through the gates of love Jesus has opened?

We have a great love available to us. We can admire it. We can adore it. We can even fill out a pledge card and invite a few people to come to church and sacrifice some hours this year for its well-being. All of these things are well and good, but they do not lift the psychological ceiling we have placed on our lives with Christ.

But if we ever take his ethics as our ethics, his dictates as our dictates, his mission as our mission, his hope as our hope, his kingdom as our kingdom, our ambitions will be far higher than they are now!

Men and women since antiquity have wrestled with the question, "What does God want from us?" Certainly God wants more than our admiration. Apparently the confining problem of adoring and admiring God under a psychological ceiling has been a concern of Christianity for a very long time. The book of James concerns itself with that problem. In exasperation, James comments that admiration without a life fixed to deeds is as lifeless as a corpse. He even evidences Rahab the harlot as someone justified by God through letting the power and hope of God get into her life.

As we think about the fatalism and pessimism in our nuclear and technological age, it is apparent that a God merely to be admired is hardly sufficient for the challenges which confront our human condition. We can admire and adore what has been done for us in the life of Christ. But that hope and power which fueled his life, that desire to see God's will done on earth as well as in heaven, must get into our lives, our businesses, our personal ambitions, and our visions for the future.

Our response to life can be no higher than the psychological ceiling we have placed on God's ability to use us for powerful acts of goodness and love. We can do no more than we believe we can do. We can have wholeness only in direct proportion to our acceptance of God's offer to us. If we can accept Christ as the pioneer of a new age, we can embrace both the visible and invisible dimensions of life. We, too, can learn to have faith in the unseen. We, too, can become pioneers for the age which will come on earth as in heaven.

---

1. My first exposure to this use of the Roger Bannister achievement came from Dr. James Bowers, former pastor of First Baptist Church, Greenwood, South Carolina.

Response To Brokenness

Luke 24:13-24
Romans 8:28-30

Dreams and visions are important in life. Every action we take in life was designed by someone. Every piece of clothing, every building, every hymnbook, every chair, every light fixture, and every automobile existed first in someone's vision. Someone had to have the idea or the dream to turn out the product. The same holds true for the way we act. As Jesus said, "The eye is the seat of the body." If you cannot dream it, cannot envision it, then you simply cannot do it.

Dreams and visions can also be crushing. Not all dreams and expectations come true. We invent certain images of ourselves, certain pictures of the way life is supposed to be, and then we are somewhat shocked at the way things do not turn out. Broken visions are the essence of our human condition.

Dr. J. Wallace Hamilton, in his book *Horns and Halos in Human Nature*, tells of one of the weirdest auctions in history. It was held in the city of Washington, DC. It was an auction of designs, actually patent models of old inventions that did not make it in the marketplace. There were 150,000 designs up for auction. There was an illuminated cat to scare away mice. There was a device to prevent snoring which consisted of a trumpet reaching from the mouth to the ear. One person designed a tube to reach from his mouth to his feet so that his breath would keep his feet warm as he slept. There was an adjustable pulpit which could be raised or lowered. You could hit a button and make the pulpit descend or ascend to illustrate a point dramatically. Obviously, at one time somebody had high hopes for each of those designs which did not make it.[1] Some died in poverty, having spent all of their money trying to sell their dream. One hundred fifty thousand broken dreams! Is there anything sadder?

If we call God the master designer of the universe, then we must view the New Testament as a book of broken dreams. It begins with a massacre of innocent children by King Herod. It is centered in the execution of its hero. And it ends with the martyred saints crying, "How long, O Lord, how long?" The crucifixion of Jesus caused serious questions to be posed in the minds of humanity. There on the cross was a man who loved his enemies, a man whose righteousness was greater than the Pharisees, a man who was rich but became poor, a man who gave his robe to those who took his cloak, a man who prayed for those who despitefully used him.[2] Yet, society crucified him, executed him. The question to ask in the presence of this awesome scene is whether such goodness is the design of the universe or forms an exception. Is life designed to be loving, serving, giving, and dying? Does that design work? Does it pay off? Is it rewarding?

We perhaps can identify with the men on the road to Emmaus who were walking and talking with each other. They told of all that had happened, how this Jesus of Nazareth, mighty in deed and word before God and all the people, had been condemned to death and crucified.

Are there any clearer words of a broken dream than theirs? "But we had hoped he was the one to redeem Israel" (Luke 24:21). Oh, we had hoped he was the one to make it. We had dreamed he would be the one. But it just didn't work out.

All of us have dreams for ourselves and our lives that just do not make it. We come back home on the Emmaus road with our dream broken in our hip pocket, a sure-fire program that fell flat, a preventive that didn't prevent, a solution that did not solve, a panacea that did not pan out. We wail the plaintive cry, "But we had hoped this would redeem us. Oh, we had hoped it would be another way."

Saint Paul wrote to the Romans. He told them that he hoped to see them on his way to Spain. Going to Spain was his grand design, his great dream, his high hope. But Paul never got to Spain. Instead, his journey ended in a prison cell in Rome. He could not pull off what he saw in his mind.

It has been very well said that *every person dreams of one life and is forced to live another.* Such appears to have been true for Jesus, and yes, even for God! From the Garden of Eden to the crucifixion, God seems to have had a grand dream for the human race but was forced to live another. Every person dreams of one life and is forced to live another.

Parents have dreams for their children. We all do. I always knew my children would be a cross between Albert Einstein and Michael Jordan. On the other hand, I'm certain that I'm not their dream of a parent, either. I knew just how I'd be as a parent in my dreams. I'd be slim, popular, handsome, and very caring and understanding. I'd be appreciative of my children's tastes in music, and kind and tolerant when they brought home poor grades. I'd spend hours communicating with my boys. We'd go down the road, arm-in-arm like Andy Taylor and Opie in Mayberry on the way to the fishing hole, and have these long, meaningful father-son talks. You dream one life and are forced to live another. This ever-present part of the human condition surfaces at every level of existence.

The college experience can be a broken dream. Every student possesses a dream of what college will be like. Mid-term grades come out and I'm certain many students go limping home on the Emmaus road with some broken dreams in their hip pockets.

Here, it seems, is the essence of our condition. If, indeed, every person dreams of one life and is forced to live another, then the manner in which one repairs that dream has to be the key to finding wholeness in the world. The essence of the crucifixion and the resurrection of Jesus Christ is not solely to be found in a personal guarantee of life after death for you and me. The resurrection of Christ is an affirmation of a certain dream for life. The schematic designs of human evil were exposed and condemned for what they were. The central claim of the New Testament is the ultimate triumph of goodness. The resurrection is the triumph of a design for life that is upheld as the fundamental principle of the universe even if the world tries to crucify it.

Consequently, Paul could affirm, "And we know that all things work together for good to them that love God, to them who are called according to his dream" (Romans 8:28). Here Paul is not saying that we all get to live the life of our dreams. A lot of things happen to us that are not good. We are indeed forced to live another kind of life at times. Paul is saying that if a person will consider all the experiences of his or her life, both the good and the bad, and bond them together with love for God, then the sum total of that life, the grand design of that person's history, will be good. As such, it is possible to believe in the sun when it is not shining, to believe in love when you cannot directly feel it, and to believe in God when God is silent for a period. Even if the world crucifies you, the design of God's universe and your life with it will ultimately triumph. The dream will triumph even if it is not immediately evident.

Sometimes it is important for us to back up from our particular experiences, hurts, angers, and pressures to reflect on the grand design of things, the larger issues. Perhaps that is why the first Gospel, Mark, was not written in finished form until almost 100 years after Jesus died and rose. Perhaps only then could the early church feel strong enough to assert that the design of love holds, stands, triumphs for all generations over the design of darkness and death.

You and I live by our dreams as much as by our particular experiences. In this world of broken dreams, in this world where we dream of one life and are forced to live another, a conclusion comes from resurrection. If God's dream for goodness triumphs, then one thing is certain.

Failure is relative to time. No one really knows when he has succeeded or failed if all he does is look at the present.[3] God's design and God's time turn a lot of failures into successes. We must measure success by God's standard of design in history, not whether or not we are immediately on the top of the world's heap. I know many people who have "arrived" and they are not very happy. I know others who look back on what they thought was a burden at the time and they now view it as having been a tremendous learning experience.

Consider Rev. Kiyoshi Tanimoto. In 1944, he was the minister of the largest Protestant congregation in southern Japan. It was in the city of Hiroshima. Tanimoto must have been proud of his large church. Then one day, a yellow flash came. Mr. Tanimoto dove instinctively into a garden and wedged himself between two huge rocks. A powerful blast of wind and fire blew over him. It knocked him unconscious. When he came to and got on his feet, the city was flat as a desert. Sixty-eight thousand human beings were killed instantly. Only thirty members of his 3,500-member church were still alive. Rev. Tanimoto began to rebuild his crucified church. He arranged for the spiritual adoption of 500 Hiroshima orphans by North American families. As a result of his work, all bomb survivors became eligible for free medical treatment. Rev. Tanimoto also created a Peace Foundation. In that Foundation's museum a little girl named Sadako placed two cranes made of folded paper. It was her belief that if a person who was ill made these little paper cranes, the person would get better. Well, Rev. Tanimoto died and little Sadako also died, after ten years of horrible suffering.[4]

Two people who loved their enemies, whose righteousness was greater than the Pharisees, who were executed by forces they did not understand, cause us to ask, "Where was the design in all of this?" What happened to the dream? They believed in the sun when all they saw was a mushroom cloud that rose six miles high in only eight minutes. They believed in love when they could not feel it, and they believed in God when God was silent for a period. Naked, bleeding, hairless, and with skin hanging loose, they went to their early graves. They dreamed of one life and were forced to live another.

Today, over half a century after their deaths, a statue stands in Hiroshima. The statue was built in memory of their deaths. It is the figure of two children on either side and another child on top, their arms outstretched to express their hope for a peaceful world. For more than fifty years, to this very day, Japanese children keep the center of that statue filled with many-colored paper cranes. God's design of love holds. It stands. It triumphs for all generations over any design of darkness and death.

Paul is absolutely correct. History has proved it in a thousand ways. If a person will consider all the experiences of his life and bond them together with love for God, then the sum total of that life will be good.

The design of God will ultimately triumph. From Bethlehem to Gethsemane to Calvary, the innocent do suffer. The good and the lonely often get what they do not deserve. But goodness never stays in the dark. The truth never stays crucified. The central theme in human history is the same as the central theme of the New Testament: *the ultimate triumph of goodness.* If we would but believe that, our lives would claim an unbelievable power and freedom.

---

1. As used by Charles L. Allen in *The Miracle of Hope* (Old Tappan, New Jersey: Fleming H. Revell Co., 1983), pp. 16-17.

2. See John Howard Yoder, *The Politics of Jesus* (Grand Rapids. Michigan: William B. Eerdmans, 1972), p. 61.

3. Ernest A. Fitzgerald, *How To Be A Successful Failure* (New York: Atheneum, 1978), pp. 6-8.

4. As told by Bruce McLeod, *City Sermons* (Burlington, Ontario, Canada: Welch Publishing Company, 1986), pp. 69-71.

VII. THE FUTURE

Endorse It!

Ezekiel 37:1-13
John 19:38-41

One of the first things you do when you move to a new place is establish a checking account with a local bank. We can all tell stories of inexperienced people and their checking account problems. I remember a student who wrote check after check, only to discover he had no money left in his account. In exasperation he explained to the teller, "But I still have some checks left."

My sister-in-law, during her first semester in college, received a notice from the bank that she was $27.60 overdrawn in her account. She calmly sat down and mailed the bank a check for $27.60.

There was a young minister in graduate school who had never had a bank account. He was sent out to preach at a small country church. At the close of the service the treasurer gave him a check. He didn't know what to do with it. The treasurer told him if he would go to the bank the next morning before he left town that he could give it to the bank and they would give him cash for it. The next morning, feeling quite important, he went to the bank and handed the check to a teller. The teller turned it over and nothing happened because nothing was written on the back. She handed it back and said, "If you will just endorse this, I will be glad to cash it."

"Endorse it!" What's that? Well, he knew it had something to do with writing. He looked around and saw other people writing on the backs of checks. He spied a desk and a pen. After thinking for a few minutes, he signed his name. When he turned it in, the teller saw that he had written diagonally across the face of the check, "I heartily endorse the sentiments herein expressed. John R. Peterson."[1]

To endorse something is to attach your name publicly to a product, to throw your sentiments to an idea — to be committed. Unlike Eastern religions which focus on the revelation of God or the gods and goddesses in nature, the Western religions (Judaism, Christianity, and Islam) believe that God operates in history. Consequently, the Christian is called upon to endorse the time and place of his or her life as the arena of God's activity. Whatever God we encounter or confirm by our reason must be verified in our experience. If we are to live in the twenty-first century then we must endorse that world as the place of God's revelation. It will not do for us to create merely a safe haven for our own spirituality and cogitate on eternal, fixed truths. If feminist reimagining of God, male movements, a re-ordered and more pluralistically composed religious landscape, and a more limited appraisal of American economic and political influence on the world is the reality of our history, then that is precisely where we must look for God's voice and God's activity. The acceptance of our human condition is in reality a part of our Christian witness as well as our hope for a more meaningful future.

We all endorse certain sentiments that come our way in life. Some entertainers and coaches earn more from their endorsements than they do from practicing their professions.

One of the saddest stories in scripture is that of Joseph of Arimathea, who came to claim Jesus' body. He was recorded as "a secret follower of Jesus." He wouldn't endorse Jesus in public but he followed him in private. He missed the essence of God's revelation to his world.

One day in Paris, Voltaire, who was generally regarded as an infidel (non-believer), was standing with a friend. A religious procession carrying a crucifix passed Voltaire. He lifted his hat as the crucifix passed. "What!" exclaimed the friend. "Are you reconciled to God?" With fine irony Voltaire replied, "We salute, but we do not speak."[2] In other words, it's nice, but don't count on me to endorse it publicly.

Some of the saddest stories in life have been those of great and talented people who, regardless of their accomplishments, just never endorsed the right thing. They never turned their lives totally over to the right power. They started out well and appeared to conquer the world. They lived life to the hilt, but then the betrayals and heartaches set in. Having never turned their lives over to Christ or any higher power, they eventually just quit on life since it did not resonate with any of their preconceived notions of what life should be like.

Such a man was found bruised and bleeding in a New York neighborhood. He was a common drunk. A passerby found him and took the drunk to Bellevue Hospital, where he died after three days. No one knew who he was. He had been admitted as John Doe. The filth, drugs, and loneliness that had been his lot were common among Bowery bums who drank themselves to death. A friend who had been looking for him for several weeks went to the city morgue and in desperation searched among the John Doe corpses. There he was, lying among the dozen other unidentified drunks. His friend gathered up all of John Doe's personal belongings: 38 cents and a scrap of paper that said, "Dear friends and gentle hearts."

As it turned out, this drunk, whose life had led to despair and rage, actually had had the soul of a genius. Long before his tragic death at age 38, John Doe had written songs that have become deeply rooted in our southern heritage. John Doe had been known as Stephen Foster. He had written "Way Down Upon the Swannee River," "Oh! Susanna," "Jeannie With the Light Brown Hair," "My Old Kentucky Home," and two hundred more wonderful songs like them. Then he gave up on life, having written so much about the past. Apparently, nostalgia for a culture long since past could not be replaced by a vision of God acting through present circumstances.

One thing we can be certain of — regardless of our talent, regardless of our education, regardless of our wealth — life at some point is going to test us. We will feel that we are *hopeless*. We are going to face some misery and considerable limits. And it doesn't matter whether we talk to the theologians or the psychiatrists, they will both tell us that people face limits in only one of three ways.

We can cry about our problems. We don't believe things will work out for us. We can languish in the tears of depression: "I knew it would be this way." We can stay in that desolate place and wallow down low, crying painful tears in the valley of our problems. We can literally cry over what we do not have. We can feel as if we are dead — we have a body, to be certain, but it's full of a dead person's bones. While others live up on the mountaintop of adventure, we can cry our tears in the valley of sorrow without working for change or insight. The elderly will be living longer and creating a host of bioethical dilemmas. The media will continue to exert a disproportionate influence on American values. Irresponsible sexuality will continue to flaunt itself in the face of the AIDS epidemic. We can languish in nostalgia, hoping for a return to a less complex world. We can even create our own little country club havens which resemble an old Kentucky home, Jeannie with the light brown hair, and way down upon the Swannee River. An abundance of candidates run for office who make us feel comfortable with our prejudices.

A second response to life's misery is to let it fester until it explodes in the anger of our self-centered cravings. We get hooked on our pessimism. We run into people who are narrow-minded and mean. We encounter prejudice and hate. We know that everyone is selfish, ruthless, and cruel. What can we expect from this crummy world, anyway? We better punch it in the nose before it punches us. Let's fight our way out of our human condition. We can take the offensive, yell reverse discrimination, close the borders to immigration, and turn on those we perceive to be the alien, the stranger, and the foreigner to our traditional cultural inheritance. And there is much support for this. The Western religions are exclusive religions and fundamentalism is worldwide. Countries ruled by dictators usually have the cleanest streets. We can employ "survival of our kind" techniques.

Gerald Kennedy tells the startling experience of a man who visited the Bell Laboratories. One of the executives had on his desk a machine that really represents the end of the line for many people. It was a small wooden casket the size of a cigar box. On its side was a single switch. Flip the switch and a hand emerges. The hand reaches down, turns off the switch and goes back into the box. When the lid comes down the buzzing stops. That's all there is to it — the machine does nothing but switch itself off.[3]

Obviously, it would seem funnier if it didn't symbolize so many human lives. There are people who wake each morning for no greater purpose than to pamper themselves, accumulate a few grown-up toys, and then switch themselves off again each evening. Then, when their battery, that old ticker called the heart, runs down, they can't even do that anymore. That's not much of a legacy to hand over to the twenty-second century.

Isaac Watts wrote a haunting poem. It went something like this:

> *There are a number of us creep*
> *Into this world, to eat and sleep;*
> *And know no reason why we're born,*
> *But only to consume the corn,*
> *Devour the cattle, fowl, and fish,*
> *And leave behind an empty dish.*
>
> *Then if their tombstone, when they die,*
> *(Doesn't) flatter and lie,*
> *There's nothing better will be said*
> *Than that "They've eat up all their bread,*
> *Drunk up their drink, and gone to bed."*

As I say, it's a haunting poem. We can indeed release all our energy eating our bread, drinking our drink, and going to bed. It's indeed possible to spend the energy of our lives loving only what we can use, worshipping only what we have bought, and believing only what we can see. And frankly, that's a waste, a tragic waste, because we never get all that energy and those years back in the future, even if we suddenly discover that life is worth living.

But there is, fortunately, a more Christian response to what life hands us at any moment within the world's history. We can surrender to one who is beyond the limited perception of our own history, endorse our lives and our times, and release the power of God which lies within the autobiography of our world.

Compared to our past American experience, white mainline Protestants may feel like strangers in Babylon in the future. In terms of our heritage, we will certainly be aliens in an unfamiliar place. Our traditional religious symbols and meanings could very well be removed from the land. We may be in exile, from the old ways, in our own country. Certainly we will no longer be the only dominant

243

religious force shaping the American experience. As we become a minority, albeit the largest minority, in our own land, we will face some of the same theological issues which faced those ancient Jews who woke up in Babylon. We will have to think through the double theme of relinquishing the old and receiving the new. The moral corruption of the clergy, the temptation toward formalism and legalism, and the appearance of the defeat of our former American way of life always call the presence of God into question. Are these other gods from the East stronger than Yahweh? Should we accommodate the New Age spirituality? Hadn't God promised us an eternal dynasty when those pilgrims sailed the ocean under the images of crossing the Red Sea into a new Israel?

While not in formal exile or slavery, we white Protestants will resemble a large ethnic group certainly cut off from its cultural surroundings. To many sitting here at the brink of the new century, the ancient prophet Ezekiel and the voices of others who have found themselves in unfamiliar surroundings may be instructive.

The prophet Ezekiel was confronted in Babylon by God. He and his people were living in a dark valley. The valley was a symbol of their situation in Babylon. It was a low place. They were surrounded by economic mountains. Their jobs were gone. They were surrounded by social and political mountains — these teachers, scholars, philosophers, and leaders had hit rock bottom — prisoners of war. They were in a valley of sorrow. Some were crying and others were getting angry over their situation. They were figuratively dead people. They were aware of their limitations, their failures, their bleak future. They were in the valley of their trouble. Ezekiel saw wheels and he was carried up and around the valley so he could see every problem. And the question was put to him, "Can these people live?" You are a scientist, but can these people live? You are an educator, but can these people live? You are a psychologist who knows all about drives and reactions and responses and tendencies. With all this knowledge, can you answer me: "Can these people live?"

"Are they going to cry? Are they going to fight? Or are they going to endorse their lives over to me?"

Big question? So those Jews turned their lives over. Right there in that valley they just endorsed their lives over to the power of the universe. They let it loose and rose above their own time and place. Through their perceived darkness and tribulation, they just endorsed their lives over to God.

That message has been let loose time and time again when humans have found themselves in a perceived valley of sorrow.

In our own nation's past, a group of people arrived upon these shores of America, and to them it was a valley. To others it was a mountaintop of possibilities. To them it was a valley of slavery. They had no thought of ever having a chance to ride in one of the great chariots or surreys that they saw their bosses riding around in. Some cried and died. Some grew angry and festered and boiled inside. And some stood in the fields of North Carolina and Alabama and Mississippi and other places and said, "I will not live in this valley of sorrow. I refuse. One day a chariot is going to swing low enough for me." They sang: "Swing low, sweet chariot, coming for to carry *me* home."

Some cried tears of depression in that valley of sorrow: "I knew it would be this way." Others tried to fight and fester their way out of that valley. But others responded differently. They endorsed their lives, and moved beyond the tears and anger of defeat.

This is not a message from me. This is a message that was let loose by Ezekiel in Babylon 2,580 years ago. It was let loose again in the cotton fields of Mississippi 140 years ago. It wound its way to the coal fields of Appalachia and was let loose again just seventy years ago. It was bottled up in the blighted ghetto of Detroit and let loose again just thirty years ago. And it is lodged in your soul now. When life throws its worst at you, what will happen to you? Will you cry? Will you fight? Or will you endorse that power of God within you to believe in so much more than your smallness and let it loose? Can you make fresh, every day, the world around you and learn to renew life in the very crises and limitations which impinge upon you? Can you view the human condition in biblical perspective?

1. As told by Earl V. Pierce in *The Supreme Beatitude* (New York: Fleming H. Revell, 1947), p. 23.

2. Ben Lacy Rose, *On Your Way Rejoicing* (New York: Carlton Press, 1991), p. 83.

3. Gerald Kennedy, *The Parables* (New York: Harper and Brothers, 1960), p. 38.

Right Woman, Right Man

Genesis 29:14-30

We have a story in the Bible that is a good reflection of the human condition. It contains a lot of successes, much failure, some shifty characters, a family squabble, a love story, and enough sex and violence to border between being rated PG-13 and R. The hero's name is Jacob. In Hebrew, the name Jacob means "the go-getter." And Jacob is a go-getter indeed. He is the boy "most likely to succeed." Jacob comes from quite a family. His mother, Rebecca, likes him more than she likes her older child, Esau. Esau isn't much of a go-getter and, you know, some mothers like to live their lives through their aggressive children. Well, Esau just likes to hunt and fish and tinker. He's quiet and steady, never had a desire to go to college. But Jacob — he's something else. He's a talker and a natty dresser. The girls all love him. He's always got a deal going and he usually pulls it off to his advantage.

The father of the two boys is an old man named Isaac. Isaac waits until late in his life to have children. He is virtually blind and he doesn't really understand the younger generation, so he's glad he can't see much of what's going on around him. But Isaac is a loving old man. Both boys are hard to raise in their teenage years, what with the age difference between them and their father. Old Isaac is the kind of man that goes on loving people no matter what they do to him. Both boys use him pretty much as they please, knowing there is nothing that will really hurt the old man. In the end he always comes around and gives them what they want.

Now, the old man has learned that he is dying. For the sake of his family he wants to tie up the loose ends of his long life. So he puts the word out for the oldest son, Esau, to come in and receive his blessing. This will be his "last will and testament." Once he gives it, it will be final. Well, Jacob gets together with his momma and they decide that Esau is just not aggressive enough to handle all that property. Esau is too lacking in administrative ability and

247

too strong in conscience to really be trusted with all that money. Heck, Esau might give it away instead of investing it wisely. Besides, Esau is a sucker. He has too much compassion. People might take advantage of him. That being the case, it might as well be Jacob who possesses the family fortune. The world is full of suckers, and since suckers are people who never know what hits them anyway, in Jacob's mind there is no law against taking advantage of Esau's stupidity. So Jacob trades some soup and bread to Esau for the privilege of going into the father's tent. He dresses just like Esau and even puts on some of Esau's smelly garments.

So the old man is now waiting in the tent for his eldest son, Esau. It's dark inside and the old man squints when Jacob walks in. "Who are you?" asks Isaac. Jacob smiles as he boldly disguises his voice and says, "I am Esau." The old man falls silent and asks again, "Are you really Esau?" Jacob lies again: "Yes, I'm Esau." Finally, the old man stretches out his arms, feels the garments and smells of the fields on them and blesses the disguised Jacob, giving him all the property.

The only person angry about the dishonesty is Esau. He rants and raves. So Jacob slips off to stay away for a while until Esau's anger can cool down.

There he goes, Jacob the go-getter, a wealthy man, thanks to being shrewd and ambitious. Jacob starts putting some miles between himself and that fool brother of his, Esau. Eventually he comes to a well in Mesopotamia. There is a big rock over the well and everyone is arguing over who is going to roll it away. But these are shepherds. They have little organizational ability — all Indians and no chief. Soon they are really arguing. Well, in steps the go-getter Jacob. He proceeds to give orders and instructions, and they roll the stone away. Jacob has come to the rescue. He's a born leader. All the thirsty people are drinking.

While this is happening, a beautiful girl named Rachel is observing the scene. Jacob looks up and his eyes bulge nearly out of his head. The woman is a knockout, a real beauty! And she is just as impressed with him. He kisses Rachel and knows that she is the woman for him. So he goes to visit her father, Laban.

Now Laban knows the boy is a person with a real future in business. Consequently Laban is determined to make a profit out of the love this Jacob has for his beautiful daughter. He drives a hard bargain. If Jacob will work for him in the family business for seven years, he can marry Rachel. Jacob jumps at the chance. His future is a promising one and the years pass in succession.

Finally, the big day comes. *Seven years* he has worked for this day and now he can claim his bride. Women in the Middle East, then as now, have their faces covered at weddings.

People from miles around come for the wedding. The vows and gifts are exchanged. Then Jacob leads this veiled bride to his tent in the darkness of the evening. They spend their wedding night there, and the next morning he wakes up to a startling discovery. He has married the wrong person. His bride is not the beautiful Rachel but the mean and cross-eyed Leah, the sister of Rachel. His father-in-law has palmed off on him the unattractive daughter.

The go-getter has become the sucker. Yet, what can he say to Laban? There is no law against taking advantage of a sucker in a dark tent who can't see well. The world is full of suckers and go-getters. Laban has done to Jacob exactly what Jacob did to Esau and Isaac. Jacob says to himself, "Hmmm ... think I'm learning a lot about life."

But Jacob still loves Rachel, so he adjusts. He reshapes his future. He agrees to work seven more years for the family business and when he agrees, Laban gives him Rachel. Now he has two wives! But the ending is a happy one. Jacob and Rachel love each other and they put up with Leah, all their days. Rachel has two children. Things go well with the first delivery and little Joseph is born. Things do not go well the second time Rachel gets pregnant. She goes again to the valley of motherhood and this time she doesn't come back. Rachel dies in childbirth but the child lives. As she is dying, Jacob names the child "Benoni," which means "the Son of My Right Hand." He has lost his right hand, the beautiful Rachel. He raises a monument and a tomb to her outside the village called Ephrath. And that's the end of the biblical story of the woman who married the right man.

What does the story tell us about the future? It tells us much. Apparently the "right man" is made, not born. Likewise the "right woman" is made, not born. If marriages are made in heaven, they are certainly worked out on earth through hard bargains and compromise, even suffering.

Secondly, I think, figuratively speaking, the story is a true one. People fall off their feet over a man or a woman, repeat the marriage vows, go home, start living together, and then discover that they did not marry the person they thought they had married. When the veil comes off, it's not always the beautiful thing you thought you'd married but this mean and unattractive thing that you've got to live with.

You think Jacob wore a good disguise when he went to see Isaac? You think Leah wore a good disguise when she covered up to marry Jacob? Most of us when we meet our future brides and future in-laws put on disguises that would put those people to shame. Jacob was the right man because he adjusted. *His love was greater than the circumstances.*

There is even a message in the seven-year bargain he had with Laban. There is no such thing as easy commitment in life. There are only bargains, and you've got to remake the bargain every day, every week, and every year, or the ideal can be called off. You wonder what kind of person it takes to stay committed for fourteen years with all those other good women around him, just for the taking. Well, Jacob was a strange mixture of *the sensual, the earthy, and the spiritual.*

He was a man who in his best moments could see more than houses, sheep and cattle, and the things of this world. He was a man who could see angels of God and ladders reaching into heaven. *The first thing that Jacob did was to bury the idols that his family accumulated and try to find God again .* Every family accumulates idols. Jacob knew that sex and earthly wealth by themselves could not sustain a family into the future. They never have and they never will.

Finally, one must ask the question: is there any virtue in being a good man and a good woman? Does it pay off in the future? Look at Jacob. He made restitution with his brother Esau, giving

Esau over two million dollars worth of property as a gift, which was far more than he stole from him in the first place. He worked fourteen years to be able to marry his wife, then she died in childbirth, leaving him with two sons to raise. He wrestled with an angel and was promised a blessing, but all he wound up with was the chance to look down on his dead wife and build her a little tomb outside the gates of Ephrath. His and Rachel's love made their hardships, trials, illusions, and visions tolerable. They didn't complain. But what did Rachel get out of it, except years of marriage, an early death in childbirth, and a huge monument beside the gates of Ephrath?

Well, the story tells us this: God always has the last word as a result of your actions, but it may not be in your lifetime. You cannot live just for your lifetime. That which God has promised comes to pass. *But it may not be in your lifetime.*

The story of Jacob and Rachel is more than the story of two suckers who finally lived right, did not chase other men and women, and sacrificed their worldly goods and time for others while holding on to a foolish belief in God and going to worship frequently as a family. That love, through hardship, illusion, and trial, was emulated by their children, grandchildren, and great-grandchildren. That love influenced the future of a family. Those descendants kept up the huge tomb and monument outside Ephrath. Finally, after many generations, the name of Ephrath was changed. The new name of the village was *Bethlehem.*

Rachel is buried just outside the main gate to Bethlehem. And one day, a descendant of those little boys she gave birth to so long ago got word that he had to return to the home place to be enrolled for taxes. So he put his pregnant wife on a donkey and they headed down toward the old tomb and monument the right man had made with his own hands for the right woman.

Right past the tomb of Rachel they walked, looking for a place to stay. Most probably they paused at the tomb of the right woman made by the right man. It must have been frightening for a young pregnant teenager to stand facing the tomb of an ancestor who had died in childbirth and contemplate her own possible future. And Joseph, aware of illusions, trials, and hardships to come in his future,

251

could at least take comfort in the fact that if Jacob could tolerate what he had to go through and still love his wife, then maybe he, too, could do the same thing.

About one block from Rachel's tomb the night air was split by the cry of a newborn baby, blood of Rachel's blood and flesh of Rachel's flesh. The young mother took her child, named him Jesus, and placed him in a manger. The Bible says the heavens split and all the angels broke into a song.

As the heavenly star shone down on the little cave and the old tomb of the woman who married the right man, I can believe that that actually happened. If you had watched the story unfold and had been an angel then, wouldn't you have sung, too?

———————————

NOTE: Two important sources provided the impetus for this message:
Frederick Buechner, "The Magnificent Defeat," pages 10-26 in *The Magnificent Defeat* (New York: Harper & Row, 1966).
See also Clarence Edward Macartney, *Great Women of the Bible* (New York: Abingdon, 1942), pp. 136-151.

Right Woman, Wrong Man

1 Samuel 25:3-25

The Scripture says it all in one sentence: *"She was an intelligent and beautiful woman, but her husband was surly and mean in his dealings."*

One fact is apparent for human beings: the human condition is composed of triumphs and mistakes. Sometimes mistakes are not limited to the insignificant aspects of life but are made in the monumental decisions as well. In fact, often the only adequate definition of an impasse or a dilemma is to say, "It was a mistake." One of the most tragic mistakes is when one occurs in marriage.

You meet a friend of former years and you make a vague allusion to her marriage. The only comment is a sad look and the statement, "It was a mistake." You sit as a minister in your office with a friend or colleague, talking about marriage. He wrings his hands, pulls out a cigarette, lights it, and leans back in the chair. With heavy eyes and a little sigh in his throat, he utters, "It was a mistake. It was just a mistake."

The Bible is a rather complete mirror of life. It would not be the complete book it is without stories about "mistakes" and the lessons we humans can learn from them. If God is God, our biblical heritage must have a word about mistakes. Consequently, we read about a man named Job who married the wrong woman. When things were going rough for Job, when his life was at its worst, his wife, instead of comforting, strengthening, and encouraging him, told him to curse God and die. She would be better off if this man who lost their money and his health just packed it in and died.

Likewise, the Bible contains the story of a woman named Abigail who married a horrible man named Nabal. It is appropriate to focus on Abigail and Nabal because the Bible devotes so much space to them. In fact, one scholar contends that there are three great, truly great speeches in the entire Bible. The greatest is the

253

Sermon on the Mount by Jesus Christ. The second greatest is the wonderful speech Judah made to Joseph in Egypt, when the still-disguised Joseph threatened to keep Benjamin as a hostage. Judah's speech made Joseph, the most polished statesman in Egypt if not the world, break down in uncontrolled tears. You and I could hardly read it today without getting tears in our eyes and lumps in our throats. But the third most eloquent speech in the Bible is the heart-rending plea the beautiful Abigail made with David to keep him from vengeance and murder.

Put yourself into the story. It was sheepshearing time in Carmel. What a time it was — three thousand of Nabal's sheep were to be shorn of their white wool. Everywhere the ground was white, like Minnesota in January, not with snow but with wool from all those sheep. Everywhere for miles around the people could hear the sound of the clippers and the bleating of the sheep. The news had spread throughout the land that Nabal was shearing his three thousand sheep. Now, in that time, people from all parts of the land came to help in the process, just as the Amish do in barn-raising. Consequently all the people in the country nearby had gathered with their picnic baskets to assist in the sheepshearing.

Small wonder, then, that word of the big event reached the ears of a revolutionary named David. David had six hundred fighting men following him. And David's men had been pretty good to Nabal's sheep. They had never stolen any of the sheep. In fact, they had protected the sheep against thieves and raiders. It was the custom in the shearing season that the man whose sheep were being sheared should give, as a token of goodwill, some nice gifts to his neighbors. Just as today when a person who has a home in a remote area will give a gift at Christmas to neighbors who have protected it from vandalism, so would a sheep owner in Nabal's day give gifts to those who had protected his sheep. The whole philosophy of the ancient Middle East revolved around such reciprocity. With that in mind, David sent some of his young men to greet Nabal and receive the usual gifts.

They found Nabal sitting under a tree. Nabal had been drinking heavily, as apparently was his custom. The men reminded Nabal of David's protection of his flock the previous year. Nabal, the drunken, mean-spirited fool, angrily shouted: "Buzz off. I'm not going to give any presents or bonuses to this David and his bunch of tramps!"

Such rebuke would make anyone mad. But when you consider how it also breached the Oriental laws of courtesy, you can imagine David's wrath. David drew out his sword, told his six hundred men to arm themselves, and declared: "Before sundown, this jerk, Nabal, and all his men will be dead." Off they went toward Carmel. David must have felt satisfied as he heard his six hundred soldiers marching behind him.

Well, Nabal was still drinking heavily. So his servant ran to Nabal's wife, Abigail, and told her how her husband had insulted David. We can be certain a number of possibilities must have run through her mind. Here was her chance to get rid of this mean, drunken fool she'd been married to all these years. But somehow she suppressed such thoughts. She summoned her servants and bade them load animals with presents for David's soldiers — raisins, cheese, bread, wine, etc. Then, Abigail got on her own donkey and led the caravan in David's direction. At the top of one of the hills the two processions met. Abigail dismounted from her beast and spoke to David as follows:

> *My Lord, let the blame be on me alone ... pay no attention to that wicked husband of mine. He is just like his name — his name is fool. I'm sorry I did not see the men you sent. Please give these gifts to your men and forgive my idiot husband's offense. You are a great man. Two wrongs do not make a right. Let no wrongdoing be found in you as long as you live.*

The great David completely melted before that speech. David turned back from his errand of revenge. And he thanked God for sending Abigail to meet him.

When Abigail returned home, Nabal was in a drunken stupor. The next day, after he had slept it off, she told him what had happened. When Nabal heard the news, he had a stroke. A few days later, he died. When David heard Nabal was dead, he began to court the beautiful widow. Soon they were married. Abigail did not live long, but she made David a wonderful wife during the formative years of his kingship. She helped keep David from many of the follies and cruelties which stained his later reign.

There are many lessons we humans can learn from Abigail. She has much to teach us in how to deal with the aftermath of great mistakes.

In the first place, she did not permit the adversity of life, the fact that she had married the wrong man, to embitter her spirit. It must have been difficult to have been married to Nabal, but she recognized Nabal as a bad person. She did not transfer her bitterness to men in general. If she had, she would have said, "Great, let them fight and kill each other. Men are devils. Let the blood pour."

Mark Twain once said, "A cat that has set down on a hot stove lid will never sit down on a hot stove lid again. But neither will she sit on a cold one again, either." *It is a tendency in life for us to take our mistakes and bad experiences and universalize them.* Such greatly reduces our capacity ever to love again. And it retards the ability of our children to love. If Abigail had transferred her experience with Nabal into a disdain for men in general, her life would have been the poorer. There was nothing wrong with men. But there was something wrong with Nabal.

In like manner, if anyone has a complaint with me, it is a complaint against me. Blame me. Talk about me. Don't knock the church, or preachers, or colleges. There is nothing wrong with the church when I make a mistake. If you let your children grow up hearing you knock the church, the preachers, teachers, and the universal concepts of respect they need to have in life, they will lose the capacity to love those things in the future. And you will lose the capacity to love those things in the future. Bear your mistakes with resignation, but do not turn it into a universal bitterness. Likewise, if you have a mistake or problem with people in the church, it's simply with those people. There is nothing wrong with the church or God if we run into a few Nabals.

Jesus was very conscious of this. He bore upon himself the sin of the world, but he knew he had to do it in such a manner that people would not become bitter with God. How poignant must have been his own sorrow when Jesus realized that he had yoked himself to a human race that was foolish. But Jesus did not universalize the disappointment he felt. Judas was a mistake, but people are not a mistake. Peter was a loudmouth, but people are not. The Pharisees and Sadducees were religious mistakes, but not all religious leaders are; that's why Jesus left us with a church and religious leaders called disciples.

There is a great message in the story of Nabal and Abigail. What do you do when you marry the wrong man? You do not universalize the experience to include all men and all marriages. What do you do when you marry the wrong woman? You do not universalize the experience to include all women and all marriages. What do you do when you run into people in life who are cruel and mean? You do not universalize the experience to include all people of that race or that profession or that age or that category. If you do, your future will be hardened. You will become pessimistic. You will become depressed. You will greatly reduce your future ability to be happy and love again.

When Jesus walked to the cross, he did not say, "God, human beings are stupid." He said, "Forgive these people, for *they* do not know what *they* are doing."

Life is composed of its triumphs and its mistakes. How do you treat them in your life as you prepare for your future?

Beyond The Years Of The Locust

Joel 1:2-12; 2:25-27
Psalm 126

Approximately five miles from the little town of Seneca, South Carolina, lies the Return Baptist Church. It seems that a particular Baptist church had a conflict. A disagreement broke out among some families within its membership. Words were exchanged — heated words — and finally almost half the congregation left and moved down the road a mile and a half. They started another church, bought land, and built a building. The people in the old congregation struggled for a few years, as did the people in the new congregation. Each went about its business in a rather routine and mundane fashion, as all Baptist organizations do.

Gradually the newer church became larger than the older church, but the people in the newer church were not all that happy. Most of the people who had precipitated the conflict had moved away from both churches within twenty years. Consequently the newer church sold its buildings to another Baptist church and moved back up the road a mile and a half to the church from which they had originally come. Shortly thereafter, they held a business meeting and they named the church the Return Baptist Church, since everyone had returned back up the road.

I asked a member of the Return Baptist Church how most people historically perceived those years when they had been split by the disagreement. His response was candid. "Oh, those were the wasted years," he said. "Those years were just lost. Those were the wasted years."

Life has its wasted years. Persons who do not understand this and hit the panic button too soon make huge mistakes when they abandon their pursuits. The people of the Old Testament understood much about life. The little book of Joel carries an amazing promise. "I will restore back to you the years which the swarming locust hath eaten" (Joel 2:25).

258

A locust swarm was a terrible thing in ancient Israel. Billions of insects six inches long would swarm and settle on the crops. They would block out the sun, destroying everything in sight. The years that the locusts came, they got everything — every blade of grass, every leaf, every shrub. The Bible says of those years, "These are the years the locust hath eaten."

It's an apt description. All of us have years in our lives that are sheer waste. These are the years that were lost. These are the years you worked for nothing; the years when your children wrenched your heart out; the years when you were stupid; the years when you had no vision; the years when your loved ones died; the years when your marriage was weakest; the years when you arrogantly thought you could make it on your own; the years when everything you tried did not seem to work. Everyone has those bitter years. "These are the years the locust hath eaten."

Edna St. Vincent Millay has a sonnet that tells a story of what to do when the locusts come upon you.[1] The sonnet speaks of an old farmer whose land has been flooded. All of his crops, all of his houses, all of the dreams, and all the work of his hands have been swept away. They are underwater. His earthly possessions are underwater. In the evening he gets in a boat and he rows away from the scene of the total desolation. His heart is heavy. His mind is numb. But the situation has in it a measure of promise; for, in the words of the concluding line, *he rows away with a twisted face and a pocketful of seeds.* Though all seems wasted, he carries in his pockets and his heart the seed of a new beginning because he knows the floodwaters will recede, and he knows that he needs the pocketful of seeds to make a new beginning in the future.

That's the assurance of Psalm 126. "He that goes forth weeping, bearing the seeds of sowing, shall come home with shouts of joy." And it's true. The greatest crops a farmer ever realizes are the crops that grow up through the land that has been fertilized by the corpses of billions of locusts. God does indeed restore the years the locust hath eaten if we carry forth in trust and patience. It all depends on what we carry away from the waste. If we can take the seeds of faith and perseverance, we can make fresh starts from anything. That is the "good news" of the Gospel.

Jesus himself had years of waste in his life. From the time he was born until the time he was twelve years old we have nothing, absolutely nothing, written about his life. Much of the time was spent hiding in Egypt from Herod. I imagine that, were you to corner Mary and Joseph and ask them, "What about the time you left Bethlehem and fled to Egypt and then had to come home and start your business over?" the response would be, "Oh, those were the wasted years. Those were the years the locust hath eaten."

In like manner, we find nothing written about Jesus from the time he was twelve years old until he began his ministry at age thirty, except for a brief account of a single incident when his parents lost him for a few days. Eighteen more years of nothing about his life loom before us. Most likely Joseph, his father, had died and Jesus had had to take care of his brothers and sisters and his widowed mother. That would have been his responsibility as the oldest Jewish child in a Jewish family.

For thirty years Jesus apparently did not make a disciple, did not preach a single sermon, and did not heal a single person. When you consider all that he did his last three years, you are tempted to think, "What a waste!" For thirty years this man, who later did so much, didn't preach a sermon; didn't heal a soul. Those were apparently the wasted years for the Kingdom of God. Those were the years the locust ate.

But out of those thirty years of struggle came a person with such sensitivity, understanding, and love that the world had never seen before. Suppose Jesus had not had those years the locust ate. Suppose Jesus' life had been one productive, affluent year after another year, year after year. Think about this. Jesus faced the great temptation in the wilderness when he began his ministry. Satan tempted him to become a carousing publicity hound and to give over to evil for personal worldly gain. Jesus resisted those temptations at age thirty. Would he have resisted them at age twenty-five? Without the years of the locust under his belt, he may have taken the easy instead of the strenuous road, and you and I would be looking for God to send someone else.

Without his ability to withstand the desertion of his friends, the treachery of Judas, the midnight trial, the taunts of his people, and the march toward Calvary, could he have persevered? Could Jesus have witnessed all that he possessed and dreamed about swept away and still rowed his personal boat through that storm toward Golgotha with the seeds of hope and love in his pocket, had he not experienced the years which the locust ate of his life? Had his daddy, Joseph, lived instead of died and left him tons of money and the family furniture business socked away in a trust fund, could Jesus have done at age twenty what he did later? Think about it.

There is no place for snap judgments in understanding how God deals with our lives, even the evil in our lives. If there is an overarching problem in life, it is the problem in our affluent society of people hitting the panic button all too soon in their vital relationships. This is why we have so many things go wrong. This is why so many people move so often from one town to the next. This is the reason behind so many resignations; the reason why separation comes to so many people; why so many people drop courses, drop plans, drop children, drop careers, and drop everything else.

The best years of a person's life, the finest crop a person produces, is the crop that comes up through the ground that is fertilized by the years of the locust.

Do you know when psychiatrists tell us are the happiest years in the life of a marriage? Believe it or not, the answer is the years following the mid-life crisis, *if* the couple stays together. After a couple has lived through the trauma of bodily changes, the death of some of their parents, the movement away from their home of their children, the limitations accompanying their career and decreased mobility and health, the level of communication, the level of respect, the level of understanding *at that point* is the highest. The finest crop is the crop that comes up after the years of the locust.

Every young person should read the story of Lot and Abraham. Lot wanted things easy, exciting, and gratifying. Lot was the original purveyor of instant coffee, instant orange juice, the fast car, the easy girlfriend, and Federal Express. None of the strenuous life for Lot — not if he had a choice, and he did. Abraham and Lot watered their flocks at the same oasis, grazed them on the same land — a family partnership. And you know how that works out. Trouble was inevitable. Their workers fought. Their families fought all the time. They had to separate.

So, Abraham called to Lot and said, "Lot, let's not fight. We have got all this land. Choose what you want. If you take the left hand, I'll take the right hand. If you take the right hand, I'll take the left hand."

Well, Lot looked around and it didn't take long to make that decision. On the left hand was the Jordan Valley, well-watered, with grass; plenty of nightclubs; lots of cities, Sodom and Gomorrah. Things were quite pleasant there; plenty of wells. To the right were the barren hills — no cities, sparse grass, scattered waterholes. Lot quickly said, "I'll take the Jordan Valley." So Abraham took to the hills and had to live there in austerity and waste. Lot avoided the years of the locust. His life was one affluent, productive year after another. Abraham lost his wife for a period of time. Actually, he had to sell her, and he even had to purchase a piece of foreign property from the Hittites to have a burial site for his wife Sarah.

The years passed and Lot died among such drunken, immoral squalor as cannot be found anywhere else in the Old Testament. Abraham battled the locusts. Finally, with a weeping heart, old Abraham buried Sarah in a Hittite cave. And he put deep in his pocket the business treaty, the real estate treaty that he carried, which was a Hittite Suzerainty-Vassal treaty. As he rode toward death, I can imagine old Abraham gathering his children and saying, "Sons and daughters, we have had it rough. The wilderness has taken everything. Your Uncle Lot got all the family money. Unlike Lot, I can't give you fertile lands and valuable property. All I have in my heart is a promise God gave me, and all I have in my pockets are these little pieces of parchment which form the international treaty that the Hittite Suzerain has with us. But it is a good way to live, so take this Suzerainty Treaty I've carried; it's all I have. I'm sorry I let you down."

Some generations later, a descendant of Abraham by the name of Moses inherited the little pocketful of parchment. And in his great hour of need Moses pulled out the treaty between old Abraham and the Hittite king. The treaty read: "Thou shalt have no other suzerains before me. Thou shalt not bow down and worship any other suzerain. Thou shalt not take the name of your protector suzerain in vain."

Moses went up the mountain where he heard a voice, and the voice said, "Moses, I am the suzerain. I am the only King. I alone am God. Go down before my people and tell them in language that they can understand, that they are already familiar with, that I am suzerain."

Moses came down with a reworked version of the commands stipulated by the old Hittite Mesopotamian International Suzerainty Vassal Treaty that he had gotten out of the pockets of Abraham. We call them the Ten Commandments.

He that goes forth weeping, bearing the seed for sowing, shall come home with shouts of joy. God always restores to you the years which the swarming locusts have eaten.

---

1. *Sonnet X, Wine From These Grapes.* Published by Harper & Brothers. Copyright, 1928, by Edna St. Vincent Millay.

Your Burning Bush

Exodus 3:1-14
Zechariah 14:7

Never have there been so many athletic contests on television as the present time. Even the most avid fan occasionally gets tired of viewing so many games. The constant barrage can become weary on the eyes. Sometimes we sit almost transfixed to the television screen.

I well remember the first professional football game I attended. I drove in the snow from Boston to New York to watch the Jets play. Frankly, I spent much of the game watching the fans instead of the players. They were a crazy lot in my section. To call them "high rollers" or the "jet set" would be an understatement. Watching those sixty- and seventy-year-old men and women try to look and act like teenagers was an experience. The women especially amazed me. Their hair was dyed blond; they wore diamond rings and necklaces that would choke a horse, and coats that resembled feeding time in a local zoo. And, my goodness, the stuff they had bought at the drug store to try to make their faces look younger. Some of their efforts to look young would have been immensely ludicrous if they were not so pathetic. The men were just as ludicrous. The weather was freezing but they wore blazers and frilly shirts unbuttoned almost down to their navels so everyone could see the hairs on their chests and the gold chains around their necks. God pity the old body that has no better safeguard against the oncoming of old age than can be found in paste, paint, and gold necklaces.

Contrary to our efforts to tax our ingenuity to the utmost to keep from growing older, the prophet Zechariah made this astounding statement: *"At evening time it shall be light"* (14:7). This assertion that the sunset can be as bright as the sunrise was no small insight.

When our society speaks of the evening of life, it means a time of weakness. Surely the evening, or the later years, is a time when the dreaded weakening of our physical and mental powers occurs. Yet this crazy Hebrew prophet and his crazy God seemed to think that the evening time of life has a radiance all its own.

To be certain, the later years in life do exhibit a weakening of physical powers. The body tends to stoop. The keen ear is no longer able to hear as well. The bright eyesight becomes dimmer. And old age is naturally lonely because so many of the friends of other years have slipped away.

Yet, the haunting words of the prophet remain — "At evening time it shall be light." Our biblical heritage contains the account of a person whose life really *began* at age eighty.

There was an old eighty-year-old shepherd who was something of a joke to the younger citizens of his land. This old boy had known better days. But for the past forty years he had done nothing but keep another man's sheep. Most probably that was all he would ever do, since he was at least eighty years old. Now, the children of Israel were in slavery at that time. If one had to project a savior or revolutionary, one would not look for it to be this old shepherd whose best days had long ago dropped into the sunset.

Certainly not. We expect little from older people except complaints, conservatism, and demands. That's probably why many people are afraid of getting old. The passing years do tend to freeze our enthusiasms and water down our courage. As a rule, old people are projected as being less daring than younger people.

Secondly, this Moses was like a lot of older people in that he had found a kind of security. He had no fear of losing his position in life. Soon his father-in-law would be gone and Moses would step into his shoes. His pension plan was set — it was as balanced as any fixed and valuable rate income could be. And everyone knows that revolutions do not come from the fat soil of security. Society has learned not to expect much from people who are both old and secure.

Perhaps the biggest reason we expect little from Moses is that he was not only old and secure, but he was an old failure.[1] He had tried to lead the Hebrew people when he was younger and he had failed miserably. Those who are most enthusiastic in their youth often wind up the wettest of wet blankets in their old age. You see, whereas the young person only *thinks* something won't work, the older person who has tried it before and failed knows for dead *certain* that it won't work.

There had been a time when Moses was an excited person. He had moved from a nameless nobody to a royal somebody. He had both power and excitement in his personality. Seeing an Egyptian bullying one of his own people, this young Moses had struck him dead. He felt that he would be viewed as a hero. But *the next day* he heard two Hebrews arguing with each other. When he sought to be a peacemaker, one of them snarled, "Who made you a judge, Mr. Big Shot? Do you propose to kill me like you killed that Egyptian?"

Can you imagine ingratitude like that? These miserable young people, for whom Moses had done so much, had no appreciation of him. "That does it," Moses inwardly raged. "You don't deserve to be free. I can't give you what you're too stupid to take. I quit. You can take your religion and shove it." He had subsequently buried himself in Midian, where for forty years he had built up a nice pension and just let the stupid ingrates stay in slavery.

Now, that's an unlikely character to turn around and lead a bunch of young crybabies out of slavery, isn't it? But something happened to Moses in the desert at age eighty. And that something is vitally important for you and me. You see, *the future of the world lies in the hands of its older people*. We preachers and teachers are sometimes wont to cast our hands over the youth and say, "Here is the future of our world. The future lies in *their* hands."

Actually, the future of every society lies in the hands of its older people. You see, the older people lay down the tracks for everyone else as to what it means to grow old and be a leader. The older people have the experience, both good and bad. The older people have the major resources of time and money. The older people *can* be more regular in their attendance patterns, in their encouragement, and in their discouragement, as well. You can only imitate that which you have seen and experienced.

When a groom is ready to marry a bride, the minister should tell him, "Look at her mother and her grandmother. That's what she *may* be like." The minister should tell the young bride, "Look at his grandfather and his father; that's what he *may* look like and act like in ten years." We can only be what we can see and imagine.

Don't take the job with a company unless the older employees have seen a burning bush, because that company isn't going anywhere. If the Kingdom is to come, in a local setting, Zechariah is right, "At evening time it shall be light."

Eighty-year-old Moses, secure in his retirement, looked up from his sheep and saw a little bush all ablaze. It did not greatly interest him. In that hot sun, even a piece of glass serves as a magnifying glass and sets brush on fire. When some of us visited Turkey we saw fire barriers all over the place. The guide explained that little pieces of glass are always starting brush fires. But what interested Moses was the fact that the bush kept burning, long after it should have burned out. There was a strange message from God behind it.

God was saying to Moses, "Moses, old fellow, you once burned like that. Once you were all aflame with enthusiasm over what was possible with God. You were once certain I had great things in store for my people. But your fire has gone out. You are still carrying on but there's no glow." And, there's nothing colder than ashes after the fire has gone out.

Secondly, Moses saw that the bush was not burning of its own resources. It burned because God was in it.[2] Moses did not have to fear failure, because if he said "yes" to God, he would not be consumed. When the children of Israel, frankly a bunch of cantankerous crybabies whose normal tone was to wail and want to turn back, criticized him, Moses did not have to fear being consumed.

It was a tremendous revelation. He did not have to depend on being appreciated, being catered to in his old age. He did not have to fear his fire going out as his friends and loved ones slipped away. There was an arm that had been locked with his when he was eighteen that would still be there when he was eighty-eight. There was one who would be unchanged and unchanging, the same yesterday, today, and forever. When sorrows would come, when the strong arm of family was dropped from around his stooped shoulders,

Moses would find an Everlasting Arm 'round him. *There was a relationship that would never be burned up.*

"You can do it," said God. "The future of my people lies in the hands of the old folks like you, Moses. You are very near home anyway. You are already near the promised land. Soon you will meet with those whom you have loved long since and lost a while. Soon you will clasp once more the hands of your loved ones for which your heart has hungered for more than a half a century. *If anyone can burn, Moses, it ought to be an older person like you.* The light of your sunset can be brighter than the light of your youth."

And Moses looked into the bush that burned before him and said, "I'll do it. I'll do it." And the world was *never*, never the same again.

There is no greater revelation than a burning bush that does not burn out, a fire burning bright that is not consumed. Moses learned the secret — *the bush which burned was Moses himself.*

Throughout human history, individuals have asked, "Why doesn't God show *me* a burning bush?" There is one in your future. Most likely you will see it when you are quite old.

---

1. See Clovis Chappell, *Surprises In The Bible* (Nashville: Abingdon, 1967), pp. 7-13.

2. *Ibid.* See also Ronald J. Calvin, ed., *The Human Chain for Divine Grace,* "Every Man Has A Burning Bush," (Philadelphia: Fortress Press, 1978), pp. 85-89; Clovis Chappell, *Home Folks* (Nashville: Cokesbury, 1926), pp. 131-143.